MA...GNERS

IN THE PUBLIC SERVICES

~ BEYOND TECHNOMAGIC

DAVID WASTELL

Nottingham University Business School

Published by:
Triarchy Press
Station Offices
Axminster
Devon. EX13 5PF
United Kingdom

+44 (0)1297 631456
info@triarchypress.com
www.triarchypress.com

A catalogue record for this book is available from the British Library.

Cover design and image by Heather Fallows ~
www.whitespacegallery.org.uk

ISBN: 978-1-908009-31-9

Contents

To Sue, Imogen and Geraldine

I must Create a System or be enslaved by another Man's
I will not Reason and Compare: my business is to Create…
Striving with Systems to deliver individuals from those Systems
William Blake, Jerusalem: the Emanation of the Giant Albion

CHAPTER 1

Design Matters for Public Managers

On November 11th 2008, the British media carried harrowing reports of the brutal death of a 17 month old boy, subsequently referred to as 'Baby Peter', in the London Borough of Haringey. Baby Peter's plight had come to public attention at the conclusion of the trial of his mother, her boyfriend and a family lodger, all convicted of causing his death. The case was seen as a catastrophic failure of the child protection system and Government reaction to public outrage was swift and dramatic. The sense of 'systemic failure' (rather than 'isolated incident') was reinforced by two disquieting features. First, Baby Peter was not an unknown child, dying outwith the protective bourn of the State; far from it, he had been seen by numerous professionals during his short life and was indeed on Haringey's Child Protection Register. Secondly, Haringey's Children's Services department had, within weeks of the child's actual death, been given a glowing report by a government inspection[1], with praise heaped egregiously upon the department's Director. Within days, Ed Balls (Secretary of State for Children, Schools and Families) ordered an emergency inspection of Haringey, arranged for the Director to be summarily sacked, and instigated a national review of child protection, to be led by Lord Laming. The latter had chaired a prior enquiry into another tragic child death, that of Victoria Climbié, which had ushered in a slew of structural reforms, all designed to keep children safer (Laming, 2003). How, therefore, could it have happened again? A further development was the setting up (January 2009) of the Social Work Task Force to conduct a 'nuts and bolts' review of the social work profession and to devise a comprehensive reform programme.

A system in crisis indeed. At this point, I will focus on the part played by a national computer system in these seismic events, the Integrated Children's System (ICS). Calling the ICS a 'computer system' is something of a misnomer; it was much more than that. It represented an attempt to redesign the entire statutory child welfare system in the UK, using

---

[1] By the Office for Standards in Training and Education (Ofsted), the national inspectorial body in England responsible for monitoring and appraising the performance of local authority children's social care departments, as well as the state school system and other services for children.

Information Technology to achieve this transformation[2]. Embodying a highly prescriptive framework specifying the precise procedural steps to be followed in handling cases, the ICS attempted to operationalise the Laming reforms in software. Standardisation and the micromanagement of process were seen as the key to quality, safety and the elimination of risk. Although the ICS had been much lauded by Government and senior managers, evidence was coming to light that it was undermining safe professional practice and paradoxically augmenting risk. Research by myself and colleagues had directly implicated it in the death of Baby Peter[3] and there were also press reports at the time highlighting the mayhem it was causing:

> UNISON[4] *wishes to draw attention to the seriousness of the problems with the Integrated Children's System. The problems appear to be fundamental, widespread and consistent enough to call into question whether the ICS is fit for purpose. ...we have reports of a number of industrial disputes or collective grievances brewing... and in many more cases staff are voting with their feet and not using the system when they can get away with it* (Unison, 2008, pp.8-9).

The miscarriage of the ICS was symptomatic of the failure of the wider system of which it was an essential and integral component. Ultimately the Social Work Task Force called for fundamental review of its design in its final report in 2009 (Gibb, 2009). In this opening chapter, I shall analyse the vicissitudes of the ICS at some length, drawing out key lessons which bear on the central argument of this book, namely that 'systems design' needs to be (re)instated as the primary task of the manager. The ICS debacle provides a cautionary tale of design at its worst, both in terms of product and process, and of the dire consequences which ensue when managers abdicate their role as designers. Linked with design is another important trend in contemporary management education, that of evidence-based practice, which I shall weave into the fabric of my argument. The gap between management research and practice is much lamented, at least by those who are aware of it. The goal of management research, like research in any applied discipline, is surely to produce useful theory. But useful for what? For design, of course.

---

2   Social work's "McDonaldization" moment (Ritzer, 2004).

3   See Broadhurst, Wastell & White, 2010; Wastell, White & Broadhurst, 2010; White, Wastell, Broadhurst & Hall, 2010.

4   UNISON is the trade union to which many UK social workers belong.

Paradise lost: tales from the trenches

Systems thinking is very much in vogue, in the public services especially (Seddon, 2008). The term embraces a gallimaufry of specific meanings, methods and affiliated sects, as we shall see. Striving for a holistic understanding of the complex causal dynamics of social organisations is its primary goal. When a specific accident or a malfunction arises, it is natural for the systems thinker to see this as a dysfunction of the system as a whole, rather than seeking to blame individuals. Child deaths, such as that of Baby Peter, are therefore construed as symptoms of defective systems design. And if the design is defective, the systems thinker will naturally ask how that system took the form it did, in other words, how was it designed? A maxim is in order: 'When a system fails or malfunctions, critically interrogate how it was designed'!

In this and the following section, I will attempt to show, from a systemic point of view, just how the ICS had produced the opposite outcome from the one its originators had looked for. My account is based on the findings of a 2 year research study[5], which exposed the pernicious impact of the ICS on front-line practice. Let us begin by noting that the ICS does not refer to a particular computer system or software package. Rather it is a national specification, comprising a workflow model, which rigidly defines the social work 'business process' in terms of a branching sequence of tasks and timescales, and a reference set of electronic forms, called the 'exemplars'. Against this specification, software suppliers had been invited to develop "compliant" software implementations (Cleaver *et al.*, 2008), and a number of ICS software products had been produced by several vendors. Although, there were inevitably some variations in quality and usability, the centrally prescribed strictures meant that the ICS had, in effect, been implemented as a national system.

The workflow model of the ICS is shown in Figure 1. It is not meant to be read in detail; rather it is used impressionistically to show how far the zeal for formal modelling has gone. The 'wiring diagram' charts the progress of a case from the initial contact, through initial and subsequent in-depth assessment phases. The shaded insert (which overlays some of the diagram) is a blow-up of the early stages of the process. The key

---

5   The study followed a so-called ethnographic approach, i.e. our findings were based on intensive, direct observation of social work practice in our various research sites (5 in all). Mentioning ethnography at this early point is noteworthy, as such immersive, 'real world' engagement is championed by the proselytisers of design in the public services and further afield, as we shall see. Our findings are presented in detail as an example of how ethnographic research is reported, using quotations to bring the story to life. Detail is important; the devil's in it after all, and not knowing the detail is why designs so often go awry.

decision here is whether to accept the contact as a referral, in which case a full initial assessment must be performed, or that advice/information alone will suffice. Each of the tasks in the model have to be carried out according the sequence given, and there can be no short cuts, no improvisation. For important phases, time-scales are prescribed, which are linked to key performance indicators. All referrals must be responded to within 24 hours and initial assessments must be completed within 7 working days, including a home visit, irrespective of contingencies. When an in-depth, core assessment is needed, this must be completed within 35 days.

Despite its lofty ambitions, evidence that the ICS's actual impact on practice had been highly disruptive was all too readily found in our research. A universal complaint related to the time taken to record cases electronically: social workers reported spending between 60% and 80% of their available time at the screen, filling in the "exemplars". Anything but exemplary, these were described as unwieldy, repetitive and difficult to complete and to read. Their lack of practical utility was even more apparent with respect to service users. The following two quotations from social workers illustrate these points:

> It is the way they have designed the forms forcing you to repeat yourself over and over again...

> The worst is, parents can't understand them. They are broken into domains and dimensions... Repetitive, loads of boxes. I have to apologise to parents.

The ICS also required that a form be completed for each individual child. For families with multiple children, this naturally invited staff, working under the exacting time pressures imposed by the system, to cut and paste data across forms. This, of course, completely negated the purpose of individual assessment and consumed excessive amounts of professional time. It was also inherently unsafe as such "cloned" information was inevitably not checked properly. The overall effect of such intensified bureaucracy had been to reduce the social work assessment task to data entry, curtailing time for visiting and thinking about the professional casework required to meet the needs of the child. Another general problem was ICS's emphasis on structured data at the expense of narrative. Practitioners reported that it was difficult to produce "a decent social history" of the family and to make sense of cases from the fragmented documentation in order to obtain a complete picture of the child. A social worker commented as follows:

> The government want us to improve our game, get to know each individual child better – but it's an absolutely impossible task... to get a feel for what's going on with the child – it's all chopped up, a complete nightmare – impossible to find the story.

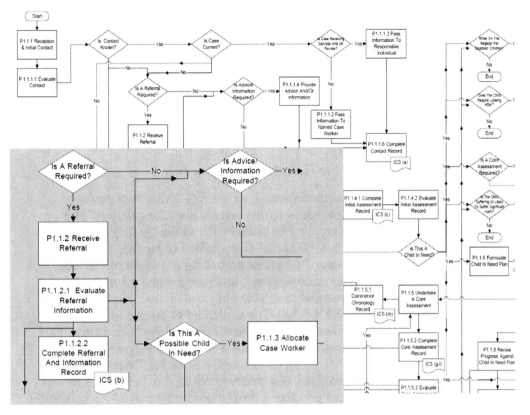

Figure 1: The referral and assessment process as officially "flowcharted"

The problem of the forms was compounded by the tortuous and inflexible workflow model; all steps had to be followed, with a form completed at each stage, however perfunctory. The electronic audit trail was all-important, as a social worker observed:

> *It's much worse since ICS. Like when you've got a child in need and you need a conference, you can't get to the conference without going through strategy discussion and 'outcome of section 47' forms. You used to just be able to write like half a side, but now you've got these terrible forms.*

The pernicious influence of the timescales and targets was ubiquitous. ICS imposes these, providing little scope for workers to exercise intelligent discretion. Worries about timescales for initial (7 days) and core assessments (35 days) had come to dominate practitioners' worlds. Although workers still managed some artful 'workarounds', they also described a strong sense of 'the system' now driving practice. As the space for professional judgments had been increasingly squeezed, key professional activities, such as assessment, had become meaningless and mechanistic. Taking short-cuts to meet targets was inevitably undermining good practice, creating what we came to call 'latent conditions for error':

> *If it's not looking that serious… sometimes you don't get all the information and the temptation is then to take a short-cut and maybe not contact the school, or because the school are on holidays you say I think I've got sufficient information to make a decision- no further action.*

The strange history of the ICS: a cautionary tale

Having given a whiff of the dysfunctions of the ICS, let us now delve into the history of its design. Although its origins are a long way off and a little difficult to descry, they may be traced back to the Quality Protects Programme, inaugurated in 1998 by the Department of Health. To ensure that social services were being "delivered according to requirements and are meeting local and national objectives", this programme prioritised the improvement of "assessment, care planning and record keeping" (Department of Health, 1998, pp.5-6). The centrality of targets and time-scales became evident in the subsequent publication of the "Government's Objectives for Social Services" which set out a range of policy objectives (Department of Health, 1999, p.22). Objective 7 is notable: "To ensure that referral and assessment processes discriminate effectively between different types and levels of need and produce a timely service response". In its sub-objectives, we see the first mention of the time-scales that were subsequently embedded in the ICS: "To complete an initial assessment and put in place case objectives, within a maximum of 7 working days of referral." The first explicit mention of the Integrated Children's System appeared the following year, in "Learning the lessons" (Department of Health, 2000a).

The ICS project was subsequently launched, heralded by a briefing paper in 2000. This is notable for its dogmatic certainty that policy aims will be achieved: the ICS is described as "an assessment planning intervention and reviewing model for all children in need… to ensure that assessment, planning and decision-making leads to good outcomes for children" (Department of Health, 2000b, p.1). A steering group for the project was set up (Department of Health, 2002). Its composition is important in the present context: 38 members are listed of whom 23 are civil servants (including the Chair), or directly linked to the civil service. There are three medical experts and four academics. The only direct link with social work practice was via one assistant director of social services and one senior manager.

Thereafter, the ICS evolved over a number of years. Although it originated in the Department of Health, it subsequently came under the wing of the

Department for Children, School and Families (DCSF). Throughout its development, design was apparently driven by a small group of senior academics and civil servants, who showed conspicuous resistance to criticism from a very early point (White, Wastell, Broadhurst & Hall, 2010). Adherence to the centrally defined specification was enforced throughout via the publication of increasingly prescriptive 'compliance criteria' elaborated in lengthy documents. Although there was an espoused emphasis on piloting and user involvement (Cleaver, *et al.*, 2008), in reality the design had been highly centralised and only weakly connected with front-line, professional practice. I recently interviewed an individual on the steering group, who commented on its modus operandi as follows. After the first couple of meetings, "it stopped and then, as far as I know, there wasn't any engagement with the operational side". For her, it was clear that the project's agenda had been ideologically pre-defined:

> There were two models, one very outcome focused, which lots of authorities liked, and the DoH one which is much more process driven, part of an inspectorial, regulatory function rather than something to help social workers make good needs assessments and plans to help kids. The word was that authorities which do not use the DoH one will suffer terribly when they're inspected, and were basically warned off. You'll fail your inspection if you don't use this one.

Negative feedback from the field appeared to have had almost no influence. A local ICS project manager, interviewed in our research, commented:

> The forms were too complicated. We spent a lot of time making the forms more user friendly. At that stage it wasn't clear that the forms couldn't be changed. This caused a lot of disappointment- staff thought they were shaping things. We kept telling them that the forms aren't user friendly. If they said, let's set up a group to look at that, then at least we'd feel listened to. But they don't – they just say it can't be changed.

There were in fact unmistakable symptoms of practitioner disquiet in the early pilot studies of the ICS, carried out by the academic team involved in its design. But these adverse reactions were dismissed as 'teething problems', mainly to be addressed through improved training. The language of the team was relentlessly that of implementation not design, and when things went wrong, unreliable IT, inefficient local authorities, or "confused practitioners" were to blame. Reporting their findings, they note that:

> ...although the change from hand-written to electronic recording will increase the time spent using IT, the findings suggest that practitioners' resentment to the change owes much to unresolved problems with IT systems and the unfamiliarity with new systems (Cleaver et al., 2008, p.177).

The following quote is particularly revealing, giving some sense of the pre-conceived worldview of the ICS team. From their point of view, failure to follow basic procedures, of recording and assessment in particular, is the root cause of all the ills of practice:

> *...the Integrated Children's System was developed in response to the findings from research, inspections and inquiry reports that highlighted weakness in practice in a number of key areas, including recording, assessment, planning and review. The recent report into the death of Victoria Climbié stressed the failure of practitioners and managers to carry out basic practice tasks* (Cleaver, et al., 2008, p.35).

Despite the negative feedback greeting its initial deployment in pilot sites, the roll-out of the ICS on a national basis commenced in early 2007. A thorough independent evaluation was carried out by an academic team based at the University of York (Shaw, *et al.*, 2009). Though expressed in careful, diplomatic language, its conclusion was stark:

> *...national IT projects such as the Integrated Children's System have often been poorly planned and actually create more difficulties for social workers than they solve, as well as diverting attention away from professional approaches to meeting the needs of children and families. We agree. ICS is promising and well-intentioned but has not shown it is fit for purpose. Its problems must be addressed* (Bell, 2008).

A similar conclusion was drawn by the Government's *Lifting the Burden's* Task Force Review early in 2008, which commented that: "[the] Integrated Children's System (ICS) moves the focus of activity towards compliance with a standardised system and away from using effective professional approaches and analysis related to meeting the needs of the client family and child" (Frater, 2008, p.9).

Despite all this criticism, the DCSF took no action to review or adapt the ICS, until six months into the deliberations of the Social Work Task Force mentioned in the chapter's opening paragraph. Nearly 3 years since its national roll-out, the shortcomings of the ICS were finally acknowledged.[6] A circular to local authorities in June 2009 announced that a fundamental review of its design was underway (Department for Children Schools and Families, 2009). The final report of the Task Force, published in December 2009, proclaimed a whole-hearted endorsement of the need for change

---

6   A survey instigated by the Task Force showed just how bad it was. Social workers were asked to indicate their level of agreement on a scale from 0 (strongly disagree) to 5 (strongly agree) with a set of statements. 369 responses were received. Asked whether the ICS enabled "safer and more thorough practice than previous paper-based recording", the level of disagreement was striking (average = 0.7). Even more so for the assertion that the ICS provided "outputs that are understandable by children, young people and families"; for this, the average score (0.3) showed strong disagreement to be almost unanimous.

(Gibb, 2009). It urged both the DCSF and local authorities "to continue to improve the ICS by… making ICS more straightforward and effective for frontline social workers in children's services" (p.10). In the months that followed, there were optimistic signs that the new design spirit was paying off. In a working group set up by one of the suppliers (which we attended) a social worker observed that the participative approach had produced "very much simpler and easy to read forms based on a family approach". Early feedback from staff using the redesigned forms in real situations was also encouraging, as affirmed by a senior manager at the same meeting:

> This is a joy to read! I've spent far too long reading ICS assessments where I'm no clearer at the end of the document as I was at the beginning what the issues were. I really think we are on the right track.

Theoretical interlude

> Practice without theory is blind. Theory without practice is sterile – Karl Marx

> There's nothing so practical as a good theory – Kurt Lewin

A key theme of this book is the integral relationship between design and another important new trend, namely the need for management, like any other form of professional activity, to be informed by evidence and research, and to be supported by a body of relevant theory. We shall consider evidence-based management (EBM) in depth in Chapter 3, but we have a natural opportunity here for a preliminary foray. We have a concrete case to dissect and it is pertinent to ask what the knowledge-base of academic research has to say about the ICS debacle. Is there a relevant body of research, what insights and explanations does it offer and what practical advice does it provide? I am pleased to report positive answers on all counts and that "academic", unlike its colloquial usage, can actually mean "quite useful really". A considerable body of germane research exists in my home field of information systems (IS) and I shall make a cursory synopsis of some key results and concepts in this section.

First, some definitions. In the opening section, I averred that systems design should be the primary managerial task. 'System' in its everyday usage elides a range of meanings,[7] but here, I have a very specific meaning in mind. By 'system', I mean 'the work system', defined by Alter (an IS scholar) as:

---

7   Often expressing some form of frustration! If a computer is anywhere in sight, and the term 'system' is invoked, it is often taken to mean 'the computer'. But in other contexts, it has a much wider connotation. Often it is used to refer to the some organisational procedure, such as the 'expenses system', or indeed the organisation as a whole. Sometimes it may refer to a body of ideas, or an institution (e.g. social work) and at the largest scale it provides a handy way of designating macro-structures, such as 'the economy' or 'the political system'.

...a system in which human participants and/or machines perform work (processes and activities) using information, technology, and other resources to produce specific products and/or services for specific internal or external customers (Alter, 2008, p.451).

In the remainder of this book, this is my default meaning for 'system'. The definition is important, especially given the vernacular ambiguity of the signifier's meaning. Often 'system' is used to denote the computer. Such conflation of the artefact with the wider system in which it is embedded is common and certainly applies when the ICS is mentioned. Not only in the everyday small talk of practitioners but in policy discourse too, the mention of ICS is taken as a reference to the artefact. Typically in modern organisations, 'work systems' will include IT components, indeed IT is often an integral part, as it was for the ICS. But the ICS is much more than a computer system; it is an all-pervasive system of work. With this larger definition in mind, it should now be clear that when I speak of managers as 'system designers' it is the work system that I have in mind; this is the proper province of the design-minded manager. I hope it is also clear why I assert this to be the manager's primary task, i.e. to configure the work-system under their jurisdiction as efficiently and effectively as possible. What else could 'management' possibly mean?

Alter goes on to distinguish a special subclass of work system, the "IT reliant work system", defined as "work systems whose efficient and/or effective operation depends on the use of IT" (Alter, 2003, p.366). He argues that the core business of the IS field should be the design of such systems, rather than the artefact itself – a position with which I broadly concur.[8] The ICS is certainly an "IT reliant work system"; moreover, its problematics would be no surprise to an IS scholar: research on the ubiquity of IS failure reaches back over 25 years to the classic papers of Markus (1983) and others, and failure rates as high as 80% have been reported at one time or another (e.g. Wastell, 1999). Failure is, of course, a complex issue; it may manifest itself in a variety of ways (Beynon-Davies, 2009): technical failure (poor usability), defective project management (cost and time over-runs), organisational failure (unrealised benefits)[9]. McMaster & Wastell (2004) further argue that the labels success and failure are often attributed over-

---

8   I adopt a wider view of IT than Alter, encompassing paper-based as well as computer-based information systems (Wastell, 2010), and indeed any other technology which can be used to record data (clay tablets, the Incan quipu etc.). So defined, all work systems are IT reliant as information is essential to the effective functioning of any form of organisation, large or small. Alter's sub-category is therefore redundant. This avoids the obvious danger of introducing a technically-specialised category of work system which managers might see as outwith their responsibility.

9   Beynon-Davies (2009) further distinguishes 'development failures' (pre-implementation problems) from 'use failures', i.e. implemented systems which are rejected as not fit for purpose.

simplistically; failure, like beauty, is in the eye of the beholder. What may be a resounding success for some, may be seen quite differently by others in the organisation. Larsen & Myers (2000) provide an example of an IT initiative in a financial services firm; accounts of its outcome critically depended on who was telling the story and they were more political declarations than statements of fact. Another example is recounted by Irani *et al.* (2001), whereby the initial vicissitudes of a major IT project in a manufacturing company ultimately paved the way for a successful in-house development.[10]

Although there are all too many 'atrocity stories' in the research literature, there are also instructive examples of success. Much IS research has inevitably sought to tease out the 'critical success factors', which, if followed, will predispose projects to achieve the desired benefits. A strong consensus has emerged, which I have attempted to summarise in Table 1. This draws on the well-known text-book of Laudon & Laudon (2004) on Management Information Systems and the influential *Chaos Report* produced every few years by the Standish Group, a respected US project management consultancy. Table 1 shows that there is a high level of accord regarding the success factors. They are predominantly managerial prerogatives, not technical ones, which indicates that the pervasiveness of IS failure reflects, at bottom, deficiencies of management. There is general agreement that users must be engaged in the development of systems and that strong commitment from the apex of the organisation is also required. Project characteristics are also important: larger projects are intrinsically riskier than less ambitious endeavours, whereas well-structured projects (clear objectives and basic requirements) are more likely to end happily. Strong project management is also an important predisposing factor. Of course, like any generalisations, there are exceptions and nuances, and certainly no guarantees[11]. User-centred methods, for instance, do not automatically produce success; indeed there is evidence that in some conditions they can hamper design work and engender less innovation (Heinbokel *et al.*, 1996).

---

10 McMaster & Wastell (2004) provide a similar example of a benighted project creating the organisation learning which enabled innovation to flourish in the aftermath. They also tell the story of another initiative which, though finally abandoned, had improved efficiency by 15% merely as a result of the efforts to implement it! Importantly, these various papers highlight the paradoxical relation of failure to design, of its germinal power to drive invention. Petroski observes for engineering in general: "Good design always takes failure into account and strives to minimise it... Given the faults of human nature, it behoves us to beware the lure of success and to listen to the lessons of failure (Petroski, 2006, p.193)."

11 Statistically, there is strong research evidence for some of these factors. For user involvement, the meta-study of Hwang & Thorn (1999) found an average correlation of 0.61 with system success.

Laudon and Laudon (2004), top 4	CHAOS top 8[12]
User involvement	User involvement
Senior management support	Senior executive support
Level of complexity/risk:	Minimised scope
• Project size	Clear business objectives
• Project structure	Firm basic requirements
• Experience with technology	Standard software infrastructure
Management of the implementation process	Formal methodology and reliable estimates
	Experienced project manager

Table 1: Critical Success Factors for Information System Development

Despite such long-standing consensus, the failure rate of IS initiatives remains stubbornly high. The ICS is one example and others are easy to find. In the UK, for example, the tribulations of the current NHS computerisation mega-project ('Connecting for Health') have been well-chronicled (Eason, 2007). Shaw, *et al.* (2009, p.10) report a survey by the British Computer Society which found that only 130 IT projects out of 1,027 were delivered on time, within cost and to specification. They remark that "computerised systems are more likely to have problems if they are ambitious and complex, and if they fail to engage their users or understand their needs". There is therefore nothing new in the miscarriage of the ICS for the IS onlooker, an old story indeed: "Another failed project, and all the critical failure factors are there: disengaged senior management, excluded users, weak project management, and so on" (Wastell 2010, p.427). Had the IS evidence-base been consulted, and acted upon, would a different outcome have ensued? There is no guarantee, of course, but events might well have turned out much better had such ideas been appreciated and informed the practice of key decision-makers. The real tragedy is not that these precepts were not heeded or not known; it seems no attempt was made even to look – not the merest glimmerings of an evidence-based approach. Instead, technology appears to have been seen as a 'magic bullet'. In this respect, the ICS is by no means unique, rather the opposite. Markus & Benjamin (1997) argue that such blind faith in technology is the predominant mindset amongst managers and executives.

Pursuing a little further this theoretical excursus, another relevant body of scholarship heaves into view, on the phenomenon of project escalation (Keil, 1995). Defining escalation (p.422) as "the continued commitment

---

12   Standish Group International (2001). Extreme Chaos.

of resources in the face of negative information", Keil identifies large-scale, long-term projects promising high pay-offs as the most vulnerable. Psychologically, the degree to which key actors feel a strong personal sense of responsibility and emotional attachment can be dangerous, igniting the reckless impulse to press forward with even greater ardour when difficulties arise. Other risk factors include the degree to which powerful external stakeholders have been led to expect success, the degree of political support for the project and the laxity of management controls. The ICS is a story of 'escalating commitment' if ever there were one! Many of Keil's (1995) noxious ingredients are there. To name a few: a "large scale, long-term project promising high pay-off", extreme emotional "over-attachment" causing negative feedback to be discounted, the impulse to continue at all costs and the general looseness of management controls. Keil offers his framework as a risk-management tool-kit for detecting and pre-empting escalation. It is hard not to see the ICS as a classic case of escalation and to lament that it was not subject to the sort of critical review that Keil recommends. If only he had been there! But he wasn't, nor sadly was his scholarship.

Other theoretical ideas are also relevant. Systems thinking, I have said, is part of the DNA of this book and systems concepts can offer useful insights into the problematics of the ICS, especially regarding the nature and management of human error. Reason (2000) argues that the analysis of errors in organisational settings should focus on general systemic weaknesses, rather than mistakes made by particular individuals on particular occasions. Through its imposition of a rigid work-flow in particular, the ICS exacerbated such "latent conditions for error", making failure more not less likely (Broadhurst, Wastell & White, 2010). Another core systems concept is the Law of Requisite Variety (Wastell, White & Broadhurst, 2010). The variety of a system is simply the number of states it can be in. Pithily the Law proclaims "Only variety absorbs variety"; in other words, the variety of the controller of a process must be such as to handle effectively the variety of the process under its control. In systems terms, the curbing of professional discretion through electronically-enacted administrative control had effected a reduction in variety. Such discretion is essential in order to get the job done especially in the public services, as the situations faced by workers "are too complex to reduce to prescribed responses" (Lipski, 1980)[13]. The implications of such over-specification for safety are made stark in Weick's classic paper on the design of "high

---

13　Making the point differently, Argyris argues that organisations are designed to achieve certain objectives, but that no *a priori* design will cover all the "specifics and uniqueness of the concrete". The specification of jobs and roles should be done as thoroughly as possible "without the specifications being so complete that they immobilize performance" (Argyris, 1999, p.54).

reliability" systems; failures inevitably occur when "the variety that exists in the system to be managed exceeds the variety in the people who must regulate it" (Weick, 1987, p.124).

An important tension is brought to the fore by the cautionary tale of the ICS, namely the tension between process and practice. By 'process', I mean a formal set of steps, often rather linear in character, whereby some output is produced; the ICS 'process model' in Figure 1 provides an example.[14] 'Practice', by contrast, refers to the activity of getting the work done, the artful performance of a craft (Wenger, 2004). Ethnographic studies have shown time and again that even work which seems highly routine is a skilled accomplishment (Gasser, 1986; Wenger, 2004); its orderliness is a product of the artful worker, not determined by the procedure manual. It is a fundamental fallacy to see process as determining practice, rather it is the artistry of practitioners, expertly negotiating situated contingencies, which produces the seeming orderliness of process. 'Working to rule' is not normally seen as a maxim for efficient performance: rules have no agency or ingenuity; it is people that make the rules work!

In the design of the ICS, process dominates all, and its calamitous impact highlights the peril of privileging process over practice, a critical error in the context of design. But we have been here before. Over ten years ago, I wrote somewhat portentously of the failure of an attempt to introduce work-flow technology to automate the seemingly simple processes of a computer help-desk in an organisation known pseudonymously as "Orchid Systems" (Wastell, 1999, p.193-4):

> ...*processes were seen as routine, recurrent activities that take inputs and produce outputs in a largely mechanical way... The study in Orchid confirms the findings of other ethnographic studies in revealing that even routine work, which appears on the surface to be mundane and procedural, involves a considerable amount of extemporisation and problem-solving which is rendered invisible in formal process models. This hidden work has been referred to as articulation*[15].

I shall conclude this interlude with another spectacular example of the failure of the 'process paradigm', this time in the private sector. In 1997, one of my PhD students (David Martin) undertook an ethnographic evaluation of a computer system 'supporting' mortgage selling in a UK financial services organisation, to be known as Blighty Bank (Martin, 2000). The aim

---

14 I've coined the portmanteau word "dystopiary" to designate the sort of nightmare world produced by such zeal for geometrical orderliness, amalgamating dystopia non-obviously with topiary (taming the wildness of natural organic growth in neat artificial figures).

15 A term taken from Gasser (1986).

of the project was to create a new mortgage interview application (MIA) ensuring that 'proper' process was followed with the hope that this would lead to time and labour savings and a higher conversion rate of potential clients to actual customers. Blighty wished to develop a tailor-made solution and engaged an international software house to produce the software. To design the MIA, a model of the ideal mortgage interview process was produced by a small team of mortgage interviewers. The specification for MIA was written, and then signed over to the software engineers.

The original date for implementation was Spring 1997, but due to a range of severe performance and usability problems it was not until late 1998 that the MIA was ready for roll out to the whole branch network. Typical problems included: repeated questions (which in the paper-based process could be skipped) and slow recovery from procedural errors. The situation was eerily reminiscent of the ICS: far from expediting the interview process, MIA had disrupted and elongated it. Passing the original delivery date, commercial pressures began to tell. At one point, 20 staff from the software house were working on the project in a desperate effort to bring it to completion; originally, delivery in 6 months had been expected by a much smaller team. Approaching final implementation nearly two years late, there came a final blow, in the form of new regulations for interviews from the Council of Mortgage Lenders coming into force. The impossibility of easily adapting the MIA to incorporate the new rules, led to the abandonment of the project. The project manager 'left', and a trouble-shooter was called in, who graphically described MIA as: "corporate haemorrhage of £17.6 million for Blighty"!

Martin concluded that once again we have further evidence that "representations of work do not capture the actual activity of work", and that if the design of software is based solely on such models it is "likely to conflict with the normal achievement of that work". He went on as below, making the case for the sort of ethnographic engagement seen in our ICS research as an indispensable design tool, a key point to which I will return in later chapters:

> Unfortunately the understanding of work was not properly contextualised and did not take into account the fact that mortgage interviewing is a flexible process structured from within, on an interview-by-interview basis. Therefore once again the call is for studies of the real-time detail of actual work to be part of the system design process[16].

So ends the blight of Blighty! Having made the case for research and evidence in the context of design, especially for an ethnographically informed understanding of practice, let us return to the real world of social work.

---

16 Quoted from the concluding paragraph of Chapter 4 of Martin (2000).

Paradise regained: there is an alternative

In this section, I offer an antidote to the tragicomedy of the ICS, a heroic tale of managers stepping up to the plate and taking control of design and innovation. As a rhetorical device, I have combined two local authorities, which are outstanding in complementary areas; not a utopia, but the best of two worlds. This literary artifice allows me to illustrate many of the key areas of managerial practice which form the core subject-matter of this book, as it would be difficult to find all the required ingredients in a single case.[17] Although fictitious, all the events described are based on real ones; the various quotations are unadulterated, paraphrasing genuine comments made in interviews with key personnel in the two real cases. The name for the fictitious local authority is Erewhon, from Samuel Butler's satire.

The story starts in 2005 with the appointment of Jean Wise (JW) as Head of Children's Services in Erewhon. Erewhon historically had a poor record across the board as a local authority with a number of services deemed to be failing (on 'special measures') including children's services. However, performance had picked up, with a grading of 'adequate' on a recent inspection. JW felt she was taking over a service which had achieved considerable improvement and had the capacity to improve more. However, all was not well, as she recalled:

> *I spent a lot of time going around places, like courts… I had judges saying things like, "Your social workers can't put a decent argument together". Front line practice was terrible. What had happened was that they were chasing government targets. These mainly measure whether you have done something in a particular time, not if what you did was good. We were playing the game with inspection.*

Of particular concern was the flight of good staff, increasingly overloaded by having to compensate for less competent colleagues and weighed down by petty bureaucracy:

> *I recall a conversation with one who I knew quite well. "I'm going", she said, "I've just spent a week in court getting us out of a mess with an adoption case and I got a note from my manager saying please tidy your desk. It's against council policy to have an untidy desk!"*

More and more agency staff were being recruited as a result, compounding further the vicious circle of disaffection and declining standards. The need for action was urgent:

---

17   In producing this pastiche, efforts have been made to modify circumstantial details in order to provide a complete disguise: "the events and characters depicted herein are fictitious and any similarity to actual persons, living or dead, or to actual events is purely coincidental"!

We had been looking for incremental improvements, but a more radical approach was needed. We needed to listen to what social workers were saying which was that they were being over-managed in the wrong areas with too much bureaucracy. That was the beginning of us thinking about a new way of delivering children's social care.

Erewhon's change programme was radical, addressing both new structures and new technology. The approach to the former was particularly noteworthy; it was based on the concept of 'the social work cell', which represented a fundamental break with the traditional structure of "the team manager and seven social workers". JW remarked that the latter:

…was always problematic because your best workers always became team managers, and the team managers always took all the decisions, but they didn't always know about the families. That's how we came up with the idea of the small social work Cell, led by a senior social worker, who like a medical consultant would be responsible for all the cases in the Cell, and we'd expect them to know the families.

As well as the cellular structure, there were other important changes in professional practice. A number of systemically-trained therapists were recruited who worked along-side the social workers. If the social worker was struggling with a case, they would come in, particularly at the point where "a family could be fixed so a teenager didn't need to come into care" (JW). Highly skilled family support was thus in place and the need to keep children with their families was pushed. To implement the new model though, drastic action was required to 'up-skill' the workforce. The need for first-class people was critical, as JW commented:

Most of what I spent my time doing was an elongated recruitment process. The final bit was the panel which I always chaired. We were ruthless. We let no-one in who we weren't sure about. Sometimes it was difficult to hold on to this as we were desperate, and I'm sure a few false negatives were made, but we were really cautious.

Although the large number of agency staff gave some easy ground for flexibility, the HR challenges were formidable. The Head of HR commented: "There was a huge HR process to manage, or we'd end up with the whole workforce against us. We had to be artful in using HR policies to achieve what we needed to achieve". With the completion of the programme eighteen months later, only 3 of the original managers and 8 social workers remained; it had been 'continual revolution'.

Parallel developments on the IT side are of interest, especially in the light of our ICS parable. The Head of IT begins this strand of the story:

> *We had a history here of home-grown IT. We had implemented our first IT system in 1999. It was document-based, using Lotus Notes. People liked the forms, but we needed a different platform using Microsoft software. It was a good system so ICS had to be an improvement.*

Taking up the story, JW observed:

> *We saw ICS as an opportunity to improve recording. Our aim was to enhance the ICS concept to make it into a good practice tool. We wanted a more narrative approach to recording, challenging the tick-boxes. The key thing was to have a report that families could understand. You need to be able to see the child in the context of the family. We wanted social workers to use the tool, something that aided analysis.*

An intensive user-centred approach was instigated to develop an in-house solution, given that no suitable commercial offering could be found. The core design team involved two practice representatives and two dedicated business analysts. A series of user workshops were also held. Tensions with the DCSF were inevitable, ultimately forcing Erewhon to withdraw from the ICS compliance regime in late 2008, losing significant funding. The sense of frustration at the repeated failure of attempts at constructive dialogue comes over strongly in the following Council minute, recording its decision to declare independence. Paraphrasing:

> *The Borough's approach differed from the Government's in our avoidance of a simple tick box approach to assessment. These differences were communicated at the time work was started. Although the Council has continued to engage with the DCSF, over the last 2 years, the DCSF's position has increasingly emphasised the need to meet detailed and extensive requirements in order to receive grant funding.*

The bespoke system, known as MyICS, has been a notable success, ultimately winning a national e-Government award, and other authorities are interested in adopting it. One social worker in Erewhon remarked "It's brilliant... it was designed in-house, and if you want anything changed, it doesn't take 6 months". The Council minute quoted above ran on as follows:

> *The system has been extremely well received by practitioners and many social work recruits have commented favourably on it in comparison with those systems used elsewhere which are difficult to use, time consuming and overly prescriptive.*

Resuming the main narrative, has the root and branch redesign work in Erewhon been successful? In terms of the all-important Ofsted audits, Erewhon has made significant progress and in 2009 was deemed to be "performing well". Here is JW again, positive but modestly circumspect, speaking in early 2010:

> *How do we know we're doing well? That's a good question. You struggle with what a good outcome is. It's complex. You've got proxies though, like the number of children who stay with their families. Having falling numbers of Looked After Children is good. You listen to what families and schools and the courts say, and you put together the bits of evidence... And you listen to what social workers say they're doing with families, and you say we're doing well here... We came up with a complete service redesign and now have social workers who want to work here.*

Technomagic

> *The transporting of the log is not an easy task... the natives resort to a magical rite which makes the canoe lighter. The builder beats the log with a bunch of dry lalang grass and utters the following spell: "Come down, rot! Come down fungus..." invoking a number of deteriorations to leave the log... the heaviness and slowness due to all these magical causes are thrown out of the log* (Malinowski, 1932, p.129).

I noted above that a common failing of managers is to see technology as a magic bullet. I will develop this point here in relation to the ICS, before going on to proffer my remedy for such a magical attitude. Although seeming opposites, technology and magic have formally much in common, as sociologists from Mauss (writing at the turn of the century) to Stivers (2001) have noted. Both are instrumental, involving the deployment of a body of practical skill and knowledge to accomplish something of social value (Mauss, 2001). The difference lies in the link between cause and effect. Whereas magic produces its effects entirely through performance, as illustrated by the so-called 'primitive' rituals of the Melanesian canoe-builders, technology accomplishes its results through direct, physical causes. Or does it? In the case of machines, such as the steam engine, yes – there is nothing magical here about cause and effect (at least to us 'moderns'!). But the metaphor of the steam engine is not a good one for so many of the technical systems of today's world. The implementation of IT will in itself not guarantee the desired outcome, however devoutly such a consummation is wished. The computer may be a machine, but the work system in which it is embedded is emphatically not, as we have seen a fortiori with the ICS.

In this second digression, I shall argue that our faith in the instrumental efficacy of technology in an increasingly complex and technologically-mediated world would seem to have much more in common with the ritualised magic of the canoe-builder beating the log with a bunch of dry lalang grass than we would like to think. The difference is only that *we* try to change the world by writing a software program or a policy document which embodies a normative idealisation of how the world should be. If magic reflects the belief that the observance of certain rites, the muttering of incantations, the avoidance of taboos and so forth, will in and of itself produce desired effects, then magic is very much a feature of the mindset of the modern world, especially the world of public policy and of business. We may not be so modern after all!

The sociology of magic

To assist in our task, let us commence with a theoretical excursion, summarising magic's key elements from Mauss's seminal treatise on magic, first published in 1902 (Mauss, 2001). For Mauss, magic is first and foremost a social phenomenon. Magic needs believers! Magicians in all societies are creatures of public opinion; their power is not an intrinsic potency, but is socially constructed by a credulous community in order to accomplish those 'outcomes' that the society seeks, bringing rain, curing illness, ensuring protection and safety. In crude terms, the magical way of problem-solving is to identify a magician with the power to solve the problems, hand over control, participate in the magical methodology, and "hey presto"!

Mauss stresses that magic in any era is always practical,[18] aimed at the achievement of change; it happens in special places, marked off physically and socially, and psychologically too (demonic possession, catalepsy, etc.). The mechanical observance of rites, both non-verbal and verbal, is fundamental, as is the role of representations (e.g. effigies, arcane diagrams, etc.) which may be abstract or concrete. Verbal rites include spells and incantations, aimed at summoning up the required supernatural forces, to achieve the desired effect. All is carefully prescribed. Mere performance of the routine is sufficient, as shown by the formulaic nature of the rites; incantations can be quite inaudible and unintelligible: enactment is all. "Between a wish and its fulfilment, in magic, there is no gap (*ibid.,* p.78)". Magical causality works by the transfer of properties via "secret sympathy… the impulse being transmitted from one to the other by what we may conceive of as an invisible ether" (Frazer, 1922, p.16). Any association of ideas would appear to suffice (even apparent opposites), e.g.

---

18 Having noted the formal resemblance of technology and magic, Mauss goes on to develop the genealogical link between the two. He argues that magic originally created the conditions for the emergence of techniques, fostering their embryonic development by endowing authority and efficacy to the efforts of early craftsmen.

the use by the Cherokee Indians of a yellow root to cure jaundice.[19] This sympathy can be imitative (the law of similarity), e.g. symbolically enacting a cure effects that cure. Alternatively, the nexus may be contagious (the law of contact), exemplified by the widespread superstition that harm may be done to an individual through damaging any severed element of that person (hair, nails etc.).

A key characteristic of magic is its incorrigible nature and the unreflective behaviour of its adherents:

> *Magic has such authority that a contrary experience does not destroy a person's belief. Even the most unfavourable facts can be turned to magic's advantage, since they can always be held to result from an error in performance of the ritual… Fortuitous coincidences are accepted as normal facts and all contradictory evidence is denied* (Mauss, 2001, pp.114-5).

Magical thinking and the ICS

Magic is defined by the accomplishment of effects, typically remotely, by the mere performance of the rite and the articulation of the spell, which specify directly or symbolically the desired change-of-state. The language of magic has an incantatory quality. The policy discourse of the ICS has much this same character. Let us examine again the opening paragraph of the first ICS briefing paper mentioned above, which sets out its core credo:

> *The Integrated Children's System will provide an assessment, planning, intervention and reviewing model for all children in need under the Children Act 1989. The Integrated Children's System is designed to ensure that assessment, planning and decision-making leads to good outcomes for children. This approach reflects a holistic understanding of children's developmental needs and the capacities of their parents, a coherent process which is focused on bringing about optimal outcomes for children* (Department of Health, 2000b, p.1).

There is no room for scepticism here, only absolute certainty and relentless positivity. The phrases "will provide" and "designed to ensure" exemplify this. There is no doubt in the minds of the ICS's architects that the implementation of their system will necessarily bring about the effects ("improved outcomes") which they seek. As I have argued elsewhere, at no point is there a carefully worked out, empirically-grounded, cause-effect argument for the benefits for ICS (Wastell & White, 2010). Instead, we have a dogma founded on an unshakeable belief that, by setting targets,

---

19   In herbalism, the doctrine of signatures provides a well-known generalisation of this principle.

monitoring performance indicators and enforcing rigorous assessment procedures, policy objectives set out in the same terms, and embodying the same internal logic, will inevitably be achieved.

One ingredient of the remedy for such magical thinking, I shall argue, is empirical evidence. To be sure, evidence is invoked by the ICS's progenitors, but with important differences. Fundamental to the ICS is its incorporation of a comprehensive new Assessment Framework, an "assessment planning intervention and reviewing model for all children in need".

> *The evidence-based knowledge that has informed the development of the Framework has been drawn from a wide range of research studies about the needs of children* (Department of Health, 2000a, p.42).

The reference to the "evidence-base" is actually risible. On closer inspection, this is revealed to be somewhat flimsy, comprising only 4 studies all without the hall-mark of academic peer review (Seden *et al.*, 2001). The first is a literature review making some general conclusions regarding assessment; the second is an interview study of the language used by social workers to describe children's needs (carried out by Department of Health officials, with no list of references); the third is a case study of assessment procedures by a team of inspectors, and the final chapter cursorily reviews findings about assessment procedures by the Social Services Inspectorate. Although the evidence-base is ritually invoked, rigorous argument, critical analysis and robust research are conspicuous by their absence. For the time-scales in particular, no empirical justification has ever been produced, not even the crudest time-and-motion study.

We have noted that a defining feature of magic is its 'incorrigibility' and the uncritical orientation of its votaries. We saw much the same in our research on the ICS. Requests to change anything were routinely ignored and nothing was ever wrong with its design; all problems were entirely attributed to implementation, just as the failed spell is blamed not on the magic itself but on the way the ceremony was performed, or some other procedural flaw (Wastell & White, 2010). The magic itself is never questioned: "The Integrated Children's System is designed to ensure that assessment, planning and decision-making lead to good outcomes for children", and ensure it will! Indeed the faith of its proponents waxed ever stronger as the tide of resistance swelled. In response to the York Report mentioned above, which damningly concluded that the ICS "has not shown it is fit for purpose" (Bell, 2008), the DCSF responded that the research was predicated on:

> *…participating local authorities' commitment to implement the ICS fully. There were, however, significant delays in the implementation process. By*

the conclusion of the evaluation the ICS had only been fully implemented in one of the sites… [therefore] the research does not provide a sound basis on which to judge the potential value of the ICS. Instead the study provides an informed assessment of the challenges which need to be overcome if this potential is to be realised (DCSF, 2008, pp.2-3).

The quote gives a strong, chilling sense of the indefeasible, circular reasoning so clearly associated by Mauss with the world of magic.[20] Ingeniously, not only are the vicissitudes of the ICS reinterpreted as implementation challenges, but these same tribulations are invoked to undermine the evaluation itself; an incorrigible but fatally deluded position. Belief in the efficacy of the magic is strengthened, paradoxically, by its very failure.

How then does technology produce its magic effects? Herein, the resonance with the mechanisms of magic is especially striking. It is as if the material properties of technology to yield material effects through efficient causes (the steam engine or indeed the computer program) are magically transferred into the social realm through the spell-like incantations of policy and the sympathetic mechanisms of both similarity and contagion. The ICS process model, presented as a flow chart with deterministic links, looks just like the blueprint for a machine; magically, the software-mediated regime thus acquires the mechanical efficacy of its material counterpart. Or so the wishful thinking goes. The sympathetic effects of technology are doubled up by the actual physical presence of computers within the workplace. As a "finite state machine", given certain inputs the computer guarantees prescribed outputs. Magically, these properties of perfect reliability will be passed on by contagion to the fallible humans who also inhabit this world.

Design – the rescue remedy

Today, what we explicitly dub magic is a form of light entertainment, which no sane person would take seriously, and has no pernicious consequences. Sadly, the same cannot be said of technomagic; ask any front-line social worker! What is to be done? Fortunately, a remedy is at hand. This book argues that the antidote to technomagic lies in a fundamental shift in the managerial mindset: away from monitoring and control, towards design. Integral to this shift is a different relationship with technology. I argue that managers need to see their main business as the designers of the workplace, of the system of work, a role in which technology has a vital part to play, as the instrument of innovation. The idea of "managing as designing" has gained some ground recently, as we shall see in the next

---

20   Memorably dubbed "oracular reasoning" by Mehan (1999).

chapter, although it is still rather an exotic notion. By design, I simply mean the creation of form, the translation of concepts and aspirations into concrete working realisations. In an organisational context, this means the design of systems made up of people, processes and technology in order to achieve the functions desired by the organisation in the service of its customers and clients. Put in more prosaic terms, it means finding the best way of organising the workplace. If this is not the primary business of management, then what on earth is?

Doing design well depends on our attitude to technology. A magical attitude will not do. Hard work is required and authentic engagement; technology is too important to leave to others. Brown & Hagel (2003) contend that the productivity paradox, the dissociation between investments in technology and actual benefits, reflects the failure of many organisations to use technology to innovate their business practices: "Companies that mechanically insert IT into their businesses ... will only destroy IT's economic value. Unfortunately, all too many companies do this" (p.2). Tellingly, those organisations which stand out in terms of the business value generated by IT are those which emphasise its innovative potential and have retained their in-house design capability, rather than relying on packed software or outsourcing. Sadly the opposite has been the trend in the UK public sector, ideologically powered by government policies such as compulsory competitive tendering (Lin, 2007). Running against the grain are those local authorities that have retained their in-house IT capability. It is significant that they have produced notably successful examples of IT-based innovation. Erewhon is one and Salford is another, as we shall see.

To conclude this chapter, a commercial example counter to the orthodoxy will be presented: Zara, the Spanish-based fashion chain.[21] In an era when clothing retailers outsource much of their manufacturing to developing countries, Zara has taken total corporate control of every part of its business, running its entire global operations (more-or-less) from a headquarters just outside La Coruña in north west Spain, including design, manufacturing and distribution. All its clothing, for instance, is produced locally from a network of small manufacturers. Information systems are critical to the Zara business model, enabling tight integration up and down its supply chain. Every day, store managers report back on what has and has not sold and this information is used to decide which product lines and colours are kept or altered and whether new lines should be created by its design team. A new design can be on the shelves in a matter of days, directly responding to the ephemeral tastes and preferences of customers, and thousands of designs are thus produced in real time over the season.

---

21 To be exact, Zara is part of the Inditex Group.

Costs are kept down by keeping inventories low and avoiding cut-price discounting of poor selling garments.

The story of IT in Zara is told in a much-celebrated Harvard Business School case study, entitled "Zara – IT for fast fashion" (McAfee, Dessain & Sjoman, 2004). I will draw on this study, supplemented by my own findings from a visit in the summer of 2008. Zara itself was founded by Amancio Ortega, with the first store opening in La Coruňa in 1975. At the time of McAfee's case study, Zara's CEO was José Ríos, originally the company's IT manager. McAfee *et al.* cite Ríos as declaiming: "The original business idea was very simple. Link customer demand to manufacturing, and link manufacturing to distribution. That is the idea we still live by" (p.3). Ríos shared Ortega's firm conviction that computers were critically important in enabling the kind of business that they wanted to build. They shared other convictions too:

> Zara needed to be able to respond very quickly to the demands of target customers, who were young, fashion-conscious city dwellers. Their tastes in clothing changed rapidly, were very hard to predict, and were also hard to influence. Zara wanted to be able to deliver such styles while they were still hot, rather than relying on the persuasiveness of its marketing to push clothes it had made some time ago (ibid., p.3).

Not only was IT critical, what was still more remarkable was how much Zara were spending on it. Reading of their success, one might expect they spent more than their rivals. Quite the opposite:[22] IT expenditure actually ran well below their sector average, only 25% at the time of the case study (McAfee *et al*, p.8). Zara had thus achieved the virtuous circle of better business value for lower cost. Part of this success derived from a minimalist attitude to technology, avoiding investment in systems which provided more features than needed. When I questioned Zara's IT manager on the purchase of packaged software from external suppliers, he opined:

> We need to keep things as simple and basic as possible, like we've been doing for 34 years now. It's not "what can we offer you", but "what do we need?". And the cost of packages is very expensive and a lot of time to adapt, which means more money. And then you need them [the suppliers]… you are joined to them. Your fate is joined to them eternally – you can't get out!

---

[22] Wal-Mart provides another rather similar example, characterised by the same combination of innovative in-house development and very low IT expenditure. For more information and illustrative examples see: http://www.informationweek.com/story/showArticle.jhtml?articleID=47902662

This sceptical, conservative attitude was clearly evidenced in the original case study by Zara's continued use of technology which was technically obsolete, principally hand-held Personal Digital Assistants (PDAs), purchased some ten years earlier. The need for their urgent upgrade was high-lighted in the case study report. Also salient was Zara's approach to software development, which was all in-house. Zara had a stable IT department, whose staff were largely recruited from local universities. The IT manager observed in my 2008 interview:

> *We have in-house people who maintain all products. It's a question of the business model – it must be so flexible, reacting all the time – you must understand what is happening or you won't be able to do it… we have tried to do things externally or to purchase applications, but it has not worked out – we need things which fit our specific business model.*

Going against convention and 'doing it yourself' can pay off handsomely, as Zara's continuing growth testifies. Continually updating their IT infrastructure is a key part of this, which recently included replacing the PDAs and developing an integrated system (Terminal Gestión Tienda) covering all aspects of store management, including point-of-sale, re-ordering, store layout and inventory management. Describing Zara's technology transition in 2007,[23] McAfee averred that he had never seen a company whose IT strategy was so well aligned with its business model and yet managed to maintain such control of IT spending. He reaffirmed that it was not technology per se, but the centralised organisational infrastructure that facilitated the speed and the quality of the design process, though the sparse but inventive use of technology continued to play an integral role.

Lest it be suspected, it is no intention of mine to lionise the private over the public sector. There is no evidence that the private sector is better at managing IT than the public; indeed, most of the research literature on IT failure is based on research in commercial organisations and the above-quoted failure rates are thus a dismal reflection of that sector. But private sector failures are just that, private; dirty secrets behind closed doors, unbeknown to shareholders, certainly not appearing in the glossy pages of the Annual Report. Zara's success is a public one, much-bruited, the topic of countless eulogistic MBA essays and class presentations, not unlike this brief account. There are certainly lessons we may profitably take away, not least the need to challenge received wisdom. Zara teaches us that local design and innovation are vital, using technology to effect desirable change, with business managers in the driving seat. Technology is not some "pixie dust… to be sprinkled over problems which then, hey presto, vanish!" (Dowty, 2008, p.398). Dowty also insists that, "the need to abandon

---

23   See McAfee, A., "Fit for purpose IT breeds profits for clothing retailer". *Computer Weekly*, 8th January 2007.

magical thinking is long overdue". Markus and Benjamin also write of the enchantment of technology across all business sectors and the need to break its spell:

> *Many IT-enabled change projects fail, despite how much is known about ensuring success… we have argued that [this] stems from mistaken beliefs about the causes of change – belief in IT as a magic bullet. IT is not a magic bullet. Change in human behavior cannot take place at a distance but requires direct personal contact between change agents and targets… Successful change takes good ideas, skill, and plain hard work – but it does not need magic* (Markus & Benjamin, 1997, pp.66-7).

The combination of "good ideas, skill and plain hard work" provide the antidote to magic; design in other words. But design itself needs to be done non-magically. Techniques for design abound, but again we find the same tendency to see tools and methods as magic potions and elixirs. This book will set out some of these approaches, but they are offered as prostheses which can assist the development of competent professional practice, not as magic bullets. The subject of magic will be deferred for the next few chapters; it will return for further perusal in the book's final section.

CHAPTER 2

MANAGING, DESIGNING AND PUBLIC SECTOR REFORM

*When it was known in Manchester that Mr. Drinkwater had engaged me,
a mere boy without experience, to take the entire direction of this new mill,
the leading people thought he had lost his senses… I at once determined to
do the best I could and began to examine the outline and detail of what was
in progress. I looked grave, inspected everything very minutely, examined
the drawings and the calculations of the machinery. I was in with the first
in the morning, and I locked up the premises at night. I continued this
silent inspection for six weeks… and during that period I did not give
one direct order about anything. But at the end of that time I felt myself
so much master of my position, as to be ready to give directions in every
department.*

The epigraph is from the autobiography of Robert Owen, management
pioneer, successful entrepreneur and social reformer of the early factory
age (Owen, 1967, pp.28-9). At the callow age of 18 (having left the family
home in the Welsh marches to seek fame and fortune in London ten years
previously,[24] in 1778) Owen had audaciously applied to manage a new mill
being established in Manchester, a mill employing the latest manufacturing
technology of the day. How he proceeded as an untutored manager in a
sticky predicament is instructive. Owen clearly saw his pre-eminent goal
as the design of the work system, to find the best way of doing things by
harnessing the new technology of the mill to its fullest potential. Far from
distancing himself from technology, he knew he needed to master it if he
were to be effective as a manager. Equally, and even more importantly,
he knew it was critical to understand thoroughly the organisation he was

---

24   I'm not sure what contemporary social services would have made of his precocious
     ambition or of the 'parenting skills' of his mum and dad, but that's another story.
     Paraphrasing from his autobiography: "Having read much of other countries and other
     proceedings… and not liking the habits and manners of a small country town, I began to
     desire a different field of action, and wished my parents to permit me to go to London.
     I was at this time about nine years and a half old, and at length, although I was a great
     favourite at home, it was promised that when I should attain my tenth year, I should be
     allowed to go" (Owen, 1967, p.9).

freshly steward of, the nature of the work and its employees. How did he proceed? 'Ethnographically' we'd call it in today's terms. Nowadays we appreciate the importance of such ethnography in design, as I have noted; Owen knew it instinctively.

And the strategy paid off handsomely. Owen epitomises designing in the field of management and his performance is a *tour de force*. As a designer, he pulled off, again using the modern argot, a spectacular piece of re-engineering. "I soon perceived the defects in the various processes and improved the quality of our manufacture. In about a year, I had… gained the means to increase the fineness of the finished thread from 120 to upwards of 300 hanks in the pound. I was now known as the first fine cotton spinner in the world" (*ibid.*, p.34-5).

Historical prologue

Owen is not alone amongst the management pioneers in seeing his primary responsibility as design. Many of the early managers were engineers, who naturally saw the design of the workplace as their principal concern. First published over a century ago, F. W. Taylor's *Shop Management* (1903) is, from cover to cover, a book quintessentially about design. Given Taylor's seminal position in the history of management thought as an area of systematically organised knowledge, I shall briefly examine his career before tracing relevant developments which unfolded over the succeeding decades.

Abandoning the promise of a legal career, Taylor was another runaway, but in his case it was the Harvard Law School from which he absconded, taking up an apprenticeship as a machinist with the Enterprise Hydraulic Works of Philadelphia in 1878. This was a life changing experience: "At Enterprise, Taylor developed an empathy for the workers' point of view. He could swear with the best of them and admired their sense of pride in their skill. However, he saw about him what he called bad industrial conditions, worker restriction of output, and lack of harmony between workers and managers" (Wren, 2005, p.122). Moving to Midvale Steel, also in Philadelphia, Taylor rose 'meteorically' from labourer to chief engineer in 6 years. Preoccupied with the practice of 'soldiering' (workers loafing, deliberately doing the minimum), Taylor began to devise his system of Task Management, which we now know as Scientific Management (interestingly, not a term he found congenial). For Taylor, it was the "explicit responsibility of the manager to design the job or task so that the greatest productivity was possible" (Wren, 2005, p.129). In a crucial move, he separated the planning of work from its performance, with the former becoming the responsibility of the celebrated Planning Department.

Other important ideas included the 'functional foreman' (the precursor of today's line manager) and the 'first class man'. The latter is particularly significant in the context of this book: "that there is a difference between the average and the first class man is known to all employers, but that the first class man can do in most cases from two to four times as much is known to few, and is fully realised only by those who have made a thorough and scientific study of the possibilities of men" (Taylor, 1903, p.6). Management's task involved "finding the work for which employees were best suited, to assist them in becoming first-class workers and to provide them with an incentive to do their best" (Wren, 2005, p.128).

Taylor also speaks to the methodology of design, with the 'Time Study' being the outstanding example. Although the subject of much opprobrious comment, the Time Study's insistence on rigorous empiricism (Taylor gives page after page of meticulous, how-to instructions in *Shop Management*) reflects a very clear position on how design work should be done, i.e. that it should be grounded on systematic direct observation rather than fancy, prejudice or ideology. For Taylor, soldiering could only be overcome "by a careful investigation of work that could then be used in setting performance standards: once workers saw that the rate was properly set, they would know it was based on facts not whims and their motivation to soldier would be reduced" (Wren, 2005, p.124).

It was the responsibility of the Planning Department to gather such facts. Taylor elucidates:

> *This information for each particular operation should be obtained by summing up the various unit times of which it consists. To do this, of course, requires the men performing this function to keep continually posted as to the best methods and appliances to use. The actual study of unit times, of course, forms the greater part of the work of the planning room* (Taylor, 1903, p.60).

The aim of the time study was "to predict with accuracy how long it should take a good man to do almost any job in the particular trade" (Taylor, 1903, p.89). Table 2 provides an example of his design methodology in action, for the work of shovelling. First, the task is broken down meticulously into its most minute parts. A formula is then developed which combines these various elements. Direct observation of task performance is then carried out and the values of the parameters are estimated by averaging repeated observations. Using this mathematical model, the time taken for carrying out the shovelling task can then be predicted across the full range of relevant circumstances. In the table, we see the calculation for shifting a cubic yard of sand 50 feet, with the resultant prediction being just short of 30 minutes.

Parameters	Formula
a = time filling a barrow with any material	B= ([a+b+d+f+ (c+e) * distance/100] * 27/L) * (1+P)
b = time preparing to wheel	
c = time wheeling barrow 100 feet	
d = time dumping and returning	Substituting observed values for parameters (minutes):
e = time returning 100 feet with barrow	B = ([a + 0.18 + 0.17 + 0.16 + (0.22 + 0.26)
f = time dropping barrow and starting to shovel	* distance/100] * 27/L) * (1.27)
P = percentage of day for rest & delays	For sand (a = 1.24) in a 2.32 cubic foot barrow over a 50 foot haul, this gives:
L = load of barrow in cubic feet	B = 29.4 minutes
B = time for moving by barrow a cubic yard of material	

Table 2: Example time study results for shovelling

What may we 'moderns' learn from this example of Taylor's design practice? One thing that immediately stands out is his insistence on the need for a 'task model' (i.e. a formal representation of the task), set out here in terms of component sub-tasks. Only when such a rigorous understanding of work has been developed, can measurements be meaningfully made. Emphasising modelling over measurement is important. "You can't manage what you can't measure" is a faddish management ukase. I am sceptical: as the ICS study shows, the act of measuring is apt to give only an illusion of control. I shall return to the critique of measurement in Chapter 3. For now, I offer an alternative formulation, set out in another maxim: 'You can't manage what you can't model; understanding is all'. The second point to note in Table 2, obvious but important, is that Taylor's model is not only empirically grounded, but its predictions always depend on the particular contingencies of the work. For different materials over different distances, different results will be yielded. Again contrasting the design practice of the ICS with that of Taylor, we note another striking difference, namely that time-scales in the former case were not based on any empirical analysis of the actual tasks performed by social workers or appreciation of contingencies. Assessments must always be completed, it will be remembered, in 7 days, irrespective of the complexity of the case, or indeed the experience of the worker. I don't think Taylor would have been impressed!

Moving from his position at Midvale, Taylor ultimately became a 'consulting engineer for management' in 1893. In his subsequent career, he attracted both fame and some notoriety. His methods often provoked controversy and there were confrontations with the labour unions. At one point, a special committee of Congress was set up to investigate a strike that had taken place in August 1911 at the Waterdown Arsenal, where his methods were being deployed. Taylor also became involved in management education and I find his attitude refreshingly sceptical (and pertinent to contemporary debates). When invited to teach Scientific Management at his old school (Harvard), Taylor apparently refused, saying his "system could only be learned in the shop" (Wren, 2005, p.137). He was finally persuaded and taught for 5 years from 1909 to 1914, though apparently refused to take any reimbursement.

Taylor was a man of his times and his methods today are often seen as inhumane and mechanistic. Lazily, for those who have doubtless never read a word of what he actually wrote, Taylorism has come to acquire opprobrious connotations. If Taylor is read, rather than decried, a different, altogether more humane figure emerges. A final quotation from *Shop Management*:

> *The employer who goes through his works with kid gloves on, and talks to his men in a condescending way has no chance whatever of ascertaining their real thoughts or feelings. Above all it is desirable that men should be talked to on their own level by those who are over them. Each man should be encouraged to discuss any trouble which he may have, either in the works or outside... Men would far rather even be blamed by their bosses, than to be passed by day after day without a word, and with no more notice than if they were part of the machinery* (Taylor, 1903, p.100).

Moving on from these early origins, the 'science of management' has burgeoned over the last century. Beginning with the notorious Hawthorne Studies, I shall briefly trace some of these developments as they have pertinence for aspects of my argument.

Controversial these studies certainly were: "no studies in the history of management have received so much publicity, been subjected to so many different interpretations, been as widely praised and thoroughly criticized" (Wren, 2005, p.279). Set in the Hawthorne plant of Western Electric, the Studies, beginning in the summer of 1925, had a modest enough objective: to appraise the effect of workplace illumination on worker productivity. Modest in size too, as groups of only five workers were involved in the initial experiments. The work itself involved the testing of assembled electro-mechanical switches (relays). The experimental group, for whom lighting levels were varied, were set to work, in a separate building from the main workforce. Contrary to expectations, output went up equally regardless of the level of illumination. The experimenters recognised that multiple factors were involved, but whatever features were varied, the trend of productivity moved steadily upwards. Various factors were pin-pointed, including the small group, the type of supervision, increased earnings, the novelty of the experiment (Wren, 2005, p.283).

Harvard professor Elton Mayo visited the Hawthorne plant to help investigate the underlying cause of the improvements. Mayo believed that industrial problems could seldom be explained by single factors, but by "the psychology of the total situation". He clearly saw that the original lighting intervention was of minimal importance: "what the company actually did for the group was to reconstruct its whole industrial situation" (Wren, 2005, p.286). Mayo conclusively identified the greater zest for work and improved morale "to be closely associated with the style of supervision". Interestingly this factor was inadvertent. The original experimenters had engaged closely with the staff in order to gather key experimental data regarding their health and happiness on the job. They were apparently relaxed and empathetic, in stark contrast with the "mean and remote" style of the regular supervisor in the assembly test room.

This linking of supervision, morale and productivity gave birth to the foundation of what became known as the human relations movement in management: "the new supervisor was to be more people-oriented, less aloof, and more skilled in handling social and personal situations" (Wren, 2005, p.287). This movement is important here as it has provided some of the key design ideas which I will review in the next chapter. Early seminal thinking derived from a management theorist, active at the time of Taylor: Mary Parker Follett. Follett's philosophy emphasised groups rather than individuals; her Group Principle argued that the potentialities of individuals remain latent until released by group life and the key requirement of leadership was therefore to bring out these differences and integrate them into a unity (Wren, 2005). Regard for facts and evidence was something Follett admired in Scientific Management and it is epitomised in her 'law of the situation', namely that "one person should not give orders to another person, but both should agree to take their orders from the situation… authority should go with knowledge and experience" (Wren, 2005, p.308). By shifting authority in this way, she believed confrontation and conflict could be avoided, thus achieving unity without friction. For Follett the work of the leader rested on "fact control" not "man control", on controlling situations not people. The leader's job was to define the aims of the organisation, to "make his co-workers see that it is not his purpose to be achieved but a common purpose, born of the desires and activities of the group" (Wren, 2005, p.310).

(Re)enter the manager-as-designer

> *Design rules! Design is about passion, emotion and attachment, and it must be at the heart of every business… Design thinking and systems thinking are one and the same. In great design, form and function come together seamlessly. Every part contributes to the whole in a way that seems inevitable. So too in a great system* (Tom Peters).[25]

What stands out when Owen's performance is compared with the debacle of the ICS is the contrast between design done well and design done ineptly. This is all the more notable given that Owen's managerial feats were accomplished over two hundred years ago, at the inception of management as a profession, and that the intervening period has seen the burgeoning of management science as a vast academic industry. This suggests one unmistakeable message: that we have seemingly learned rather little!

Management as an academic subject represents a diverse range of ideas, differentiated into various distinctive sub-disciplines. 'Organisation design' is one of those areas, itself a sprawling and eclectic field. The reader might be forgiven for expecting this to be a fertile source of ideas for this book, indeed the very existence of such a field would seem to obviate the need for this small volume. Though there are some ideas that we can draw on, this is not the case. This disconnection reflects what Karl Weick called 'the trap' in the phrase 'organisational design', that design can be both noun and verb. It is the former which predominates in practice: "when people in organisations talk about the design of the organisation, they tend to equate it with things like organisational charts… to focus on structures rather than processes" (Weick, 1995, p.348). The vast bulk of theory and research on organisation design shows this same bias, concerning itself with design at the macro level (what structures work in what circumstances) rather than the practical process of designing at the micro level. As Yoo *et al.* note, the orthodox theory of organisation design "offers little help to organisations that need to create novel and unique solutions" (Yoo, Boland & Lyytinen, 2006, p.215). Although a congeries of structures has been proposed over the years, some with tantalisingly exotic names (such as the 'front-back hybrid'), Yoo *et al.* argue that the very idea of choice amongst 'ready-made' alternatives is fundamentally misguided. It loses the idea of design as form-giving: designing an organisation is not like buying an 'off-the-peg' suit!

It is not the place of this book to review this literature, which has been well done by seminal texts such as Daft (2009). The work of a couple of figures in this canon will be highlighted though. One important theorist is Jay Galbraith. Galbraith defines organisation design as "the continuous

---

25   Peters (2005, p.54).

monitoring and assessing of the fit between goals, structures and rewards; the creation and choice of alternative actions when there is no fit; and the implementation of the chosen design" (Galbraith, 1977, p.7). The "design problem" involves finding a coherent solution in three areas: strategy (defining the organisation's objectives); integration of individuals within the organisation (selection, training and rewards); and 'organising mode'.

This last refers to the division of the primary task of the organisation into sub-tasks and their integration into a smoothly functioning whole, through hierarchies of authority, rules, information systems, etc. Task uncertainty is the critical variable here, which Galbraith defines as: "the difference between the amount of information required to perform the task and the amount of information already possessed" (Galbraith, 1977, pp.36-7). Various strategies are available to cope with task uncertainty including managing the environment to reduce uncertainty and the reduction of levels of required performance to create "slack resources". More fundamental changes could also be considered, such as shifting from specialised functional structures to self-contained units. In general, as uncertainty increases, "fewer situations can be programmed in advance and more exceptions arise which must be referred up the hierarchy" (Galbraith, 1977, p.44). To avoid over-loading the hierarchy, discretion at the point of action must be increased, through "professionalisation" of the workforce, shifting from "control based on supervision and surveillance to control based on the selection of responsible workers" (Galbraith, 1977, p.45). Sadly, the architects of the ICS seem not to have appreciated these fundamental theoretical precepts of organisational design!

The Nobel laureate Herb Simon is another markworthy figure and, in particular, his slim volume *The Sciences of the Artificial*, first published in 1966. Simon famously defines design as "courses of action aimed at changing existing situations into preferred ones" (Simon, 1966, p.55). Managers, like architects and engineers, are "form-givers", shaping organisations and economic processes. They are concerned with "not how things are but how they might be, in short with design".[26] In advocating the case for design, Simon bemoaned the ascendancy of pure science in professional schools:

---

26   Schön (1987, pp.41-2) has a more critical take on Simon. Although acknowledging that Simon regarded designing as fundamental, Schön comments that "he saw designing as a form of problem solving in its purest form, optimisation, thereby ignoring situations of uncertainty, uniqueness and conflict where instrumental problem solving occupies a secondary place and problem setting, a primary one. In its most generic sense, designing consists in making representations of things to be built... designers put things together and make new artefacts. They juggle variables, reconcile conflicting values, and manoeuvre around constraint..."

> *Design is the core of all professional training. Schools of engineering, architecture, business... medicine are all centrally concerned with the process of design... It is ironic that in this century the natural sciences have driven the sciences of the artificial from professional school curricula... Medical schools have become schools of biological sciences; business schools have become schools of finite mathematics (ibid., p.56).*

Simon went on to call for a new curriculum for management education based on design. His advocacy is especially important here. In 2004, two academics at the Weatherhead School of Management (Case Western University), Dick Boland and Fred Collopy, convened a rather unusual colloquium, which formed the initial stimulus for this book. They brought together a "stellar collection of scholars, artists and managers to explore the implications of taking the manager's role and responsibility more seriously" (Boland & Collopy, 2004, p. xii). Simon's work was an important inspiration; *The Sciences of the Artificial* is eulogised as "one of the finest examples we have of the design attitude for managers" (p.8).

The proceedings of that august gathering were published as a book, comprising a collection of nearly 40 papers. In the opening chapter, Boland and Collopy contrast two paradigms of management practice and education. They characterise the current orthodoxy as the 'decision attitude': "concerned with the various techniques and methods managers use in making choices, starting from the assumption that a good set of options is already available" (Boland & Collopy, 2004, p.6). In contrast, they proclaim the 'design attitude' in the following, rather romantic-heroic, terms:

> *A design attitude views each project as an opportunity to question basic assumptions, a resolve to leave the world a better place. Designers relish the lack of predetermined outcomes, the opportunity to go back to those assumptions that have become invisible and unnoticed, looking for the real thing we are trying to accomplish, unvarnished by years of organizational habit. A design attitude fosters a problem-solving process that remains liquid and open, celebrating path-creating ideas about new ways to use technology and new work processes (ibid., pp.9-10).*

If managers adopted such a design attitude, the world of business "would be different and better, [managers] would approach problems with a sensibility that swept in the broadest array of influences to shape inspiring and energising design for products, services and processes that are both profitable and humanly satisfying" (*ibid.*, p.1). Presciently, they observed that "exotic methods of financial analysis do not create value" (p.7). What is needed is the manager "as an idea generator who gives form to new possibilities with a well-developed vocabulary of design" (p.8).

Although no revolution in management education has yet taken place (an issue to which I will return in the final chapter), Boland and Collopy are not alone as advocates of the cause of design. Interviewed in 2006, Roger Martin (Dean of the Rotman School of Management, Toronto) observed that "business schools are under intense criticism and, in the view of some, have reached a point of crisis. Both academics and management practitioners criticise MBA programmes for their lack of relevance to practitioners" (Dunne and Martin, 2006, p.512). And the remedy? Nothing less than a fundamental reformulation of management education: "we are on the cusp of a design revolution in business… today's business people don't need to understand designers better, they need to become designers" (*ibid.*, p.513).

Richard Farson, author and management guru,[27] provides more sound and fury but important points to boot. Farson argues that design is ubiquitous for the manager. In a Discussion Paper,[28] he contends: "Design is the creation of form. Everything that a manager deals with has form – buildings, offices, meetings, procedures, workflows and systems" (p.1). Technology and design go hand in hand for Farson, as they do for me. He argues that technology presents "a completely new way to design our organisations". Yet he bemoans that, "Most executives ignore systems design. As a result, neither IT nor systems design has reached its potential" (p.7). He recognises, like Tom Peters in my opening quotation, the strong link between design and systems thinking, that design entails the recognition of complexity, inter-dependency and the potential for unintended consequences. Farson urges managers to be 'social architects', asking such questions as: How can I restructure this group to elicit more innovation? How can I arrange this workspace more sympathetically to raise morale?

Standing back from the rhetoric, I concede that the concept of the manager-as-designer is not one that most managers would readily recognise, nor is it an appellation that they would spontaneously use to describe their professional practice.[29] Designing is not one of Mintzberg's celebrated clutch of managerial roles: figurehead, leader, monitor, disseminator, spokesman, disturbance handler and so on (Mintzberg, 1989). Nonetheless, much of the mundane practice of managers may generically be described as design work. I would argue that middle managers in particular have a critical role to play as designers. To them falls the primary responsibility for configuring that part of the organisation for which they are responsible

---

27 Author of such entertainingly provocative texts as *Management of the Absurd* (Farson, 1996).

28 The quotes from Farson are extracted from his pamphlet *Management by Design* at http://www.wbsi.org/farson/com_mgtbydesignr.htm

29 Nor is managing as designing an idea in vogue in scholarly writings about the managerial role and has yet to gain much currency amongst management researchers.

and for its ongoing redesign in response to changing contingencies. Floyd & Wooldridge (1997) characterise a key role of the middle manager as "the implementation of deliberative strategy". This is defined as the translation of corporate strategy into action plans and individual objectives; in other words, giving material form to higher level aspirations, i.e. design work.

Penrose (1980) defines the primary function of management as organisational, entailing the creation, maintenance and enhancement of administrative systems which transform resources into productive outputs. The role combines the imperatives for both continuity and innovation which are in conflict, producing what has been called the "paradox of administration" (Whitely, 1989). Writing in a systems' vein, Tate (2009) has recently made the same distinction, describing two conceptualisations of the managerial role: System 1 (Delivering today) and System 2 (Securing tomorrow). System 1 designates maintenance of the current operational system, ensuring deadlines and targets are met and so on: "managing what we think we know we know". In contrast, System 2 is a Leadership system, concerned with making sure "that the future is better than today. It concerns what we know we don't know, and calls for innovation" (*ibid.,* p.216). The tension between these two systems is generally resolved in favour of System 1: "The more senior a manager's position, the more time they should be devoting to System 2 [but] System 2 is often absent or spasmodic, unrecognised and not formalised in managers' jobs" (*ibid.,* p.216).

The design agenda in management can be seen as an attempt to shift this balance in favour of innovation, i.e. System 2. But it is important to stress that the design attitude embraces more than innovation – it covers continuity too. Good designers naturally pay critical attention to current designs, how well these are working; they are concerned with keeping form and function in harmonious alignment by the monitoring and adjustment of current designs, as well as reflecting on opportunities for more profound change. Design is a larger concept than innovation: it subsumes both systems 1 and 2 and thereby encompasses much more of the routine practice of management.

The reform of public services

> *Slowly, gradually, Gladstone and his contemporaries dismantled the ancient structures of "Old Corruption" and asserted the values of citizenship, equity and service. By the end of the nineteenth century, the patronage-ridden, nepotistic state of 100 years before had been effectively replaced by an efficient, 'rational', modernizing state equipped with a remarkably corruption-free Parliament and a bureaucracy recruited and promoted on merit* (Marquand, 2004, p.46).

Change in the public services is nothing new, but the last two decades do seem to have been particularly turbulent, not just in the UK but across the international scene. In this section, I shall attempt to provide an overview of these developments. In doing so, I will frame my account using the language and ideas of key political scholars. An interesting characteristic of their worldview is its 'Grand Narrative' character (Lyotard, 1979), the propensity to portray history in terms of large-scale, programmatic movements, fractured by convulsive paradigm shifts. The narrative thus tells of the demise of one paradigm, the traditional bureaucratic model and its usurping by a new regime, which goes by the generic rubric the New Public Management (NPM). Its origins can be traced back to the neo-liberal regimes in the UK and US of the 1980s, reaching full spate a decade or so later. NPM is argued by many scholars to form a coherent programme, although its manifestation varies over time and from country to country. But NPM itself is now seen to be fraying and faltering, and a new order is in gestation. In this section, I shall briefly trace out the main lineaments of this period of flux, locating within this the progressive emergence of an agenda giving central place to technology and innovation.

New Public Management

With the benefit of hindsight, Denhardt & Denhardt (2003) fittingly dub the pre-NPM regime, the 'Old Public Management'. As critics of NPM they speak rather approvingly of its 'core ideas', which they summarise as follows: that the primary function of government is the direct delivery of services; that public administrators should play a limited role in policy-making, their primary responsibility being service delivery; that public programmes are best administered through hierarchical organisations, guided by the cardinal values of efficiency and rationality; and finally that the role of the public administrator is that of "organizing, staffing, directing, coordinating, reporting and planning" (Denhardt & Denhardt, 2003, p.12). Although OPM has "served well, even if imperfect", they describe it as "under increasing attack, especially by proponents of what we will call the New Public Management" (*ibid.*, p.12). Denhardt and Denhardt characterise NPM "as a cluster of contemporary ideas, which have at their core to use private sector and business approaches in the public sector" (*ibid.*, p.13).

Writing in a similar vein, Hood (1995, p.93-4) also describes the embattled position of the *ancien régime*, which:

> ...*put heavy stress on two basic doctrines....to keep the public sector sharply distinct from the private sector in terms of continuity, ethos, methods of doing business... [and] to maintain buffers against political and managerial discretion by means of an elaborate structure of procedural rules. This organizational model attracts more derision than analysis today.*

Hood also characterises the fault-line with the past in similar terms: "The basis of NPM lay in… lessening or removing differences between the public and the private sector and shifting the emphasis from process accountability towards a greater element of accountability in terms of results." (Hood, 1995, p.94). In this brave new world, public managers were challenged to find new and innovative ways to achieve results or to privatise; they were urged "to steer, not row".

Although broad continuities and general themes can be made out, NPM is by no means an intellectual monolith. Writing in 2005, Dunleavy *et al.* comment on the progressive evolution of NPM since its inception and subsequent diffusion across many "influential advanced countries", including the UK, US, Canada, Australia, New Zealand and the Netherlands (Dunleavy *et al.*, 2005). Despite being a "slippery label… with different conceptualizations stressing different things" (*ibid.*, p.469) they claim that three chief "integrating themes" can be descried: *Disaggregation* (splitting up bureaucracies, "flexibilisation"); *Competition* (purchaser/provider separation, quasi-markets); and *Incentivisation* (rewarding performance based on pecuniary incentives). The underlying complexity of NPM is revealed when the authors drill down into these themes to unearth what can only be described as a rather incontinent rag-bag of "NPM-badged ideas, a whole string of specific inventions and extensions of policy technologies that have continuously expanded the NPM wave and kept it moving and changing configuration" (*ibid.*, p.470). A total of 34 distinct components are itemised at this "second tier". For example, within Disaggregation, we have: purchaser-provider separation, quasi-government agencies, improved performance measurement and league tables. Within the Competition theme, elements include: quasi-markets, voucher schemes, outsourcing, market-testing and user control; and within Incentivisation: light touch regulation, private finance initiative (PFI) and performance-related pay.

In the US, the NPM cause was given momentum by the reforming zeal of Osbourne and Gaebler in their best-selling book, *Reinventing Government* (1993). Journalist and former city manager, they expounded a set of principles through which government, adjudged to have failed in the eyes of the public, could be rejuvenated only through the spirit of "public management entrepreneurship". The language is apocalyptic: "Public fury alternates with apathy. Our cities succumb to mounting crime and poverty. Our public schools are the worst in the world. Our health-care system is out of control. Our proudest cities are virtually bankrupt" (Osborne & Gaebler, 1993, p.2). Nothing less than an "American Perestroika" will answer the scale of the crisis!

Several vignettes set out in the opening chapter illustrate what they had in mind. Herewith a synopsis of the first (extracted from pages 2 to 5) which is set in Visilia (California), Gaebler's own bailiwick.

> *Once upon a time on a hot Thursday in August 1985, a third-level parks and recreation employee got a call from a friend in Los Angeles. It transpired that the Olympic committee was selling its swimming pool, an all-aluminium pool that would survive an earthquake. Buying it second-hand would cost half the amount of a new model, and two local colleges enthusiastically wanted it. But a non-refundable check for $60k was needed. What did the employee do: he got in his car and took a check down that afternoon. How could that be? Normally, the school district would need at least two weeks to get approval for a such a special appropriation. The answer was simple. Gaebler had introduced a radically new budget system, the "Expenditure Control Budget", which enabled departments to save unspent monies. Sufficient savings were in place. Knowing that entrepreneurial behavior was valued, there were no qualms about seizing the opportunity. "It's something you'd find in private enterprise," said the admiring school superintendent. "You don't have the bureaucracy you have to deal with in most governments".*

Built on such an 'evidence-base', the book sets out a series of principles whereby government and the public service may be transformed. Befitting such self-styled zealots, these have the tone of commandments: "We hope the vision we have laid out will empower you to reinvent your government" (*ibid*, 1993, p.331). And the specific injunctions of the vision? The exhortations, ten (inevitably) in number, included: Catalytic Government (steering not rowing); Community-owned Government (empowering not serving); Mission-driven Government (transforming rule-driven organisations); Results-oriented Government (funding outcomes, not inputs); Customer-driven Government (meeting customer needs, not the bureaucracy); Anticipatory Government (prevention not cure), and so on.

To what extent did such efforts to 'reinvent government' work? Goodsell (1994) recounts that when Clinton took office after the 1992 election, Osbourne proposed that a "reinventing-government group" should be set up in the White House and that a one-page "vision statement" should be hung above the desk of every agency head! Nothing so dramatic occurred; instead, a more modest National Performance Review was set in train to create a government that "works better for less". Some good ideas were produced (such as decentralising personnel administration, two year budgeting, simplifying procurement) and Kettl (2000) concluded it had "saved a significant amount of money, brought substantial management reforms, and promoted a more performance-based discussion about the functions of government". But this was hardly revolutionary stuff. As Goodsell notes:

> *This is because most of the reinventions have already been invented. For years, American bureaucracy has been contracting out; improving management; bidding for services; engaging in partnerships. As far as being innovative, competitive and entrepreneurial, these qualities have always been exhibited by the best of our public executives. The remaining specifics offered by Osbourne and Gaebler… will hardly "revolutionise" American public administration. But they won't ruin it either* (Goodsell, 1994, p.179).

Switching to the UK, NPM's lineage can be traced back to the Thatcher era of the 1980s. Thatcherism included attempts to introduce managerialism into health service, the creation of an internal market and other measures, such as compulsory competitive tendering, also aimed at introducing market-based discipline. Here we shall be mainly concerned with reforms from 1997 onwards, following the resounding election victory of New Labour, under the leadership of Tony Blair. The Party's manifesto had articulated a bold commitment to "modernise" government at all levels. Although there were differences in terminology and nuance from the foregoing neoliberal agenda, infatuation with the methods of private business became, if anything, stronger. Of the various strands of NPM, Dillow (2007) argues managerialism to be the defining feature of New Labour's approach to public administration. Its ideological contours, traced by Chard & Ayre (2010), are: that a central elite know best; that strong top-down management is the key to quality and performance; that workers are self-interested and inefficient; that the standardisation of processes and explicit targets drive quality, which is also ensured by rigorous micro-management using performance indicators (PIs). Going back to our ICS exemplar, the managerial mindset is clearly seen, etched deeply in the design of its software.

New Labour's reform agenda was manifest in several related policy initiatives. Work on the 'Best Value' (BV) performance management regime (Martin & Hartley, 2000) began early in the new administration's term, being ultimately enacted through the 1999 Local Government Act. The same year also saw publication of an important policy paper, *Modernising Government*, which challenged all public sector organisations (including local government) to deliver efficient and responsive "citizen-centred services". IT was seen as critical to achieving these aims, and the concept of "information age government" in the UK (e-Government as it became known) was born. This ushered in a remarkable period of public sector reform, with electronic technologies at the very heart of the effort to reform government and the public services. The ambitiousness of the national e-Government agenda was reflected in the best value target (BVPI 157) to "electronically enable" 100% of relevant services initially by 2008, subsequently accelerated to 2005.

Various national initiatives subsequently lent force to the e-Government programme in local government. A so-called 'Pathfinder' initiative was launched in 2001 with £25 million of new funding set aside for local authorities (LAs) able to demonstrate a leading position in relation to some aspect of e-Government. 140 LAs bid for funding and 25 Pathfinders were appointed in April 2001. The following year saw the publication of a National Strategy for Local e-Government (ODPM, 2002). A talismanic faith in technology as the instrument of change continued unabated over the following years. The hyperbole became, if anything, more excitable, with e-government eventually giving way to "Transformational government: enabled by technology", the sloganistic title of a Cabinet Office report in 2005. The following quote has been extracted from the start of that document:

> Twenty First Century Government is enabled by technology – policy is inspired by it, business change is delivered by it… Moreover modern governments with serious transformational intent see technology as a strategic asset and not just a tactical tool. So this strategy's vision is about better using technology to deliver public services and policy outcomes that have an impact on citizens' daily lives: through greater choice and personalisation, delivering better public services, such as health, education and pensions; benefiting communities by reducing burdens on front line staff…

NPM and managerialism: RIP?

The term 'paradigm' was originally used to designate the set of practices defining a scientific discipline at a particular period (Kuhn, 1962), but has now been generalised to apply to any domain of human endeavour. Paradigms exert a profound effect on practice and thinking, delimiting what is to be observed, the kind of questions that can be asked and how the results of investigations should be interpreted. Ludwik Fleck (1932) coined the cognate idea of the 'thought collective', defined as "as a community of persons mutually exchanging ideas or maintaining intellectual interaction" (Fleck, 1979, p.39). Fleck designates the set of beliefs, values and cognitions common to members of a given collective as its 'thought style': "The individual within the collective is never, or hardly ever, conscious of the prevailing thought style, which exerts an absolutely compulsive force upon his thinking and with which it is not possible to be at variance (p.41)"

What then of the NPM paradigm, now well into its third decade; how well is it doing? Not surprisingly, the academic literature is bustling with debate. Dunleavy *et al.* (2005) have no doubt, declaring NPM "dead in the water". They appraise each of the component elements within each theme, adjudging whether the trend has been wholly/partially reversed, has substantially stalled or is still actively spreading. Table 3 summarises the results of their analysis. For most elements, the diagnosis is poor. For the quasi-market, for instance, they note its "decisive scrapping" in the UK National Health Service in the late 1990s due to disproportionate 'back-office' bureaucracy. An even more dramatic example of failure is the UK's Private Finance Initiative, where the critique has been coruscating. In the context of the health service, PFI has been lampooned as "one hospital for the price of two"[30] and careful financial analysis shows just how bad this ill-thought-out deal has been. Shaoul *et al*, for instance, have estimated that the additional cost of private finance for the hospital PFI programme (worth £8.7 billion) could be as high as £480 million per annum (Shaoul, Stafford & Stapleton, 2008).[31] Dunleavy *et al.* conclude this sorry story as follows: "Few PFI advocates now anticipate large-scale cost savings compared with conventional procurements, and criticisms continue that the British government is overpaying for PFI projects on an heroic scale" (*ibid.*, p.473).

Theme	wholly/partially reversed	substantially stalled	actively spreading, not questioned
Disaggregation	8	1	2
Competition	2	6	2
Incentivisation	3	6	4

Table 3: *Summary of NPM implementation*

Considering NPM as a whole, with less than 25% of its elements still standing, Dunleavy *et al.* pronounce their pessimistic verdict (Table 3). Others are more sanguine. Hood and Peters invite us to consider how a "bureaucratic Rip van Winkle" awaking in the new century "after

---

30 Cuthbert, J. and Cuthbert, M. (2008). The Implications of Evidence Released Through Freedom of Information on the Projected Returns from the New Royal Infirmary of Edinburgh and Certain Other PFI Schemes. Written evidence to the Scottish Parliament Finance Committee. Available at: www.scottish.parliament.uk/s3/committees/finance

31 This additional 'risk premium' is typically justified on the grounds of the risk transferred to the private sector. However, as Shaoul *et al.* point out, such savings are notional, based on estimates rather than actualities, and have been proven hollow. Other intrinsic problems with PFI include: the ability of 'monopoly suppliers' to crank up costs, the lack of transparency of 'off-balance sheet' accounts, tax minimisation tactics by PFI consortia, and budgetary inflexibilities which, in times of financial stress, will augment the pressure to cut jobs as the only management option.

twenty years of slumber" would be dazzled by "the products of the NPM industry… the variety of themes, approaches, and terminology produced by an eclectic mix of consultants, conventional scholars, senior public servants, politicians, and spin doctors" (Hood & Peters, 2004, p.267). Whilst acknowledging that NPM is "middle-aged" and has generated "unintended consequences", Hood and Peters attribute these paradoxical effects to the agenda's complexity, optimistically concluding that "the identification of paradoxes associated with NPM offers an opportunity to enhance understanding of administrative reform as a process" (*ibid.*, p.279).

Critics and obituarists alike of NPM have naturally set off in search of another new paradigm. Osborne (2006), for instance, argues that NPM is a transitory arrangement, a stepping stone between the bureaucratic traditions of public administration and the coming of the age of "New Public Governance". NPG involves "a plural state, where multiple inter-dependent actors contribute to the delivery of services… its focus is on inter-organizational relationships and the governance of processes, and it stresses service effectiveness and outcomes" (Osbourne, 2006, p.384). For their part, Dunleavy *et al.* hail the advent of "Digital-era Governance", characterised by three main themes: reintegration, needs-based holism and digitalisation. Techno-utopian celebration of new technology seems to be the unifying theme of their brave new world, rather than an intellectually coherent set of ideas. As an example, whilst it is justifiable to recognise the potential of IT to enable more agile government or to reengineer processes, the idea of the public agency "becoming its website" seems overly fervid, at best.

No fans of NPM, Denhardt and Denhardt (2003) talk about its replacement by the New Public Service, a framework which emphasises citizenship, civil society and humanism. Reversing many of the key precepts of NPM, its core doctrines are set out in a countervailing set of commandments, fighting fire with fire! These include: Serve Citizens, not Customers; Seek the Public Interest; Think Strategically, Act Democratically; Serve rather than Steer; Value People not just Productivity. Alford & Hughes (2008) provide another prescription. Denouncing both NPM and its bureaucratic predecessor for their "one best way" orientation, they argue for a "public value pragmatism". By this they mean a contingency approach, whereby the optimum "managerial arrangement" for service delivery (in-house, 'arms-length' agency, partnering, or classical out-sourcing) should be sought through positing four key questions: Would the external provider be cheaper or more effective? Is there a competitive market? How easy is it to monitor the service? Is the level of trust and cooperation sufficient? Drawing on Moore (1995), the aim should be to deliver optimum 'public value', defined as "value that is consumed collectively by the citizenry, rather than individually". Alford and Hughes put forward their framework in a heuristic spirit, to suggest what the "design rules" might look like and to inform further research. I will return to public value and its relationship with design later in this section.

Finally, the scepticism of Paul du Gay should also be mentioned. In his seminal *In Praise of Bureaucracy (2000)*, he mounts an erudite and shrewdly perceptive critique of the reinvention project and how it rests on fragile rhetorical grounds. All depends on an "epochal discourse", in which change is seen as self-evidently good, with the "new" (the decentred, entrepreneurial corporation) inherently contrasting favourably with the "old" (the rigid, hierarchical bureaucracy). The turbulence of the times is integral to this discourse; given the omnipresence of change, surely only the entrepreneurial will do, it has a historical inevitability. Du Gay sees a "religious and romantic" fervour driving those who would bring down the old order; the new prophets deploy "the religious language of visions, missions and the like" (du Gay, 2000, p.67), in which "charismatic authority" is emphasised.

As a counterpoint, du Gay highlights the virtues of the bureau, extolling the positive ethical qualities of the public bureaucrat, with his abnegation of personal preference and sense of duty standing above ties of class and kin. He quotes Max Weber approvingly: "This is the ethos of office… To be above parties, in truth to remain outside the struggle for power, is the official's role, while this struggle for personal power… is the lifeblood of the politician as well as of the entrepreneur" (*ibid.*, 78-9). Du Gay warns of dangers of the shift from bureaucratic to entrepreneurial forms of management:

> …the eradication of formal rules, regulations and procedures and their replacement by informal networks and an emphasis on individual creativity and deal-making [places] considerable responsibility on the shoulders of individuals for their own advancement. With the struggle for personal power an increasing feature of entrepreneurial conduct, it should come as no surprise to learn that forms of personal patronage are far from on the wane (*ibid.*, p.69).

Du Gay concludes by expressing anxiety that such entrepreneurship risks making public administration into something it is not. Its rules and procedures were not developed to inhibit entrepreneurship, rather to ensure probity, fairness and reliability, for which they may be a "price worth paying". To critique bureaucracy for its failure to operate more like a business is to mistake its role:

It is misguided to announce the death of the ethos of bureaucratic office. Many of its key features as they came into existence a century or so ago remain as or more essential to the provision of good government today as they did then. These features include the possession of enough skill, status and independence to offer frank and fearless advice to achieve purposes impartially, responsibly and with energy. Representative democracy still needs the bureaucratic office (ibid., p.146).

Is NPM dead? Is a paradigm change underway? It would seem there is no settled consensus amongst the theoreticians of the Academy. We have, however, sampled but a fraction of the plethora of pertinent academic research. This ranges from the high-level and abstract (typified by the papers cited in this section) to more concrete appraisals of policy implementation in specific domains, such as our ICS research[32]. As a designer, my preference is for research at the micro-level. The ICS provides a microcosm of NPM in action and we have seen how the performance management regime it operationalised worked counter-productively, not to afford greater protection for children, but to undermine safe professional practice. The tragic death of Baby Peter shows all too clearly the dysfunctional effect of target and indicators ('targetitis'). Baby Peter also brings into serious question another key aspect of NPM dogma, namely the vogue for partnership working, the multi-agency approach. Who could be against working collaboratively? Yet Baby Peter was seen by over 60 professionals during his short tragic life[33]. Why then is multi-agency working so lionised? A little systems thinking would suggest a more cautious appraisal of its benefits. Will it not tend to dilute responsibility rather than engender fruitful collaboration? The problem is that this is not what the policy-makers wanted to see[34]. It is not enough to invoke the idea of the multi-agency collaboration to make it operate effectively. Again, the policy mantras have the aura of magic about them. As Lymbery astutely observes:

Effective collaborative working is hard to achieve, particularly in the light of the vast differences in power and culture between various occupational groupings, and the inherently competitive nature of professions jostling

---

32 There is also a significant industry of what could be called implementation research, funded by government sources, often producing lengthy, glossy reports. This can be critical, in the limited sense of critiquing methods of implementation and making recommendations for improvement, rather than questioning underlying policy dogma.

33 Most worryingly of all, he was seen by a consultant paediatrician shortly before his death, who failed to spot his broken back and damaged ribs!

34 The idea of multi-agency teams is now well-ensconced in children's social care (e.g. the 'team around the child'), but typically these are 'scratch teams", i.e. not really teams at all. No-one would expect a scratch team to perform well, but policy-makers seem unaware of this important nuance.

> *for territory... These issues cannot be resolved unless they are properly understood; a rhetorical appeal to the unmitigated benefits of 'partnership' alone will not produce more effective joint working* (Lymbery, 2006, p.119).

Given the amorphous, protean character of NPM, let us address the more tractable question: has managerialism had its day? Perhaps; but once a paradigm or thought-style takes hold, it can be difficult to dislodge. The ICS debacle shows how powerful the managerial mindset can be for the denizens of its thought collective. We have seen how the progenitors of the ICS were so much in thrall to their managerialist paradigm that even the manifest problems the ICS was encountering in the field were hubristically re-interpreted as consistent with their preconceptions: disquiet was seen as resistance from a recalcitrant work-force, resisting "modernisation". Such resistance only confirmed the need for more micro-managerial control, it did not call it into question!

Opinion has, however, steadily turned against important components of managerialism; targets in particular have become themselves a target, for journalists and academics alike (Bevan & Hood, 2006; Chard & Ayre, 2010). The thought style is certainly fraying, although paradigms can be remarkably resilient (Kuhn, 1962). Apologists are apt to see failings not as fatal flaws, but as temporary problems, remediable as knowledge and understanding progress. Lord Laming is the high-priest of managerialism in social care. In his most recent report, whilst recognising the deficiencies of the regime he had devised, he perversely goes on to prescribe more of the same, a larger dose indeed (Laming, 2009). The proverbial "man with a hammer"! Nonetheless, there are clear signs that managerialism is nearing its demise, at least in its present guise. The incoming coalition government in the UK – elected in 2010 – firmly set itself the task of dismantling the centralised, command-and-control state of its predecessor. Given the origins of managerialism in the former conservative regime of Margaret Thatcher, there is a delicious irony in this.

Managing to improve public services

> *The global focus on improving public services... has resulted in a significant period of reform and experimentation. At the heart of these initiatives is the idea that improvements to the ways public services can be governed, managed and delivered will produce improved outcomes for citizens* (Hartley et al., 2008, p.3).

So opens a recent book which reviews the results of a "bold experiment" by one of the UK research councils to develop a knowledge-base of theory and practice to help public managers to "cope effectively with the complexity and multiplicity of these centrally instigated changes, alongside local and in-house initiatives" (p.3). A strong theme of the book is the conviction that social science can help policy-makers and managers, that there is a need for "a fuller, better theorised and more contextualised understanding both of innovation and its contribution to improvement" (p.197). These are bold ambitions, which touch on several strands of my argument, and I shall summarise some of the book's main ideas which seem most relevant here.

The opening chapter stresses the "distinctive features" of public service organisations, that they do not choose their market, have to provide services for all, operate in areas of "market failure", are subject to political control and are actuated to deliver "public goods" of a complex nature, which cannot be reduced to the simple financial bottom line of the commercial organization. These features enjoin that "generic management theories and techniques may require modification to fit services which are complex, obligatory or in the public eye" (p.9).

Three subsequent chapters in the book seem particularly germane in the present context. Chapter 7, for instance, considers the nature of innovation, defining it as a "step-change" rather than incremental development (Hartley, 2008). Whilst extant research, being based on the private-sector, has tended to address the development and adoption of novel products, innovation in the public services is typically characterised by the development of new services, modes of delivery or more efficient forms of internal organisation. Hartley notes that many innovations fail along the "innovation journey" and that the failure rate is likely to be higher in the public sector. The relationship between improvement and innovation is key. Hartley points out that low levels of innovation can be associated with either low or high improvement, and equally that high innovation may or may not lead to tangible improvement. She also notes the "increasing role of users in creating innovation" (p.203):

> ... [the] classic public service model of innovation as designed by policy makers and implemented by managers is not the sole approach. Increasingly, innovation is as much bottom-up (p.202).

The following chapter addresses the relationship between innovation and improvement empirically (Walker & Damanpour, 2008). Using external performance data[35] complemented by a questionnaire survey of perceived

---

35   Extracted from Best Value reviews in 2002 and 2004. Best Value is a performance management regime which ran for a number of years in the UK. A Comprehensive Performance Assessment appraised each local authority in terms of its performance along a range of dimensions, including value for money, customer satisfaction and capacity for improvement. All services areas were assessed, with a score assigned on a scale from 1 (lowest) to 4 (highest).

internal performance in a sample of nearly 100 authorities, a dataset of ingenious, though crude, indicators was assembled. Service and process innovation were distinguished. Examining the correlations between innovation and performance over the three year period, two significant correlations were found, between process innovation and internal improvement two years later, and between service innovation and external performance the following year. Though the picture is a complex one, "the results generally support the notion that innovation has a positive effect on organizational performance" (p.231).

In the penultimate chapter, Wallace and Fertig begin by reiterating "the need for social-science-informed theoretical development to address the increasing complexity of public service change" (Wallace & Fertig, 2008, p.258). The chapter puts forward a "practical planning framework" for developing "knowledge-for-understanding", i.e. for thinking about complex change processes[36]. Three aspects need to be addressed: change management (coordination, planning, culture building); complexity (number of elements and stakeholders); and stage (initiation, implementation and institutionalisation). The complexity of programmes of change compared to single initiatives is emphasised, which points up "orchestration" as a key leadership quality: "orchestrating a change entails implementing it alongside other changes and the rest of the on-going work". Orchestration is contrasted approvingly with charismatic leadership, as being "more realistic than clinging to an over-optimistic sense of the leader's ability to choose the direction of change and control its course" (p.269). Wallace and Fertig propose what they call an ironic perspective "as a sensitising device" to highlight the empirical gap between change intentions and outcomes and, hence, the limited manageability of public service change programmes. The ironic perspective highlights the limits of managerial agency in the face of a complex world of diverse rationalities and incompatible goals, where action aimed in one direction can evoke unintended consequences building pressure towards the opposite pole.

Public Sector Reform: designing services for public value

> *The history of the modern era has been a long string of failed or abandoned designs… Designs are fraught with risks; as modern times went by, an ever larger part of the designing zeal was to detoxicate or remove from sight*

---

36 Though the ideas presented are abstract, practical proposals are made to operationalise the framework, including a national leadership development programme aimed at: "identifying and supporting development of those in a position to act as change orchestrators based at different administrative levels… focusing training support on effective coping with ambiguity and the limited manageability of change… fostering emergent change through local innovativeness" (p.203).

the collateral damage done by past designing. Designing becomes its own paramount cause, an intrinsically wasteful endeavour (Bauman, 2004, pp.23-4).

This book is about design and it is fitting to round off this section with some general reflections on the reform developments sketched above from the perspective of design, addressing also current academic debate regarding public management. What are the important messages to take away? Some motifs are clear. The need for relevant theory is one. I concur with Hartley that this should be specialised for the public services, but as an interim strategy, the existing evidence-base can furnish much of utility and critical value. The need for practical tools for managers is another message, allied with a more mature concept of management, transcending the narcissistic fantasy of the charismatic leader. The need for an ironic perspective is also welcome; irony is the perfect antidote to magical thinking!

Above all, what stands out from the perspective of design is the massive failure of the top-down, dogma-driven approach to reform. This, for me, is the real significance of Table 3. The death of NPM is a somewhat moot point; what is not debatable is the scale of failure, with over 75% of 'design concepts' having come to grief, some at enormous financial cost (not just at the time but for many years to come in the case of PFI). Many years ago, the philosopher Karl Popper warned of the dangers of top-down design or "utopian engineering" as he called it, distinguished by "a dangerous dogmatic attachment to a blue-print". It is the blue-print approach which is in the dock here, design as a noun, the conceit that there are pre-existing solutions which can be simply picked off the shelf and implemented. Popper's antidote to dogma-driven design was the piecemeal approach, the execution of small scale experiments with continuous adjustments in which "we can make mistakes and learn from our mistakes", i.e. designing as an open, form-giving process. I am not as pessimistic as Bauman in this section's epigraph. It is not "design zeal" which is at fault, but the way design is done in the sphere of public services. Popper again:

The piecemeal method might lead to the happy situation where politicians look out for their own mistakes instead of trying to prove they have always been right. This would mean the introduction of scientific method into politics, since the whole secret of scientific method is a readiness to learn from mistakes (Popper, 1995, p.163).

Finally, I will make a direct connection between my case for design and recent developments in the theory of public management, specifically with the concept of Public Value, mentioned briefly above. This is an "idea whose time has come" in the words of two of its leading proselytisers (Bennington & Moore, 2011), or as Seddon put it, "Public Value is all the rage" (Seddon, 2008, p.163). A brief exploration of this idea is important as it focuses attention on the ends, rather than the means, of design. In conventional product design contexts, designers aim to produce artefacts which pleasingly marry form and function: the Aga stove, the Duralex glass, the Vespa scooter, to name but a few design icons. But in the wider remit of design addressed here, what should be the aim of system design for the manager? Whilst the "resolve to leave the world a better place" is laudable enough, can we be more specific? Management means making choices not least because resources are limited and mandates must be gained; why should one design be followed and another dropped? The need for a concept of value is thus integral to the design attitude. In commercial organisations, this is relatively tractable: to create shareholder value, which can ultimately be operationalised in monetary terms, such as an increase in profit and therefore dividends. Even here, the methodological difficulties are formidable, and financial concepts such as 'return on investment' go only go so far.[37] But in the public sphere, the definition of value is tougher still.

The idea of Public Value was first elaborated in 1995 by Mark Moore at Harvard's Kennedy School of Government, around the time of NPM's apogee in the US. Interest in the UK practitioner community sparked off in the early 2000s with the publication of a Cabinet Office report, *Creating Public Value* (Mulgan, 2011) and academic enthusiasm has now also "erupted vigorously", albeit late in the day (Bennington & Moore, 2011). Moore's aim was to provide "a conceptual framework that would be practically useful to public managers… to encourage strategic thinking and entrepreneurial action to tackle complex problems in the community" (Bennington & Moore, 2011, p.1). In a design context, it is the implicit link with innovation which is particularly relevant; Moore describes public managers as "not just as inward-looking bureaucratic clerks, but as stewards of public assets with restless value-seeking imaginations…" (*ibid.*, p.3). Given the increased complexity of public services and social problems a decade and a half later, together with the raised expectations of citizens, "the emphasis that public value theory places on innovation seems even more important for the future than in the past" (Moore & Bennington, 2011, p.270).

What does the theory say? Its core idea is that an alignment of three elements is vital for the creation of public value (the so-called "strategic triangle"): first, public value must be defined (i.e. strategic goals and outcomes); secondly, the "authorising environment" must be put in place

---

37   The Balanced Scorecard, for instance, was developed to provide a more holistic concept of value, embracing organisational learning and customer satisfaction, as well as financial and efficiency benefits (Kaplan & Norton, 2006).

to legitimise and sustain the necessary strategic action (i.e. the required coalition must be built of stakeholders from all sectors, including the community); and thirdly, operational capacity must be created, harnessing resources from outside as well as inside the organisation (again including the community). Public value itself cannot be operationalised in any prescriptive, universal way, though it is essential in any concrete initiative to define the "public value outcomes" that are sought. This is for several reasons: to facilitate public debate about policy priorities and the direction of desirable change, to define the specific goal(s) for a given initiative and, finally, to measure actual improvement. Always what should be measured is the collective benefit, i.e. the benison for society as a whole. Citizens gain from their participation in an enriched commonwealth (the greater good); it is not a matter of whether individuals gain directly on a personal basis ("value consumed collectively"). It is also important that managers should consider not only value creation, but (crucially to my mind) the possibility of value destruction too, by infelicitous decisions. It is acknowledged that measuring such outcomes is itself a significant intellectual challenge (Mulgan, 2011); seldom will monetary proxies suffice and the choice of what to measure will necessarily depend on the sector (e.g. the Quality Adjusted Life Year – QALY – in health, 'fear of crime' in community safety, etc.).

An important feature of public value theory is its emphasis on community engagement, i.e. that public value is 'co-produced' with the active assistance of actors (partners and clients) outside the official agencies. The innovative public manager must look beyond the internal resources he directly controls, devoting time and effort:

> ...trying to mobilize and deploy the latent capacity of potential partners... Perhaps, for example, a school superintendent could boost student achievement more by strengthening connections with parents than she could by overseeing operations within the schools (Moore & Bennington, 2011, p.268).

Looking again at the detritus of NPM, how does the balance-sheet stand in terms of public value, between value created and value destroyed? The question is rhetorical of course, just as it is when the ICS project is interrogated with the same searching question: net value gained or destroyed? Certainly, public value outcomes were invoked in its justification, but the actual outcomes seem quite the reverse. The synergy between the design attitude and public value theory should now be clear: the latter provides the strategic framework and the former the means of implementation, operationalising the theory in the everyday practice of public managers. Only by doing design well (i.e. not magically) will public value be accomplished: "Managing as designing for public value" – that should be the credo. And so, to more practical matters.

Design in the Big Society

> *Public services lie at the heart of the new Government's vision of a Big Society, and giving schools, hospitals and police forces greater freedom from central control is central to this vision. To translate this vision into a practical reality that can improve services even at a time of restrained spending is a challenge the Design Council believes needs to be addressed by working innovatively and by using creative thinking and new approaches as well as new technologies.*[38]

Whether NPM works, or is obsolete, whether it is perfectible or an evil scourge, are not our central questions. This book is concerned with magic, technology and design. NPM is just another form of technology, albeit a complex one; whether it works or not will depend on how it is implemented on the ground by human actors. This is where design comes in, as I have said, and it is time to re-join our main narrative. In this section, I will make a brief appraisal of how the design attitude stands in contemporary public services. I believe we are at a turning point, paradoxically due to the very adversity in which we find ourselves. At the time of writing, UK public services stand at a point of profound change. The 'Big Society' has arrived and all are struggling, the die-hard Statists on the Left, the liberal enthusiasts of small government on the Right, to work out exactly what it means: Big-endians and Little-endians alike! Time will tell. Design is always relevant, but the chances are that it could be even more relevant in the times ahead. Now, what was that proverb about "the mother of invention"?

Grass-roots innovation

But where is this innovation to come from? In the large bureaucracies that typify the public sector this is an old problem. In his influential book, *Small is Beautiful*, first published in 1973, E.F. Schumacher reflected on his experience as Economic Adviser to the UK National Coal Board, a vast nationalised industry at the time (Schumacher, 1993). He talked about the difficulty of innovation in big organisations, of the danger of men becoming "small cogs in a vast machine". It is worth summarising some of his insights. Through a set of principles, he set out his remedy. The first, that of subsidiarity, called for organisations to be divided into semi-autonomous units ("quasi-firms"). Although well-established functions can be addressed by "directives, rules and regulation", Schumacher pertinently asked "what about new developments, new creative ideas? What about progress, the

---

38 From the UK Design Council website, http://www.designcouncil.org.uk accessed November 2010. The Design Council is a body funded by the UK government to promote the cause of design, a role it has performed for over 60 years. Its recent work in the public service sphere is noteworthy.

entrepreneurial activity par excellence?" (*ibid.*, p.210). The challenge for senior management is to specify, but not too much: "good government is always government by exception" (*ibid.*, p.206). Schumacher's final principle, The Middle Axiom, captures this wisdom. For instance, when opening up new coalfaces, minimum standards of profitability were set down but local autonomy was protected. If any local unit decided to open up a coalface falling short, then it could do so, provided a justification could be given. Schumacher continues:

> *This was a true and effective way of applying the Principle of the Middle Axiom, and it had an almost magical effect. To preach is easy, so also is issuing instructions. The Centre had found a way of going beyond mere exhortation, yet without in any way diminishing the freedom and responsibility of lower formations (ibid., p.212).*

The best ideas literally do emerge, it would seem, at the coal-face! More recent research in the public services has confirmed this, showing mid-level managers and front-line staff to be the most fertile source of innovative ideas and proposals, far out-pacing elected officials and agency heads (Borins, 1998). In his study of change in the US procurement services, Kelman also speaks of front-line dissatisfaction as an important engine for change; all that needs to be done to "unleash change" is "to activate the discontented" (Kelman, 2005). In his study, discontentment revolved around lack of autonomy caused by too many rules and sign-offs, and the need to give better value by focusing on results. In a similar vein, Blond writes that "front-line staff frequently confront problems or become aware of opportunities long before strategic managers… bringing decision-making and service design to the point of delivery can generate vast savings for any service" (Blond, 2010, p.254). Drawing on Seddon (2008), he provides examples where "empowering employees and their managers to design against local demand has resulted in efficiency gains of over 400%" (p.256). He cites the case of one authority where capacity for housing repairs had increased from 137 jobs per day to 220 in 4 months, with savings amounting to "a staggering 20-40% of costs".

One of the arguments for private-sector superiority, driving the NPM bandwagon, is its much-vaunted capacity for innovation. Reviewing the literature, however, Goodsell challenges this orthodoxy: "studies of technology diffusion… show that the public sector is not always that much different from, let alone slower than, the private sector" (Goodsell, 1994, p.68). Goodsell cites research done in the US Coast Guard demonstrating many innovative examples of the adoption of new technologies. My ethnographic peregrinations in social services have shown that local innovation abounds in the public services, as witnessed by the following remark of a team leader in children services in one of our ICS research sites:

> *Systems and processes are vital here as we need to turn things around quickly… Jonathon has come up with a brilliant case load system… it could benefit everyone. Suzanne has also evolved a check-list she uses before closing cases. Between these two systems we could make some big improvements.*

With the aim of stimulating such local innovation, the Design Council in the UK has taken a markworthy lead. In the early 2000s, it set up a small, interdisciplinary R&D team, known enigmatically as RED, which carried out a series of design projects in health, energy conservation and citizenship. Of note was RED's development of a methodology known as "Transformation Design" (Burns, Cottam, Vanstone & Winhall, 2006). RED notably styled itself as:

> *…a "do tank" that develops innovative thinking and practice. RED challenges accepted thinking. Innovation is required to re-connect public services to people and the everyday problems that they face. RED harnesses the creativity of users and front line workers to co-create new public services that better address these complex problems. We place the user at the centre of the design process rapidly proto-typing our ideas to generate user feedback. (ibid., p.2).*

In early 2009, the Design Council launched its "Public Services by Design" initiative, proclaiming that: "public services must be designed to meet the complex needs of users while delivering cost efficiencies".[39] Recognising that "many public service providers lack the knowledge and skills to use design as a strategic approach to innovation", the initiative aimed to help develop capacity for public sector organisations to "manage their creative processes and find innovative solutions for service delivery". The need for a design methodology was emphasised: "evidence shows that design methodologies can drive innovation in public services". Methodology was held to benefit innovation in a number of ways: developing more personalised services through more user control; harnessing the knowledge of frontline staff via collaborative design; managing risk by prototyping new ideas; improving efficiency and value for money. Through a number of live public sector projects, practical design solutions were developed for a range of complex problems in local areas. For example, one design team worked with Gateshead Primary Care Trust to improve sexual health screening and treatment services.

In summary, in the contemporary public services, design has never seemed so important, part of the zeitgeist even, whatever the future holds. Nor is design seen as the prerogative of senior executives or remote technocratic

---

39 Quotations taken from the Council's website, http://www.designcouncil.org.uk accessed in March 2009.

elites; the grass roots must be engaged and there is also a recognised need for methodology. These motifs are core themes of this book and will occupy much of what I will have to say. To set the scene, another case study will be recounted, of management-as-design in action, which is relevant in multiple ways: first, that it gives some insight into the 'street level' response to the macro-level policy developments in the early New Labour era in the UK; second, it provides a dramatic example of local service innovation, as we see a beleaguered IT department reinvent itself to 'get out of jail'; third, the case gives the opportunity to reflect on the conditions for successful innovation; and fourth, central to the reinvention effort was the development of a design and innovation methodology, which we shall inspect at length in Chapter 4.

A case study from the trenches

The setting for the story is Salford City Council (SCC), with the action beginning in 1999, centred on its IT services department (ITSD). At this time, ITSD was staffed by around 20 professionals organised in a number of specialist teams (e.g. training, software development, PC support). The story[40] begins shortly after the 'failure' of a project known as CAPELLA, a collaboration led by the head of ITSD (Mike Willetts, MW) in concert with two local academics, Tom McMaster (Salford University) and myself, then at Manchester University.

CAPELLA had begun in 1997, its aim being to implement an integrated set of software engineering tools (CASE) in order to improve software productivity and quality within ITSD. CAPELLA had foundered because staff were uncommitted to using the toolkit, which became seen as increasingly marginal to the urgent, practical problems they were dealing with (e.g. Year 2K). Of particular salience was a key conclusion of CAPELLA's final report: "The Council is not a strategic animal, services are driven by operational needs. It's hard for IT to provide business benefits in this context. We need to be seen as a critical lever for change". The need for ITSD to adopt a more business-oriented approach had also been articulated in the City's Information Society Strategy, *People not Technology*, published earlier that year. The Strategy's aim was to harness the potential of IT to improve the social and economic well-being of the people of Salford. Significantly, it proposed the adoption of a BPR (Business Process Reengineering) approach which would "align ICT systems to support best quality service delivery". The report advocated continued collaboration with academic partners as the way forward. At a national level, there were also potent forces at work. New Labour had come to power, committed to

---

40   Reconstructed from contemporaneous documents, notes made at the time and the author's memory, supplemented by interviews with key actors carried out in 2005. The quotations in the text are taken from the latter.

modernise government at all levels, and the phenomenon of "electronic government" was beginning to take shape.

The decision was thus made to develop an in-house BPR approach (to be known as SPRINT) rather than adopting an existing methodology. Work commenced immediately with the formation of a small team led by MW, which also comprised myself and another local academic (Peter Kawalek) and several of ITSD's software professionals, including one section leader (Ewen Locke, EL). It is important to re-emphasise the vulnerable position in which ITSD found itself at that time. Reflecting on the original motivation for SPRINT, MW commented:

> *We were largely a traditional, technically orientated IT department, our people were predominantly technology people. We did try to understand the Council's strategic agenda but our alignment was vague. We were seen as people who built software, put PCs on desks and installed networks rather than adding strategic value.*

More starkly, EL observed:

> *We went through a strange phase in the olden days. Departments increasingly thought they could do things for themselves, they could buy their own system and didn't need ITSD. This was leading us to stagnation in the way we were moving, we had no role or identity. We were feeling very marginal at the time.*

One directorate, Environmental Services, had gone so far as to declare UDI regarding its computing provision, and key projects had been lost elsewhere, e.g. a major system in housing.

Work began and a draft methodology was produced in the autumn of 1999; the acronym SPRINT was coined at this point (Salford Process Reengineering Involving New Technology). In mid-October, a paper was presented by MW to the Council's senior management team, proselytising the concept of BPR and emphasising its strategic importance. The paper recommended the formal adoption of SPRINT and its deployment on a comprehensive programme of reengineering projects. The paper was accepted, including the recommendation to constitute an internal BPR team to carry forward the work. Significantly, no new resources were requested by MW. He later reflected: "I prefer the skunk-works approach. Having too many resources can be a problem. There's something heroic in not having enough resources. We actually made a saving. We created the BPR team from internal people".

The first project carried out was key in developing the methodology. It focused on clerical support for the committee-based decision-making structures operational within SCC at that time. Work began in late October and concluded in January 2000 with the production of an innovative reengineering concept, described in Chapter 4. Far from mere office automation of the clerical function (as originally envisaged), the creation of a new Knowledge Management function was proposed: one that focused on supporting elected representatives in policy research and decision-making.

Two further projects were quickly instigated, in the housing and treasury departments. The achievements in the former were limited; treasury, in contrast, was a notable success. A key problem facing that department was the high number of unanswered telephone queries for its Revenues and Benefits service (R&B), and it had also performed very poorly in an external audit. The BPR work here was enthusiastically led by the manager running R&B, with all levels of staff participating vigorously. The main recommendation was to create a dedicated "Customer Contact" facility for Treasury, which subsequently went live in mid-2000. The transformation in Treasury's housing benefit service was ultimately reflected in the award of a 4-star rating.

Turning back to ITSD, morale had significantly lifted in the summer of 2000. EL commented:

> *Things came together nicely. SPRINT arrived at the right time, and there were also areas in the authority that needed major change. We saw the situation as an opportunity to flex our muscles. SPRINT helped to crystallize our new role... then the crisis came in Council Tax and then e-Government. There was a lot of change going on at the time... we were needed.*

Further BPR projects were launched over that summer, and two other developments became increasingly influential over the ensuing 12 months. First was the appearance of a threat to outsource the IT function. Though real and serious, this was turned to good effect. MW observed:

> *We worked hard to convince management that we needed to reflect more on it, and give the in-house service more chance to get in shape. We were re-positioning anyway, but SPRINT allowed me to say to management that we're addressing our weaknesses, that they should "trust the in-house service". Internally it did give a sense of urgency. There was a burning platform, and I wanted people to understand this.*

The BPR team leader added:

> *Outsourcing made us realise that there was no future in the classic IT development area. This encouraged people to join the team and do something different. We saw outsourcing as a very real threat, and people*

> *got into BPR as a way of fending it off. We felt that when we had an*
> *established BPR process, we'd be seen as valuable.*

To buy time, ITSD called for an independent assessment to be carried out by
a local Business School. Although the threat persisted for over a year, ITSD's
resistance prevailed and by the time the external report was published the
threat had effectively gone away. The second important development was
the announcement of the national e-Government Pathfinder initiative in
early 2001. A collaborative bid involving the fledgling Customer Contact
Centre was submitted and was successful:

> *We were lucky enough to get it, one of 25 – it was all about building*
> *the SPRINT toolkit and developing it. Two years later, it would have*
> *had nothing like the impact, and two years earlier, they wouldn't have*
> *recognised its significance. Yes, all the stars did align, the customer service*
> *emphasis, the whole front-line agenda alongside the e-Government agenda.*
> *The time was perfect – it was serendipity* (MW).

£500,000 of funding was obtained with two inter-linked aims. The first was
to 'productise' SPRINT as a resource for the local government community
as a whole. The development of bespoke CRM (Customer Relationship
Management) software was the second element. This home-grown system
subsequently became known as Citizen. A re-organisation of ITSD also
commenced in the summer of 2001, in part triggered by the Pathfinder
success. The more routine activities were split off into a separate section and
a new organisational entity was created, emblematically christened 'Salford
Advance', subsuming the BPR team, a small R&D Group and training. The
Contact Centre was also established around the same time as a corporate
'customer services' function, entitled 'Salford Direct'. It subsequently
enjoyed an impressive period of growth, assimilating a range of additional
services.

Salford Advance was formally established in November 2001, and was a
clear step towards realising MW's strategic vision for IT:

> *Advance was born in November 2001. We took IT services apart and*
> *rebuilt it. Salford Advance was about change management, putting*
> *together BPR, e-Government, training and support under one umbrella*
> *and aligned with the change agenda. I wanted something free from*
> *encumbrances, so we put a bubble around Advance: it was a new entity, it*
> *was about the future. We took a bunch of guys out of the main organisation*
> *and gave them a new purpose.*

Over the Pathfinder year, SPRINT was internally deployed on a further
cohort of projects and over 40 other local authorities were "mentored".

Autumn of 2002 saw a crisis erupt in Housing, namely a highly unfavourable Best Value review. This precipitated a return by the BPR team to Housing, turning crisis to opportunity:

> *Eventually they had a real crisis, a zero in the Best Value review. The [Housing] management team was replaced and there were threats that their budget would be taken away. Senior management [of SCC] realised that if they had taken on board the BPR proposals back in 2000 then the crisis could have been avoided. They asked for copies of all the work and the outstanding actions (MW).*

From this point our story rolls quickly forward to its denouement. Late 2002 saw the publication of a fully revised version of SPRINT and, over the following 18 months, a further set of BPR projects was initiated. Many of these were rather limited and the lack of senior level buy-in was highlighted in a BPR Team report, which commented "It appeared that project sponsors would commission a piece of BPR work without necessarily having the commitment to develop it beyond a piece of business analysis". Despite this, the SPRINT team operated as artfully as ever:

> *...it's the devil's own job to get higher level people involved, to set up the full SPRINT team as the methodology says. But we have to be pragmatic, we can't say we're not doing anything unless it's set up properly as a BPR project. You've got to do the project you've got, hoping it will turn into the project that you want. It's better to achieve something than nothing (EL).*

Growing external interest, fuelled by Pathfinder, saw the creation of a SPRINT User Group, which held its first meeting in May 2004. Interviewed in 2005, MW was notably bullish; in his view a seat at the "top table" had finally been achieved and SPRINT had been pivotal.

> *SPRINT helped profoundly to re-position IT as a true enabler of business transformation. We're now on the top table. The Chief Exec now recognises that BPR is key to achieving strategic aims and objectives. It's put us on the strategic change management map. We're even on the treasurer's radar now... we're seen as the Ghost-busters, the ones that can fill the hole. We now make a real difference to delivering the Council's agenda. We know what's going on and we're shaping it.*

MW went on to reflect on the long and tortuous road that the "re-positioning" had taken, of the key role of external events (e.g. the crisis in Housing) and the need for an opportunistic response:

> *Organisations are slow to change. Something can be seen as innovative, but it takes time to understand it. It drifts away, comes back. Yes, there were difficult days, and we fought guerrilla warfare to sustain things. We*

> *just kept producing reports, doing good work. Housing was critical. This gave BPR a real push. We're now in everyone's consciousness, but you can't rest on your laurels. Things change – the chief executive leaves next year and everything could change. You think you've got it all nailed down, but you're always in the eye of a storm – if you move an inch one way or the other you'll be blown off course.*

An updated review of the BPR programme was carried out at that time. A cumulative total of 22 projects had been carried out and, although many projects had had limited implementation, the long-term learning benefits of the BPR work were being increasingly appreciated. EL's observation in the quote below is typical of his sanguine view of "failed implementations" as "learning successes". Indeed, he goes to opine that the failure to achieve substantial on-the-ground change in the wider organisation had paradoxically been a boon, the key to SPRINT's strategic success. EL reflected that: "We're now seeing the links. We don't do implementation, but lots of small, disparate non-implementation projects which have helped to build this picture, and it's been essential to creating our more strategic role".

Our story comes to a natural conclusion in 2005, with the wining of a national e-Government award. The Council's website proclaimed:

> *The council's ICT services were praised at the national e-Government Awards in London, which are deemed the yardstick for UK excellence in innovative government services. Salford was particularly singled out for its joined-up approach to transforming front-line and back office services enabled through improvements in council processes and implementation of computer systems and so making council services to citizens and businesses more effective and efficient.*

Theoretical coda: design as bricolage, leaders as tricksters

In this final section, I shall reflect on what may be learned regarding design, innovation and organisational change in the public services from the history of ITSD's phoenix-like resurrection. We have witnessed the department's spectacular rise from a 'techie' group facing the threat of extinction to a place in the strategic vanguard of the organisation. How may we account for this *tour de force*? From a conventional stand-point, two familiar 'success factors' immediately stand out. In Chapter 1 (Table 1), I reviewed the various generic factors which can be regarded as critical to the success of any organisational intervention. The two top factors are the commitment of senior managers and the willing participation of staff. Both these pre-conditions were clearly met in ITSD. The project was led passionately by the head of ITSD, who operated throughout as a "transformational leader" (Bass, 1985). The approach was also intensely participative. The development of SPRINT was an integral part of the process and a core group of practitioners were engaged throughout in its design; the methodology was not imposed from without, but developed endogenously by practitioners and academics working in close collaboration.

But this analysis is only part of the story. Other key factors were clearly at work. Kotter (1995) argues that the universal spur for organisational innovation is a "sense of urgency", the cliché of the "burning platform"; without such a sense of crisis, inertia will tend to prevail and any mobilisation for change will quickly peter out. To a degree, the crisis facing ITSD at the end of the 1990s was still theoretical. There were clear warning signals but the threat of outsourcing had yet to come and the e-Government agenda was still embryonic. Nonetheless, times were clearly a-changing and ITSD's traditional, technology-focused *Weltanschauung* was perceptibly out of joint with the brave new world of modernised public services. The Information Society Strategy presented a powerful challenge to reach for a new role, at the fore of the City's strategic agenda. The impending crisis could have been discounted: a defensive process of denial might have set in, with ITSD ignoring the emerging imperatives. Instead, the challenges were viewed positively, as an opportunity for growth; the time was ripe for action. Seeger *et al.* (2005) refer to such a positive orientation to adversity as a "discourse of renewal". They identify several characteristic features of this discourse: an optimistic attitude to the future rather than defensive rumination; a focus on constructing new technical faculties, methods and procedures; and an improvisational pragmatism emphasising expediency and flexibility. ITSD had renewal discourse in spades: a 'never say die' positivity, the determination to create a distinctive new technical capacity and, above all, an unquenchable spirit of opportunism and extemporisation.

Let me develop further the latter point, as there are unorthodox messages about leadership, design and organisational change to be read in ITSD's renaissance. The conventional model of change in the management literature is characterised by Kawalek as top-down, linear and planned, i.e. a defined "change initiative" (Kawalek, 2007). An idea occurs, a plan is put in place, stakeholders are identified, the ground prepared, work begins, progress is measured, the change is completed and lessons are learned. Kotter's eight-step "road map" is perhaps the best known of such top-down models (Kotter, 1995). But the orthodox model is not without its critics. Karl Weick, something of an iconoclast, provides an elegantly trenchant critique of its fundamental assumptions (Weick, 1995). He argues that it is founded on a misconceived concept of "organisational design", deriving from a false analogy with architectural design. He encapsulates the latter in the following axioms: "that a design is a blueprint constructed at a single point in time, that designs produce order through intention, and that design produces planned change" (p.348).

Weick argues that organisational design is a quite different process from architectural design: it is dynamic and continuous, partly pre-planned and top-down, but also emergent, spontaneous and organic, more like a recipe than a blueprint. There is no fixed initial concept: designs are continuously reconstructed, order produced by attention not intention, i.e. by imposing meaning on an on-going stream of social activity. What we call design, he argues, is the codification of "unplanned change after the fact".

Weick suggests a different metaphor, that of *improvisational theatre*. The essence of improvisation is "making do", the creation of order in the moment, in the act of performance: "resourcefulness is more crucial than resources – [using] whatever resources and repertoire one has to perform whatever task one faces" (p.346). Weick argues that bricolage[41] is the quintessence of leadership: "the main function of any leader is to draw organisation out of the raw materials of life… fixing things on the spot through a creative vision of what is available and what might be done" (pp.352-3). Leaders are tricksters, "people who improvise". Interpreters not decision-makers, they make sense of a confusing world thereby opening up courses for coherent action. From the bricolage perspective, Weick argues that conventional efforts to improve organisational design inevitably founder for several key reasons: "people are too detached and do not see their present situation in sufficient detail"; their past experience is limited; they are unwilling to make do with what they have, being preoccupied with a "decision rationality" (not the rationality of "making do"); and by striving for ideal solutions they are "unable to appreciate the aesthetics of imperfection" (p.353).

Weick's heterodox account of change throws into sharp relief the leadership style provided by MW and the central part it played. He was the prime orator of the renewal rhetoric and it was his sense-making which created a clear vision of the need for change and for the development of a BPR capability. The improvisation and resourcefulness celebrated by Weick were conspicuous. It is important to recognise that there was no top-down mandate for change, nor were new resources made available. Resources no, but resourcefulness in abundance: examples abound of opportunism

---

41   The use of the term in this context is borrowed from the French anthropologist, Claude Levi-Strauss. Weick invokes the vignette of "Willie's Tractor" to epitomise the "genius" of the bricoleur. Willie is a mechanic in a small backwoods garage in upstate New York; the eponymous tractor has been improvised from "a 1929 International truck rear axle and seat, a 15 horse-power motor from a hay baler, front wheels from a Chevrolet car… and a gas tank from an outboard motor". Nonetheless, it could "pull enormous loads in super low, yet travel up to 40 miles per hour" (p.352).

and improvisation in the leadership provided by the Head of ITSD, at least matching his visionary rhetoric. These include: his shrewdness in exploiting crises, the tactical alignment of SPRINT with the emergent Contact Centre, the artful deflection of the outsourcing threat and the audacity to conjure from "slack resource" both a BPR capacity and a major change programme. The survival of ITSD also depended on the determination of its staff to reinvent themselves, to take up the challenge of a new and enlarged role, a role only they foresaw with any clarity.

To conclude, in the story of ITSD's resurrection we have an instructive counterweight to the tacit managerialism of mainstream scholarship on change, which emphasises the supremacy of senior managers and top-down intervention. Against this, the innovation we witnessed in ITSD was spontaneous, bottom-up and emergent, and we have glimpsed the leadership qualities of ingenuity and artfulness that are required if such grass-roots innovation is to be brought off. ITSD's renaissance has a subversive edge, showing the limits of hierarchical power, de-stabilising the conceit that design is the sole prerogative of senior managers and their proxies. The heroes in our story were ordinary mortals, the accomplishments their own.[42] The emergence of SPRINT exemplifies innovation thriving on hardship and the reinvention of ITSD was the product of this same adversity. Had there been a conscious, top-down initiative "to build capacity for design and innovation", the outcome might well have been very different, with the additional bureaucracy and resources engendering sclerosis and rigidity rather than innovation and entrepreneurship. Any such external intervention might well have been resisted anyway.

The role of adventitious historical contingencies cannot be overemphasised. The 'special' conditions in ITSD were many and various, both positive and negative: its vulnerability in 1999, the threat of outsourcing, the academic research relationship, the advent of e-government, the spirit of extemporisation and opportunism, the availability of external funding, the lack of internal funding, the timely occurrence of service failures in other departments. Above all, it was an endogenous movement. ITSD's reinvention, and the capacity for design and innovation thereby created for the organisation as a whole, sprang from a unique configuration of chance, contingency and human virtuosity.

---

42 Law (1994) observes that histories of organisational change fall into two main categories: stories that tell of evolutionary change (quietly orchestrated by thoughtful, administratively-minded managers) and stories that emphasise crises and radical change. The latter are like Norse sagas, peopled with heroes, discontinuities and qualitative leaps. The present history (as I have told it in this chapter) belongs in the latter genre. Crises and heroes, the titanic struggle of the small against the powerful, are key motifs.

CHAPTER 3

THE KNOWLEDGE-BASE OF DESIGN

Evidence-based management – the very idea!

> *A bold new way of thinking has taken the medical establishment by storm in the past decade: the idea that decisions in medical care should be based on the latest and best knowledge of what actually works* (Pfeffer & Sutton, 2006, p.63).

With these hyperbolic words, Pfeffer and Sutton usher in what they see as a revolutionary new paradigm in the practice of management, the idea that it should be evidence-based, emulating professional practice in other domains, medicine in particular. Pfeffer and Sutton contend that managers would "practice their craft more effectively if they are routinely guided by the best logic and evidence, and if they relentlessly keep updating their assumptions, knowledge and skills… managers and companies that come closest already enjoy a pronounced competitive advantage" (p.64). Rousseau & McCarthy (2007) are also proselytisers; they define Evidence-Based Management (EBM) as "managerial decisions and organizational practices [being] informed by the best available scientific evidence… [enabling] well-informed managers to develop substantive expertise throughout their careers as opposed to faddish and unsystematic beliefs" (p.84). Leaving aside the natural scepticism such evangelism stirs,[43] here I shall adopt a positive stance, as I believe EBM and managing-as-designing have much in common and there are natural synergies to develop and exploit. Given its seminal position, I will set out Pfeffer and Sutton's argument at some length.

The paper begins by lamenting the way that professionals of all stamps traditionally make decisions, i.e. based on prior experience and strengths, compounded by dogma, belief, ideology and the blandishments of snake-oil 'sales reps'. All too often, the 'default solution' is evoked; it worked before and fits so well with what they already know. Pfeffer and Sutton

---

43 And indeed the significant body of critical research problematising the evidence-based movement across a range of fields, such as crime policy (Wastell, 2005).

also highlight the endemic problem of "uncritical emulation", the simple mimicking of high-performing role models. Though this can lead to gains, without local adaption and deep understanding, these will perforce be limited; and indeed there can be major losses, where critical features of the original organisation are not present in the imitator, such that the new practice fails and further ground is lost. Performance-related pay is used as a detailed example, in the form of the Forced Ranking System, whereby top-performing executives are given outsize rewards, the middle 70% are "targeted for development" and the bottom 10% are counselled or fired. In some companies, this method has seemingly succeeded and is strongly promoted by management consultancies. Yet when the evidence is interrogated, the effectiveness of forced ranking is shown to depend critically on the degree to which work relies on cooperation. Pfeffer and Sutton are unable to find a single study supporting its value in settings where collaboration, coordination and information sharing are crucial to performance. Indeed, in the automobile industry there is strong evidence to the contrary, that lean and flexible production systems, which emphasise teams and job rotation, build better cars at lower cost.

Pfeffer and Sutton acknowledge that becoming evidence-based is no primrose path. They cite a range of barriers: there's too much evidence (hundreds of journals and thousands of business books) and not enough "good evidence" to boot; often the evidence doesn't quite fit the local circumstances; scientific papers are arcane and obscure; and "stories are more persuasive" anyway. Several prescriptions are proffered for leaders to nurture the evidence-based approach in their organisations. For example, to demand evidence when new courses of action are being proposed and always to examine forensically the logic behind proposals: "When people in the organization see senior executives spending time and mental energy to unpack the underlying assumptions for some policy, practice or intervention, they absorb a new cultural norm" (p.71). Another tip is to treat the organisation as an "unfinished prototype". They elaborate as follows: "the best evidence is to be found at home, in the company's own data and experience... Companies that want to promote more EBM should get in the habit of running trial programs, pilot studies, small experiments" (p.71). Finally, businesses are adjured to esteem wisdom and intellectually curiosity: "EBM is conducted best not by know-it-alls but by managers who profoundly appreciate how much they do not know" (p.72). Cultivating the right balance of "humility and decisiveness" will be challenging, but can be facilitated by supporting "professional education with a commitment equal to that of other professions", such as medicine.

And will being evidence-based make a difference? The experience of medicine is invoked by Pfeffer and Sutton, which they claim shows "conclusively that patients receiving care that is indicated by evidence-based medicine experience better outcomes" (p.72). Although no specific studies are actually cited[44] (which is somewhat ironic) undismayed they proclaim that "the theoretical argument strikes us as ironclad... We have a huge body of peer-reviewed studies that provide simple and powerful advice about how to run organizations [and] if found and used this advice would have an immediate positive effect" (p.72). Despite the paucity of concrete evidence, I do not doubt their "theoretical faith" in EBM and have already provided my own "thought-experiment" in Chapter 1 which shows how theory could have averted the calamity of the ICS. I will now provide another cautionary tale from the beginning of my career, when I worked in the late 1970s on a collaborative project with British Telecom, the nationalised precursor of BT (Brown, Wastell & Copeman, 1982).

British Telecom at that time had recently completed a major modernisation programme in its telephone switch-rooms, phasing out the old 'cord board technology'. This had involved operators connecting calls by physically inserting plugs into sockets and then dialling the 'called party' in an attempt to make the call. The sockets were arranged on tall vertical panels which made up a long continuous bank, in front of which the operators sat.[45] This technology had remained virtually unchanged since the dawn of telephony; it was crude, the switch-rooms were noisy and operators had no view of anything else, except the panel which reared up in front of them. Its replacement, the CSS1 cordless switchboard, had been designed with considerable ergonomic care: all the various controls were arranged on a modern looking console within easy reach of the comfortably seated operator, who looked out over a spacious, carpeted office. Yet despite all this design effort, there was evidence of job dissatisfaction and impaired work performance, with 'Time to Answer' targets not being met. This had necessitated an increase in staffing levels of 8% to maintain the same level of performance as the old cord board!

The research itself took place at an interesting intellectual juncture, coming after an efflorescence of research on job satisfaction and motivation, within the Human Relations tradition we looked at in the last chapter. The Job Characteristics Model of Hackman and Oldham was particularly influential (Hackman & Oldham, 1976). It held that job performance and satisfaction were related to five job characteristics: skill variety, task identity, task significance, autonomy and feedback. Our diagnostic analysis showed that

---

44 This is not untypical. As one reads Pfeffer and Sutton, one meets claim after claim, all sounding eminently plausible, but typically backed up by anecdotal rather than hard evidence.

45 Most calls, of course, at the time were connected automatically – the switchboard would be rung only if callers were experiencing difficulties, or an operator service was needed (e.g. a transfer charge call).

the quality of the work in the new environment was deficient in all areas. The CSS1 board had partially automated the operators' task, reducing the first three elements. For example, skill variety had been reduced by limiting the opportunities to seek alternative routings for 'difficult' calls. Autonomy had also been eroded: work in the new regime was 'forced-paced', driven by a queuing system, whereas on the old switchboards operators had complete discretion over which call to take and when. Finally, feedback had been attenuated in various ways, some unwitting: e.g. by making the switch-room a quiet place to work, auditory cues about the busy-ness of the work group had been removed. Diagnosing failure is one thing, what about positive action? Whilst the argument is hypothetical, my strong conviction is that had the Job Characteristics Model informed design, a much better result could well have been achieved. Certainly the design work would have been more nuanced, considered and rigorous.

The synergies between EBM and design are potentially very strong. When Pfeffer and Sutton talk of organisations as "unfinished prototypes" and espouse the need for experimentation, this is 'design talk' *par excellence*. Design, I would argue, provides the natural domain for putting EBM into practice. In the hurly-burly of everyday work, the exigencies of decision-making mean there is often scant time for reflection, for consulting the evidence-base. Design work, however, is not like everyday practice, it typically takes place over a longer duration, allowing ample room for reflection and research. This is the natural ground for EBM to take root and flourish. And in turn, effective design should always be informed by the best evidence. Local knowledge is critical, i.e. the sort of systematic understanding of actual work practices which we saw Robert Owen so diligently seeking out (Chapter 2). But there is also room for the evidence-based manager to look further afield, to study other organisations facing similar issues and, above all, there is time and opportunity to consult the knowledge-base of management scholarship.

Examples: Goal setting theory and IT strategic alignment

> *The first principle of evidence-based teaching is to educate people on principles founded upon a convergent body of research... enabling their professional practice to reliably yield desired results.*

So write Rousseau and McCarthy (p.85) in setting out the prospectus for evidence-based practice in management, contrasting its backward position relative to the evidence-based movement in medicine and education. If EBM is to prosper, the first requirement is the presence of a "convergent body of research". They nominate 'goal setting theory' (GST) as their candidate exemplar. It would seem to fit the bill. The canon is indeed substantial. In a recent review, Locke & Latham (2002) point to a "35 year odyssey" of research on GST, from which they distil a number of stable generalisations.

Table 4 presents a partial summary of the knowledge-base, mixing key ideas from Locke and Latham with further principles cited by Rousseau and McCarthy. Although the exhibit is a mixture of the bromidic and the more nuanced (not quite up to the standards of the evidence-base in medicine, it has to be said), it is useful nonetheless, especially where the principles challenge common sense. Yes, there is a direct link between the setting of performance goals and job performance (principle 1), but this is "modulated" in various important ways. Principle 5 in effect says that self-set goals are critical in determining task performance and that assigned (i.e. external) goals only exert influence if they are embraced as legitimate. Principle 4 makes an important distinction between complex jobs and simple ones, stating that 'learning goals' are more effective for the former.[46] It is certainly a shame that the designers of the ICS had not read any goal-setting theory, especially precepts 4, 5 and especially 6. This might have suggested different design principles, such as measuring the quality of analysis of a case (learning goal) rather than setting a rigid, control-oriented goal (do this in 7 working days whatever the complexity).

1. Specific goals are more effective motivators of performance than general goals. Challenging goals are more effective motivators than less challenging goals.
2. If the path to the goal is not a matter of using automatised skills, people draw from a repertoire of skills that they have used previously in related contexts, and they apply them to the present situation.
3. People with high self-efficacy are more likely than those with low self-efficacy to develop effective task strategies.
4. When people are confronted with a task that is complex for them, urging them to do their best sometimes leads to better strategies than setting a specific difficult performance goal. A better approach is to set specific challenging learning goals, such as to discover a certain number of different strategies to master the task.
5. Assigned goal effects are mediated by personal or self-set goals that people choose in response to the assignment, as well as by self-efficacy. Goal acceptance is critical to goal achievement when goals are not set by the employee.
6. Prevention or control-oriented goals (with a ceiling or natural limit, such as 100% safety or zero defects) create vigilance and negative emotion in employees, whereas promotion or growth-oriented goals promote eagerness and positive emotion.

Table 4: Key ideas from Goal Setting Theory.[47]

46 Locke and Latham provide cogent experimental evidence of the efficacy of this principle. A group of business students playing a simulated business game who were set the learning goal of understanding how the simulation worked, financially outperformed students set the task of making the most money.

47 Paraphrased from Locke and Latham (2002), and Rousseau and McCarthy (2007).

GST provides one exemplar; I will examine another now in more depth. Elsewhere, I have argued that my field, that of Information Systems, furnishes a "formidable knowledge-base of tools, theories and critique" relevant to any manager, once the primary task of management is reformulated as system design (Wastell, 2010, p.427). To evaluate this claim critically, I will turn to a topic, that of 'IT strategic alignment' which is arguably the best candidate for the title 'convergent body of research' in my field. Certainly, the evidence-base is substantial. Chan and Reich (2007) unearthed 150 journal articles in their recent review of research going back two decades or more. In a parallel article, they ask the pertinent question "what have we learned?"

First, a definition is needed of 'IT strategic alignment'. Although definitions inevitably abound, that proffered by Reich and Benbasat (2000) would command the support of many. They define alignment as the degree to which the mission, objectives and plans contained in the organisation's business strategy are shared and supported by the IT strategy. Or, more simply, "Good alignment means applying IS/IT in an appropriate and timely way and in harmony with business strategies, goals and needs" (Luftman & Brier, 1999). The question of alignment is not an esoteric one; quite the contrary. The US-based Society for Information Management (SIM) conducts an annual survey of the pressing concerns of Chief Information Officers. For many years, this has identified 'strategic alignment' as a top priority issue; in the 2006 survey it was their foremost concern, and again in 2008.

The need for alignment is, of course, a general organisational problem.[48] Kaplan & Norton (2006, p.3) aver:

> *The greatest gap between the practices of Hall of Fame organizations occurs for organization alignment… and this indicates that alignment, much like the synchronism achieved by a high-performance rowing crew, produces dramatic benefits. Understanding how to create alignment in organisations is a big deal, one capable of significant payoffs for all types of enterprises.*

They go on to propose their well-known 'Balanced Scorecard' as a technique for achieving alignment across the whole organisation. Although alignment is a generic issue, it has nonetheless attracted disproportionate attention

---

48 Parsons (1956), for instance, views organisations as social systems, devoted to the attainment of goals. Alignment is key: "Primacy of orientation to the attainment of a specific goal is the defining characteristic of an organisation (p.64)". Rather more ironically, I recently described alignment as a "totalizing myth of the organization as a happy family, a perfect society in which the manager/worker divide has been forever sutured and all work for the common good" (Wastell, 2007).

in my field. Why this is so, I am unsure.[49] There is a smattering of research addressing alignment in other business disciplines, but I am not aware of any other area of management research where it has been addressed in such a concerted fashion. This has resulted in the accumulation of a substantial and coherent corpus of research. This is the scholarship that Chan and Reich have recently reviewed and which affords an opportunity to test the 'fitness for purpose' of the IS knowledge-base (Chan & Reich, 2007).

Chan and Reich begin by usefully identifying a number of key challenges in attaining 'IT business alignment': that corporate strategy may itself be unknown; that IT is seen as costly, 'low status' and is poorly understood; and that alignment is a 'moving target'. They then deal with conceptual complications arising in the research literature, such as the confusion between strategic and structural alignment.[50] Further methodological problems follow, including how to measure alignment. Then follows a plethora of research strategies, which can be divided into two main camps, those focused on cross-sectional correlations between "antecedents and outcomes" and those looking in more detail at longitudinal processes. The all-important question is then addressed of the link between alignment and firm performance: 4 papers are cited as showing a correlation with increased profits and a further study indicates that this depends on the business strategy. Two studies show no relationship, or even a negative one, but this contradictory result is attributed to the quality of the research ("lack of control variables") rather than constituting reliable evidence!

The paper's conclusions begin with "Future research directions", including the need for new research approaches, better measures and new "theoretical underpinnings". Finally, there is a section entitled "Implications for practitioners: key takeaways". Significantly, this makes up only 1.5 pages out of the 19 pages of the whole article. I have summarised these "takeaways" in Table 5, quoting from the original article with minimal paraphrase. Incidentally, it is interesting that only 20 specific papers from the total collection are used in drawing up this final review and that these are cited to make individual points, rather than clustering around consensual positions. Chan and Reich conclude:

> ...*we observe that alignment remains an important but elusive goal. Research is moving towards a more nuanced approach to definitions, measures, models, and prescriptions regarding alignment. Much is well understood but there is more to learn. We hope that this summary provides helpful information for future explorers and managers of alignment* (p.312).

---

49   We may speculate that the IT profession is uniquely renegade and there may indeed be special factors, such as the technical nature of their work, but I have no definitive answer.

50   The latter denotes the fit between how the IT function is organised relative to the rest of the business (e.g. decentralised vs. centralised).

The table shows, prima facie, that there is some practically useful knowledge to be gleaned for the reflective manager; the problem, as Pfeffer and Sutton rightly said, is finding it and then applying it in the local context. Chan and Reich's review in many ways exemplifies many of the endemic problems of academic research and its failure to penetrate management practice. Although the intellectual feat is impressive, the reader will have gathered that the paper is not for the practitioner. It is very much the academic community taking stock of what it has learned, rather than the learning which has been disseminated into the sublunary world of practice, where after two decades the problem of alignment continues apparently unabated. What is needed is a different dissemination approach and ethos, to make the knowledge accessible and actionable for the practitioner community; this will entail a richer narrative medium, including exceptions, alternatives and caveats, backed up by illustrative applications. I shall return to this general problem, of how to suture the gap between research and practice, in the final chapter.

General principle	Selected comments
Share responsibility for alignment	Alignment should be a joint responsibility between IT and business executives. The CEO is in the best position to facilitate alignment. His ultimate job is to make the organisation see itself as a broader community that shares core values. Executives and line managers should concentrate on improving the relationships between the business and IT functional areas, working toward mutual cooperation and participation in strategy development and prioritising projects effectively
Share knowledge	Organisations need to educate their IT professionals to be more business-oriented. Organisations should put junior business managers on project teams that deal with IT implementations so they get IT experience early in their careers. Systems analysts must learn about the deep structure of business, perhaps by following their applications into line units when they are implemented. The importance of regular communication between IT and business people at all levels cannot be over-emphasised.
Build the right culture and informal structures	Creating alignment is not just a matter of changing the CIO (Chief Information Officer) or implementing an IT steering committee. Over the long term, the culture and stories within the organisation must move from those of failure and defeat to those of mastery and success. Research shows how transfers of people can affect the culture of IT competence throughout an organisation. Organisations should consider cross-functional moves as a part of their organisational development.

Focus on the essentials	The following factors contribute to a well-integrated business and IT strategy: a CIO who spends productive time with business colleagues; an executive team that develops informed expectations for an IT-enabled enterprise; clear and appropriate IT governance; and taking an IT portfolio-management approach to balance risk and return.
Educate and equip – provide tools to demonstrate IT benefits	In order to increase alignment, CIOs should educate management about competitors' use of IT. IT executives should mount educational campaigns to educate senior executives about the benefits of IT alignment. Business managers and IT personnel need to measure IT effectiveness in order to demonstrate measurable improvements and bring about closer alignment.
Manage the IT budget	IT executives should think about where their business is going and ask whether their current IT spending can get them there. Business executives should manage IT investments just like any other investment – with an eye on the business case. Business and IS executives need to guard against choosing costly transition paths in managing IT resources [and] be careful not to radically change some aspects of IT strategy, while neglecting others.
Embrace change	When organisations face shifts in the business environment, a new or enhanced business strategy should be simultaneously implemented with a revamped IT strategy and a redesign of IT structure. IT management is similar to walking a tightrope, which balances IT innovation and business transformation simultaneously. IT should adapt and improvise in order to bring value to the firm and meet key strategic objectives.

Table 5: *The Evidence-base of IT business alignment*

The knowledge-base of Table 5 is expressed in broad generalities which invite further perusal and I will conclude by picking out a couple of papers for the interested reader. The two I make most use of in my teaching are: Luftman and Brier (1999) and Reich and Benbasat (2000). Both are highly readable. The former provides a simple list of "enablers" of alignment, supplemented by a range of practical measures which organisations can adopt to enhance alignment. Reich and Benbasat make a useful distinction between short- and long-term alignment, and identify four factors as "determining" the former (shared domain knowledge, a track record of IT success, strong communication and planning links) which are neatly illustrated through a set of mini-cases. The reader may also be interested in the views of the Chief Information Officer of a major financial services organisation regarding alignment, who I interviewed some years ago; some key extracts from that interview are set out in Appendix 1 (some perceptive comments on innovation and its impediments are also included).

The present chapter is about the relevance of the knowledge-base of scholarship to management practice. Although the prospects may not seem entirely convincing at this point, I'm glad to say that the options are not exhausted. In my field of Information Systems, there is a rich vein of research that follows a different course to conventional social science and I will turn to it now. Hevner *et al.* (2004) distinguish two broad approaches in IS research: 'behavioural science' and 'design science'. The aim of 'behavioralists' is to develop psychosocial theories that "explain or predict organisational and human phenomena" surrounding the application of technology. Design science, in contrast, seeks to develop a corpus of practically-oriented knowledge through which "the design, implementation, management, and use of information systems can be effectively and efficiently accomplished" (Hevner et al., p.77). Much of the IS research we have seen thus far belongs in the former category and this is indeed the dominant genre, though less so than in management research in general. In IS, design science may be a minority paradigm, but it is a long-standing and vigorous one; we have been spectacularly prolific in the production of tools and methods, though not so many of these have made the cross-over into practical application. In the remainder of this chapter, I shall review some important ideas and methods, beginning with sociotechnical systems design, which links directly with the human relations movement reviewed in the last chapter.

Sociotechnical design

> The persistence of socially ineffective structures at the coal-face is likely to be a major factor in preventing a rise of morale and in increasing labour turnover. The immediate problems are to develop formal small-group organisations... But it is difficult to see how these problems are to be solved effectively without ensuring that each of these groups has a satisfying sub-whole as its work task, and some scope for flexibility in work-pace (Trist & Bamforth, 1951, pp.37-8).

Though the above quotation could have been uttered in modern social services (with the coal-face reference a metaphorical one) we are back to the real coal face, over sixty years ago. The quote is from a paper by Eric Trist (a consultant psychologist and social researcher) and Ken Bamforth (a former miner with 18 years' experience, who, supported by his trade union, had taken a degree at Leeds University). Both men worked for the Tavistock Institute for Human Relations (Bamforth as an Industrial Fellow), an organisation set up in 1946 directly after the second world war, bringing together an eclectic assortment of researchers and consultants seeking to apply their therapeutic tools and techniques to alleviate the industrial problems of the post-war epoch. In 1947, the Institute founded the journal Human Relations, in which Trist and Bamforth's piece was published. The Institute still flourishes: its website[51] confidently proclaims:

> *The Institute is engaged with evaluation and action research, organisational development and change consultancy. Our staff work creatively with people involved in innovative activities, working across boundaries or in difficult situations. We combine research and analytical skills with practical help in devising solutions and in following through to implementation.*

The pioneering work of the Tavistock is no mere historical bauble. Its formation represents the origin of an important design movement that became known as sociotechnical systems design (STSD). STSD has been especially prominent and influential within the IS field. In my view, it continues to be as relevant to the industrial problems of today as it was at its inception, but sadly its precepts are not widely appreciated. Its wisdom needs to be better known – a revival is in order and, indeed, one is underway, involving a group of scholars and practitioners led by Chris Clegg at the Centre for Socio-Technical Systems Design, at Leeds Business School. As a long-time aficionado, I am proud to be part of this. In our recently published manifesto we set out our core argument in the following simple proposition: "80% of IT projects are known to fail. Adopting a socio-technical approach will help them to succeed in the future."[52] The reader will not be surprised to learn that the ICS was one of our disaster stories.

The IS scholar and sociotechnical advocate, Enid Mumford has provided a very useful summary of the historical development of sociotechnical thinking from the Tavistock days onwards (Mumford, 2003). She is also very well known for the development of her own particular variety of STSD, the ETHICS methodology (Mumford, 2003). Other overviews may be found in de Sitter *et al.* (1997) and Pava (1983). The following brief notes are a synthesis of these various sources.

The ultimate origins of sociotechnical theory take us back to the historical prologue in the previous chapter, resuming the story where we broke off with the advent of the human relations movement. Many important intellectual developments ensued over the subsequent decades (including the work of key thinkers such as Barnard, Maslow, Pareto, Simon, Lewin,

---

51   http://www.tavinstitute.org. Accessed December 2010
52   See http://www.wastell.org/STSD_Manifesto.pdf

Fayol, Parsons) as management established itself as an academic discipline, leading to the period which Wren describes as the "modern era" (Wren, 2005). But let us abridge this retrospective and shift directly to the birth of the Tavistock. In her book, Mumford maps out the international development of sociotechnical thinking, across Europe, the US and India. Developments in the UK were an important strand and Mumford describes some of the early projects (precursors of the sociotechnical approach) including the work of Trist and Bamforth with the National Coal Board (Trist & Bamforth, 1951). I will dwell on this early example at some length; the parallels with modern children's social care are intriguing and important. Keep in mind contemporary developments in social work, specifically the ICS and the parallel events in Erewhon, as you read this.

The focus of Trist and Bamforth's work was the mechanisation of the mining industry, specifically the introduction of moving conveyor belts, in imitation of the methods which had transformed factory production. Traditionally, miners had operated in small groups; the coal was 'hand got' by working with picks and shovels, and groups had collective responsibility for a given section of the coal face. They had close relations with each other, often being members of the same family; supervision was internal, having the quality of 'responsible autonomy' (Trist and Bamforth, 1951, p.6). The new technology of the conveyor belt ushered in a new form of work organisation: the so-called 'long-wall method of coal getting'. This involved a more complex division of labour: Shot-firers began the day's work using explosives to break up an extended stretch of the coal; fillers then loaded the conveyor belt with the loose coal to transport it out of the mine; in the afternoon, the conveyor movers arrived to dismantle and reassemble the belt at the new coal-face; packers then arrived in the evening to remove pit-props from the worked face. Coal production had thus moved from a small-group, multi-skilled activity to an "unsocial series of specialist activities which allowed little opportunity for interpersonal interaction".

Trist and Bamforth regarded the long-wall method as a "technological system expressive of the prevailing outlook of mass production" (*ibid.*, p.5). They made a critical distinction between "bad conditions" and "bad work":

> *"Bad conditions" tend to instigate "bad work"… The result is a tendency for circular causal processes of a disruptive character to be touched off. The system is always to an extent working against the threat of its own breakdown, so that tension and anxiety are created* (Trist & Bamforth, 1951, p.21).

Trist and Bamforth highlighted the very different situation of the mine to the factory. In the latter, all can be readily standardised, with control over the production process taken to a high level and contingencies managed to a minimum. The work environment of the factory is a stable one, but not so the mine. The underground situation is always changing, as the face advances by detonation and re-propping: "the activity of the ground has always to be dealt with and the ability to contend with this comprises the common fund of underground skill shared alike by all experienced face workers" (*ibid.*, p.23). Low productivity (Galbraith's 'slack resource') had inevitably evolved as "the only adaptive method of handling a complicated, rigid, and large-scale work system, borrowed with too little modification from the radically different situation of the factory" (*ibid.*, p.23).

To improve productivity and health and to alleviate stress, Trist and Bamforth recommended reinstating as much as possible of the original organic form of work, with fillers, conveyor movers and packers working in small, multi-skilled teams. All would be paid the same and have overall responsibility for managing their section of the face. Although this work-group concept ultimately proved highly influential in subsequent sociotechnical experiments in many other industries, developments in the UK coal industry were prematurely halted by resistance from the unions and the long-wall method was itself soon made redundant by new mining technology that automatically cut the face and loaded the coal.

In such early projects, we see STSD emerging as a counter-discourse to the Tayloristic 'logic of efficiency' which dominates management orthodoxy. Like any body of thought, it had absorbed important cognate ideas, especially from the Human Relations movement. Pava (1983) describes the fifties as a period of "gradual development" for STSD. Work continued with the Coal Board and projects further afield were undertaken, drawing on Tavistock ideas, including an Indian textile factory. In 1959, Fred Emery published the *Characteristics of Socio-Technical Systems*, which attempted to formulate the approach as "an analytical method that propelled sociotechnical design as something more than a vague admonition to match technology with people" (Pava, 1983, p.35). Emery's 9-step method involved techniques for environment and stakeholder analysis, variance analysis for sequential processes and social analysis based on examining different work roles.

Further important projects took place throughout the 1960s, including a major sociotechnical undertaking with Shell (Mumford, 2003). STSD's core idea, that technical and human factors need to be "jointly optimised", provided the theoretical driving force for the project, which apparently ran for many years. Opportunities for sociotechnical intervention also arose in Norway, where economic growth had stagnated and industrial modernisation was lagging (Pava, 1983). In response, the Norwegian Technical University led a grass-roots programme of sociotechnical design projects, several of which were launched and led to positive results.

According to Pava, this success aroused much interest in Sweden and, by 1973, over 700 similar projects had been set in train in its Scandinavian neighbour. By the end of the 1970s, Mumford writes that "sociotechnical ideas were becoming accepted. Projects were spreading from manufacturing to service industries" (Mumford, 2003, p.22). In her view, STSD had become something of a social movement, "a fertile environment for the development of new policies and values". The Council for the Quality of Working Life, for instance, was set up as an international group during this time.

Since those heady days, sociotechnical ideas have continued to be influential, although marginal. In retrospect, the 1970s seem less the dawn of a golden age, than the age itself. But the ideas are still alive, with the work of Mumford in particular having held some sway, especially in Information Systems. Most management texts will have a desultory mention or two; Daft, for instance, gives over a couple of pages, acknowledging the origin of STSD in the work of the Tavistock (Daft, 2004, pp.270-72). He proffers cursory examples of change projects where STSD precepts have been applied, noting that the core idea of joint optimisation of "technology and structure to meet the needs of people as well as efficiency, [has] improved performance, safety, quality, absenteeism and turnover" (Daft, 2004, p.271).

Interest though has tended to wane and academic publications have correspondingly declined, although there have been notable developments such as Clegg's updating of the sociotechnical desiderata (Clegg, 2000). A special issue of *Human Relations* devoted to STSD was also published in 1997 (volume 50, number 5), containing an excellent article by de Sitter *et al.* (1997). They identify mounting uncertainty and complexity as key challenges for organisations, for which two broad options are available. The first is to increase internal complexity, through the creation of more staff functions and processes and, therefore, more sophisticated management control structures. They dub this the strategy of "complex organisations and simple jobs". The second response takes the opposite tack, reducing control and coordination by the creation of self-contained units. Fragmented tasks are to be combined into larger wholes, thinking to be re-united with doing; in other words, a strategy of "simple organisations and complex jobs". The authors go on to elaborate their Integral Organisation Renewal (IOR) methodology in detail, but unfortunately no empirical case material is provided.

Principles of sociotechnical design

Inevitably variants proliferate, but some shared, foundational ideas of STSD can be identified (Mumford, 2003) which I will now try to summarise. First, that organisations should be seen as open systems, i.e. subject to the influence of an external environment to which they must adapt. Secondly, this work system should be regarded for analytical purposes as comprising two sub-systems, the 'technical' (the production technology, the formal work process, the skills required etc.) and the 'social' (comprising the human elements: individual and group behaviours, organisational and group culture, communication effectiveness, motivational levels and so forth). Joint optimisation is always the aim, meaning the search for a combination wherein the technical and the social systems are designed to fit the needs of one another, striving for the best balance between what workers need and want, and the technical requirements of the organisation for effective performance. Analysis of the technical processes focuses on the identification of groups of tasks which comprise 'unit operations', to be made the responsibility of the work-group. The concept of 'variance' is key, i.e. "problem areas where what did happen deviated from what should happen" (Mumford, 2003, p.23). Dealing more effectively with such variances becomes the focal concern of the (re)design effort.

Cherns (1976) codified the general principles of STSD as follows:

- Minimum Critical Specification (no more should be specified than is absolutely essential)

- The Sociotechnical Criterion (variances must be controlled as close to their point of origin as possible)

- The Multi-functionality Principle (work needs a redundancy of functions for adaptability and learning)

- Information (information should be available where it is needed for action)

- Support Congruence (systems of social support should be devised to reinforce desired social behaviour)

- Design and Human Values (high quality work requires stimulating jobs with opportunities to learn, a degree of autonomy and social support)

- Incompleteness (the recognition that design is an open-ended iterative process).

Two rather different examples of STSD approaches will now be reviewed.

Two examples of STSD

Mumford describes her influential methodology, Effective Technical and Human Implementation of Computer-based Systems (ETHICS), as having three principal objectives. The first is participative design. She argues that involving people in the design of their own work is more likely to lead to gains in both job satisfaction and efficiency, and to greater motivation and commitment when the new system is ultimately implemented. Second, that 'quality of work life' standards should be set as well as the usual performance and efficiency objectives: "Unless these are made explicit, and the technical system designed to achieve these, the human impact will be unpredictable... [with possible] undesirable consequences such as a routinization or deskilling of work, or an increase in stress" (Mumford, 2003, p.268). Finally, the technical system must be surrounded by a "compatible, well-functioning organisational system [including] the design of work procedures, individual jobs and work group activities; the specification of roles and responsibilities; and an ability to meet the needs of the customer" (ibid., p.268).

ETHICS involves a number of steps and tools to assist "logical thinking", though Mumford stresses that these are offered not as a "design straight jacket", but as a helpful guide, which will reinforce designers' morale and assist in communication. She emphasises the flexibility of ETHICS; it can be used on small and large projects alike and potential users are invited to "follow the process as set out, or pick-and-mix, or just use parts of it" (*ibid.*, p267). The steps are as follows. First, a clear need for change must be established, including discussion of present problems and potential opportunities for improvement, including the exploitation of new technology. Step 2 focuses on identifying the boundaries of the system (who will be affected, and so on), followed by a detailed analysis of existing arrangements (benefits and problems etc.). Key strategic objectives then need to be stipulated, followed by a thorough analysis of efficiency based on variance control (Step 5). Step 6 involves a questionnaire analysis of job satisfaction, covering knowledge/psychological and efficiency/competence needs, in terms of individual and group values. The future must also be explicitly considered, to ensure the system will continue to serve the organisation's purposes (Step 7). Based on the combined diagnosis of efficiency, job satisfaction and future needs, objectives are set in each category, to provide the basis for the design of the new system (Step 8).

The stage is now set for detailed Organisational and Technical design: "Ideally, new technology should fit an improved organisational design. Design groups are recommended to consider a number of options: team-working, multi-skilling, increasing decision-making authority" (*ibid.*, p.271). Mumford has a special interest in Information Technology and her methodology is often seen as an IT design approach (although this portrayal is far too narrow; hers is a method for designing the workplace as a whole). She notes the difference between the 1970s, when many IT systems were bespoke and ETHICS directly informed the design of software, and the more recent situation where off-the-shelf packages are procured. In the latter context, she argues ETHICS "to be of value in a different way. It enabled users to state their needs clearly and to test available software against their project objectives" (*ibid.*, p.272). Implementation then proceeds in Step 10, and here she reiterates the benefits of participation for easing the change process and facilitating the assimilation of new technical processes. Evaluation, the final step, is vital, with both early and later monitoring to check that "efficiency, job satisfaction and future change" objectives are being met.

Our second exhibit, the STSD methodology of Calvin Pava, has some particularly striking and genuinely innovative features (Pava, 1986; Pava, 1983).[53] Pava's main interest is in 'office work', broadly construed as white-collar, professional 'knowledge-work', such as software design. His primary criticism of conventional STSD is that it can only deal with routine processes, i.e. work which typically follows a "linear, sequential conversion process", with one step inexorably following the previous.[54] In contrast, non-routine work, the work done by skilled professionals and managers, addresses unstructured or semi-structured problems; it is driven by "plausible but imprecise information inputs, varying degrees of detail, extended or unfixed time horizons", and is characterised by fairly broad discretion (Pava, 1983, p.48). For Pava, this distinction is fundamental. Unlike routine work, its non-routine counterpart is characterised by:

- multiple concurrent conversion processes (i.e. the management of many activities at the same time)

- non-routine conversion flow ("a disjointed zigzag process" of problem-solving on uncertain, shifting terrain)

- vocational separatism (professionals are educated experts with a high degree of autonomy, qualities which do not readily fit the classical work-group concept).

---

53 Incidentally, Pava notes Emery's concern that his method could become "something of a fetish" even though never intended as "a universally applicable methodology" (Pava, 1986, p.203).

54 The ICS process model exemplifies this kind of work, though as we have seen it affords an invalid representation; social work is anything but routine.

Pava sees non-routine work as consisting of multiple, overlapping 'deliberations' carried on by flexible and fluid networks of individuals ('discretionary coalitions'). Deliberations are defined as "reflective and communicative behaviours" concerning equivocal, problematic topics; deliberations in software work (one of his examples) might include: 'requirements capture' and 'system specification'. In social work, assessment would be an example.

As all method-makers do, Pava sets out his own step-by-step guide, using software development as an example. Pava's technical analysis involves identifying relevant deliberations, examining the "organisational fora" in which they take place and mapping out the various parties involved. Each deliberation is analysed in depth, in order to extract its various elementary activities, looking in particular for important "information gaps". Pava's social analysis entails depiction of the role network for each deliberation, identifying who interacts with whom, attempting to summarise the "characteristic values" for each party, i.e. its primary concerns ("orientations"). Three types of inter-role relationship are distinguished, ranging from unity (strongly aligned) through convergence to contention, where there is significant conflict. Again, the key to improving performance is to optimise the joint design of the technical subsystem (the deliberations) and the social subsystem (the role networks). Pava suggests, as example interventions, human resource measures to support the formation of effective coalitions (e.g. job rotation, team-based pay schemes) and technical innovations to support deliberations (e.g. computer conferencing). Although his system is notable conceptually and hypothetical illustrations are provided, I am unfortunately unaware of any serious attempts to put it into practice.

Post-script: STSD and the ICS

Before moving to our next general category of design technique, it is instructive to consider explicitly the relevance of sociotechnical ideas to the ICS. In our various papers, we have argued at several points that the remedy for the ICS's failings was not the Luddite abandonment of new technology, but a different approach to design, based on sociotechnical precepts (e.g. Broadhurst *et al.*, 2010; White *et al.*, 2011). We accentuated STSD's core principles of user participation, minimum critical specification and the optimisation of local autonomy. Above all, we argued that it was essential to focus the design of systems on the needs of users, founded on a rigorous understanding of their working practices. This is vital primarily to gain reliable knowledge for designing new tools and processes, but also because, without such involvement, the risks of alienation and resistance would be aggravated. We noted parallels between the ICS debacle and problems encountered by other large-scale IT projects in the UK public sector, such as the gargantuan National Programme for Information Technology (NPfIT) in the health service. In doing so, we highlighted the argument of Eason that NPfIT had generally followed a "push strategy, thrusting new technology into the healthcare practices of the NHS" (Eason, 2007, p.258), leaving little room for local design. Eason makes a similar case in his own work for a flexible sociotechnical approach fostering local diversity, based squarely on user needs. We thoroughly concurred; had an STSD approach been followed in children's social care, a much better system could well have been developed, one that supported practice rather than disrupting it (Wastell & White, 2010).

Soft Systems Methodology

The second methodology which we shall examine at length is Soft Systems Methodology (SSM), again with many votaries in the IS field. Let me stress, though, that SSM is not specifically an IS design method; it is generic and can be applied in any context, just like STSD. SSM was developed by Peter Checkland of Lancaster University; it is known well in the UK but also has a strong international following. It is described copiously in a series of books written by Checkland and various co-authors (e.g. Checkland, 1981; Checkland & Scholes, 1990) and its pedigree is long. Checkland describes how SSM developed through 25 years of action research, aimed at dealing holistically with "messy real-world situations" using systems thinking (Checkland & Holwell, 2005). The empirical grounding of SSM is impressive. Checkland speaks of "several hundred systems studies carried out by Lancaster teams" (*ibid.*, p.12); the research, though based in the university, has always been conducted externally, working with "managers of all kinds and at all levels try[ing] to cope with the complexity of life's rich pageant".

Checkland makes an important distinction between 'hard' and 'soft' systems. Hard systems are typified by those dealt with by engineers, ranging across the spectrum of complexity from a domestic thermostat at one pole to a petrochemical plant at the other. Such systems can be rigorously defined and specified and can ultimately be realised as physical entities. Their design and optimisation is assisted by formal methods from mathematics and operations research; alternatives can be modelled and choices made on the basis of defined technical criteria. However, in many problematic situations faced by managers, such an engineering approach is not appropriate; indeed in such 'soft' situations it is the very inability to stipulate objectives, or even to define what the system really is, which "caused the situation to be regarded as problematic in the first place" (*ibid.*, p.12). Even situations which may seem to be simple, are not as simple as it may seem at first sight. Checkland gives the example of Concorde. Could the Concorde project simply be regarded as a system to create the first supersonic airliner? Or perhaps, as the name implies, it was 'really' a system to persuade the French that the British could be good European partners, nailing the myth of perfidious Albion. Or should it be seen as a system to develop UK aviation expertise? Of course, it was arguably all these things. What matters is that the project (i.e. the system) would be designed differently depending on the relative priorities. If the second definition were the overwhelming priority, then there would be no ultimate need even to deliver a working product!

Spurred by these considerations, Checkland developed a new approach, based on "the fact that all real-world management problems have at least one thing in common: they contain people interested in taking purposeful action" (*ibid.*, p.13). Checkland coined the concept of the Human Activity System (HAS) to designate the web of activities linked together such that the whole set accomplishes some defined goal. Notations for producing diagrammatic representations of such 'soft systems' were developed. These can be seen as blueprints for how the world 'might be', their role being to help in problem-setting, i.e. helping understand what the problem is and aiding in its solution or amelioration. Human activity systems are not real, stresses Checkland, they are conceptual, existing only in people's heads, ways of 'making sense' of how things are and how they could be.

SSM assumes a fluid social world, one which persists and changes, "continuously socially created in never-ending social processes". Just as for Concorde, there will always be different interpretations and opinions as to what is really going on, or what should be done: as many different worlds as there are participants and spectators. To accommodate such complexity, Checkland has a brilliantly simple solution: build a model for each relevant perspective! Checkland adopts the German word Weltanschauung (world-view) to refer to these different orientations. It is the immanent Weltanschauung which makes:

> ...a particular model meaningful, since the purposeful action which one observer perceives as freedom fighting will be perceived as terrorism by another observer with a different taken-for-granted image of the world (*ibid.*, p.13).

Checkland also adopts the term 'holon' from Arthur Koestler for abstract entities which are autonomous wholes and, like Russian dolls, potentially part of larger wholes. An example is urgently needed, methinks! Figure 2a shows a simple HAS.

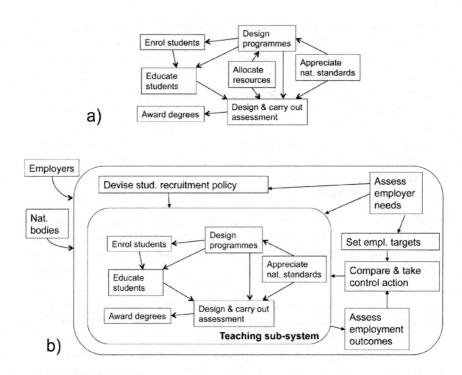

Figure 2: *An example conceptual model for a university system*

The hypothetical context (visible in Figure 2b) is higher education and the problem being addressed is the need to produce students with qualifications suited to the needs of potential employers. The notation is simplicity itself; bubbles denote activities and links indicate logical dependency, i.e. if A is dependent on B, this means that without B, A could not be done.

A set of activities is shown in Figure 2a. The activities certainly seem to be relevant to the issue at hand. But is this a system? It might seem so, but it is not. To see why, let me recapitulate the meaning of the ubiquitous term 'system' in the technical sense in which Checkland uses it and in which it is used more broadly in the world of systems thinking. Crudely, a system has the following characteristics: it is goal driven, purposefully transforming inputs to desired outputs, and feed-back loops are present (performance measures) to ensure that goals are achieved. Systems also operate in a defined environment, to which they are 'open'; they are encased by a permeable boundary and are capable of adaptation to changing circumstances, ensuring viability. None of the above properties is present in Figure 2a: there are no goals or feedback loops, there is no boundary and hence no environment, no means of control or adaptation. In short, no more than a 'headless chicken'. Clearly, more design work needs to be done to produce a fit-for-purpose system; this is where SSM comes in.

Like all methodologies, again we have a formal step model of how to do it (seven stages in all) but Checkland is clear that this is for expository and teaching purposes only, i.e. for the novice. Once basic competency has been acquired, the formal process becomes internalised and used in a much more flexible and fluid fashion. Checkland uses a sporting analogy:

> ...initially the thinking of the apprentices was SSM oriented. Everything that was done started from a reference to the methodology. It was noticeable that by the end of the work... [they were] using SSM more as a set of internalised guidelines which helped the attack on complex problems. The schoolboy batsman learning his craft thinks consciously about getting his left foot to the pitch of a good length ball, keeping his elbow up and swinging his bat through a vertical arc. Only when he has stopped thinking consciously about these things ... can he begin to be a real batsman (Checkland & Scholes, 1990).

The seven steps of SSM are shown in Figure 3.

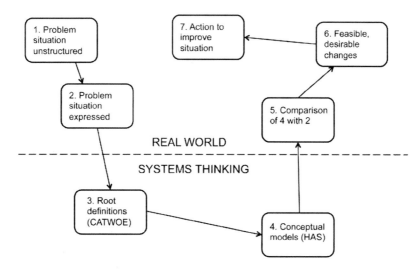

Figure 3: Overview of Soft Systems Methodology

Steps 1 and 2 take place in the 'real world'; they reflect the need for the SSM practitioner to understand fully, not the problem as such, but the problem situation, i.e. the organisational setting in which the problem is located. This 'zooming out' is critical for the reason already stated, i.e. the problem is imperfectly known; it guards against the danger of superficial diagnosis, with the real malaise going undetected. A deep understanding is thus sought in these early stages, to be articulated by drawing a 'Rich Picture', i.e. a detailed pictorial representation of the problem situation. There is no handy syntax for this: Rich Pictures are free-hand sketches or doodles and can contain as much pictorial and symbolic information as the author chooses.

An example is provided in Figure 4. Interestingly, it was produced by a member of IT Services at Salford,[55] around the mid-period of SPRINT's development, i.e. contemporaneously with the history recounted at the end of Chapter 2. Ominously the wind of change is shown at the top left, in the form of central government pressure. Internally, the vicissitudes of an overloaded bureaucracy are depicted with piles of paper and jangling telephones, and e-government is portrayed in the form of a threatening e-commerce train.

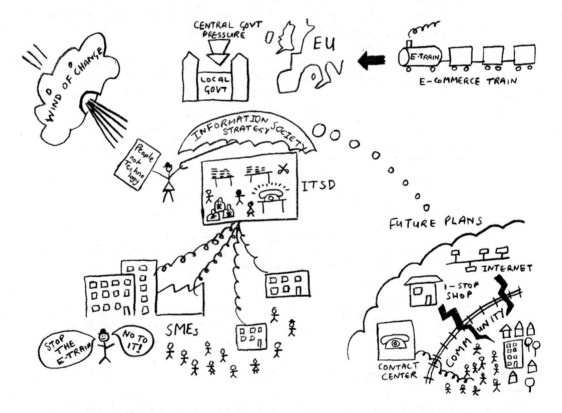

Figure 4: *Example of a rich picture*

---

55   Re-drawn from the original Rich Picture sketched by Maria Roberts of the Salford BPR team.

88

The most striking image is that of the *Information Society Initiative* as a protective umbrella in the centre, with future plans shown in the thought bubble on the bottom right. Like Figure 4, a good rich picture typically shows up different factions in the organisation, the presence of political conflict, important physical features (crowded offices, etc.), relevant internal and external threats and possible crises. The finished picture may be useful to others, but its real value is the way it forces the creator to think deeply about the problem situation, to understand it well enough for pictorial representation. Rich pictures may be an artistic challenge for some, but the real test is anthropological. If you're stuck for what to draw, that probably means you don't understand what's going on!

At this point, the analyst leaves the real world and moves into the world of systems thinking (Figure 3). It is time to build conceptual systems, which will inform the problem-solving process when the analyst re-emerges, blinking, from the grotto of 'pure reason'. Elaborating a HAS is a two stage process. From her real-world research, the analyst will have identified a number of relevant but, as yet, inchoate ways of thinking about the problem situation. Let us return to our university example. We shall assume that the original problem concerned the need to increase student recruitment. One idea emerging from, for instance, the interview with the Director of Teaching, would be to increase the employability of graduates. Sitting in her systems grotto, the analyst attempts to formalise this idea, first by formulating a 'root definition' for a HAS which would achieve this function. Six elements, represented by the so-called CATWOE mnemonic, must be specified. The essence of good design is of form following function, so let us begin with the transformation (T); systems are functional entities after all. In this toy example, the analyst decides to formulate the transformation as follows: the HAS takes candidate students (input) transforming them into marketable degree holders (output). The remaining elements of the root definition are as follows: the Customers (C) are the students, the Actors (A) are the university staff, the Owner (O) of the HAS is the university governing body, and the *Weltanschauung* or worldview (W) which makes sense of this system is the belief that awarding degrees is a good way of demonstrating the qualities of candidates to employers. The CATWOE formula also requires that relevant features of the environment (E) be addressed, for example national educational and assessment standards. Together these various elements can be combined to give the following root definition boiled down to a single sentence: "a system to award degrees (in accord with national standards) to demonstrate the capabilities of candidates to potential employers".

A "detailed" activity model is then built in stage 4, informed by the CATWOE. The analyst's first attempt was not very good. She tries again, aiming for a "viable system" that will fit the bill. Her second attempt, Figure

2b, is much better! There are boundaries, goals and feedback loops. Above all, we see the teaching system (of Figure 2a) embedded in a management system, which determines employer needs, sets recruitment policies and sets targets for the system's success in terms of employment outcomes. Irrelevant activities have also been pruned, i.e. the resource allocation process (it is not critical to specify this, such logistics can be assumed). Now this system would have a chance of working!

At this point, we re-join reality; the method in the madness is ready to be revealed. The activity model is not the real-world, it is a hypothetical world, which can be compared with the real one, to generate ideas for action. This is the crux of SSM. With "a handful of models of this kind, of purposeful activity built from a declared point of view" (Checkland & Holwell, 2005, p.13), a coherent debate can now be held about the problem situation and what can be done to improve things. This is the so-called comparison stage of the methodology (stage 5). The different models could reflect nuanced variations around a common theme (of increasing employability), but some radically different perspectives may have materialised in the analyst's peregrinations. For instance, the university might seek to improve its recruitment by enhancing its research profile. Here quite a different HAS would be relevant, dealing with funding-body priorities, the appraisal of research strengths and those of competitors, the development and management of a research strategy, and so on.

As noted, the purpose of the debate so stimulated is to enable the organisation to think collectively about desirable and feasible changes which could be made to move things forward (step 6). In the present case, setting up a system for appraising employer needs and graduate outcomes could be one such practical option, to be implemented in the final stage. Occasionally, an overall consensus may be found but, in general, Checkland acknowledges that this debate will involve finding accommodations between divergent interests, hence "feasible" as well as "desirable". Organisational politics, like all politics, is the art of the possible. Nor is action the end of the process: rather action is where the learning really begins; as Kurt Lewin quipped, "if you truly want to understand something, try to change it!" Checkland neatly sums up the over-riding philosophy of SSM as follows:

> *SSM emerged as a learning system. In principle the learning may go on and on, and to end a systems study is to take an arbitrary step, since problematical situations will continue to evolve and will never be free of differences of interest, opinions and values* (Checkland & Holwell, 2005, p.14).

Systems thinking – Senge and Seddon

> *Paradox is the technique for seizing the conflicting aspects of any problem. Paradox coalesces or telescopes various facets of a complex process in a single instant.* (Marshall McLuhan, *The Book of Probes*).[56]

At this point, we will move beyond the domain of IS to consider additional design tools of a generic nature, potentially useful to the manager-as-designer. In this section, I will examine further techniques and concepts within the systems thinking fold, which focus on the dynamic behaviour of systems. We will begin with the seminal work of Peter Senge on the 'Learning Organisation', highlighting the central part systems thinking plays within this (Senge, 1990).

Senge heralds five "component technologies" as the vital ingredients "in building organisations that can truly learn" (Senge, 1990). The first four are:

Personal mastery: "the discipline of continually clarifying and deepening our personal vision, of focusing our energies, of developing patience, and of seeing reality objectively" (*ibid.*, p.7).

Mental models: "deeply ingrained assumptions, generalisations that influence how we understand the world and take action... The discipline of working with mental models starts with turning the mirror inward, learning to unearth our internal pictures of the world and hold them rigorously to scrutiny" (p.9).

Building shared vision: "If any one idea about leadership has inspired organisations for thousands of years, it's the capacity to hold a shared picture of the future we work to create" (p.9).

Team learning: "When teams are truly learning, not only are they producing extraordinary results but the individuals are growing more rapidly than could have occurred otherwise" (p.10).

To these four elements, Senge adds the all-important fifth, that of *systems thinking*, "the discipline that integrates the disciplines, fusing them into a coherent body" (p.12). Systems thinking is:

> *The discipline for seeing wholes... Today we need systems thinking more than ever because we are being overwhelmed by complexity... Systems*

---

56   Two other pertinent 'probes' in the same ironical vein: "Effects are perceived, causes are conceived. Effects always precede causes in the actual development order" and "Every process pushed far enough tends to reverse or flip suddenly. CHIASMUS – the reversal of a process caused by increasing its speed, scope or size". For a publication applying the concept of chiasmus to the design failure of the ICS, see Wastell, White & Broadhurst (2009).

thinking is a discipline for seeing the structures that underlie complex situations (Senge, 1990, pp.68-9).

In common with this book's argument, Senge also sees leaders as designers *par excellence*, but acknowledges that this view of the leader as designer is not one which most managers would recognise. Senge offers the metaphor of the organisation as an ocean liner: "the neglected leadership role is the designer of the ship... It's fruitless to be the leader in an organization that is poorly designed. Isn't it interesting that so few managers think of the ship's designer when they think of the leader's role" (*ibid.*, p.341). Senge contrasts the conventional view of the leader with the more modest figure of the designer: "those who aspire to lead out of a desire for control, or to gain fame, will find little to attract them to the quiet design work of leadership", although deep satisfaction will be gained "in empowering others and being part of an organisation capable of producing results that people truly care about" (p.341). The design work of leaders includes "designing an organisation's policies, strategies and systems... integrating the five component technologies".

For Senge, what is required in the world of business is a fundamental shift in the managerial mindset (denoted by the Greek word metanoia). He proposes a number of practical techniques whereby this reorientation can be facilitated, focused on the development of each of the 5 disciplines. Here we shall be principally concerned with his concept of systems thinking, for which he proposes a simple tool called 'structural modelling'. Senge defines structure in a specific technical way, quite distinct from the conventional architectural sense in which the term is used with reference to organisations (i.e. static descriptions such as the organisation chart). In systems thinking, structure refers to the pattern of dynamic relationships amongst key components (variables) of the organisation. Senge employs the infamous 'beer game simulation' (a scenario involving actors up and down a supply chain ordering, selling, producing, distributing and warehousing a new beer) to demonstrate how the structural properties of systems dominate over the agency of individual human actors. Even when experienced managers play the game, unstable patterns of boom and bust are produced, despite the fact that consumer demand remains stable throughout. The oscillations derive from the lags between cause and effect, the dominance of local knowledge and the failure to understand the dynamics of the system as a whole. Above all, what the beer game teaches is that structure is more important than individual behaviour: "when placed in the same system, people, however different, tend to produce similar results" (Senge, 1990, p.42).

For Senge, the primary task of 'systems analysis' is to understand such 'dynamic complexity'. This involves learning to recognise generic patterns of system behaviour ('archetypes') which recur again and again ('circles of causality'). Distinguishing two forms of feedback is critical: *reinforcing (amplifying) feedback*, when a small change builds on itself, causing a self-fuelling escalation in the original effect; and *balancing feedback*, which operates whenever there are goals or targets that serve to regulate behaviour.[57] Whereas the former intrinsically produces instability, including exponential growth and possible catastrophe (such as the self-confirming prophecy of a bank run), the latter produces stability. Being able to identify these two forms of feedback and appreciating how they interact is the key to understanding organisational behaviour. The presence of lags (i.e. delays between causes and effects) is of central importance; it is such lags which make the management of complex systems so difficult.[58] The so-called 'shrink-swell' effect, for instance, refers to the delay between interventions to improve performance and the realisation of demonstrable gains. An initial dip is inevitable, as the innovation is assimilated. It will always take time for new ways of working to be learned and incorporated, before the benefits are tangibly seen; the danger is that if managers do not understand such delays (or work under a management regime which makes no such allowances) then precipitous decisions may be taken, e.g. to abandon the new approach and try something else, again with the same dysfunctional effect. That way lies instability, decline and failure.

Figure 5 provides an pertinent example of such systems thinking, using my version of Senge's notation. I have used the example of forced ranking from Chapter 2 to consider the full range of the possible effects of this management intervention. Key variables are shown in boxes and the arrows linking them show the potential causal influences which can be imagined. Angular arrow heads show positive links whilst blunt terminals show inhibitory influences, where an increase in one variable (e.g. morale) produces a decrease in its dependent (e.g. staff turnover), and vice versa. Feedback loops are not explicitly shown. Senge provides some specific notation for distinguishing reinforcing and amplifying feedback; here such loops have been left implicit. They can readily be identified though. Setting targets for individual performance, for instance, provides an instance of balancing feedback, acting to stabilise the individual's behaviour at a particular level, assuming the level is within practicable reach.

---

57 Positive and negative feedback are the more usual engineering terms for these two forms of systemic behaviour.

58 As the psychologist Dietrich Dorner (Dorner, 1996) has also shown in a set of ingenious experiments. Using an economic simulation tool, he revealed various 'pathological' methods used by subjects for coping with complexity, such as the tendency to focus narrowly on single variables (*encystment*) or to flit erratically from one aspect to another (*thematic vagabonding*). In an earlier paper, the effects of stress were addressed; elevated stress was shown to engender cruder 'system management' strategies, based on reactive rather than proactive control (Dorner & Pfeifer, 1993).

Looking at the system in Figure 5 as a whole, the crunch question is: what will be the overall outcome of forced ranking? The flow emphasised in the thicker links, through individual ambition and performance to enhanced organisational performance, is what we want to happen. The rest of the reticule of causal ramifications draws attention to all of the other possible effects when the system is considered as a whole, many of which have the tendency to counteract and undermine the desired effect. And the net result? The only plausible answer here is that we cannot tell... and that is the point! It will depend on how the various forces work together and come into 'dynamic equilibrium', assuming that the system ultimately settles down to a stable pattern of behaviour. The aim of systems thinking is first and foremost to attempt to grasp the complexity of such organisational dynamics and the presence of possible unintended consequences. Drawing diagrams such as Figure 5 can be helpful, but it is the mode of thinking that is important.

There is currently much interest in system thinking of this kind in the UK public sector. Eileen Munro, for instance, has championed the systems approach in the context of child welfare (Munro, 2005) and was leading a national review of child protection services at the time of writing. Her work is directly pertinent here, given our opening depiction of the child protection system as a "system in crisis". Paraphrasing from the Review's interim report:

> *A systems approach will help this Review to avoid looking at parts of the child protection system in isolation, and to analyse how the system functions as a whole. Social workers accept many previous reforms were well intended but their interaction and cumulative effect on frontline practice have had unintended consequences. The Review will use systems theory first to explain what has happened, providing a strong basis to build the Review's understanding. Second, the intention is to use systems theory to look forward, helping design an improved approach* (p.10).[59]

'Systems dynamics' diagrams akin to Figure 5 feature prominently in the interim report, especially to highlight unintended adverse consequences ('ripple effects') of targets and excessive "procedural prescription" on professional discretion and staff morale. Munro's models illustrate how overemphasising compliance can reduce job satisfaction, leading to elevated staff turnover, which in turn will tend to reduce the experience level of staff, which itself will operate to lower the public status of the profession. And so unfolds the systemic reading, showing how policy reforms aimed at enhancing practice, can produce opposing, counter-productive effects.

---

[59] E. Munro (2010). *The Munro Review of Child Protection Part One: A Systems Analysis.* Published October 2010 by the Department for Education. See: http://www.education.gov. uk/munroreview/downloads/TheMunroReviewofChildProtection-Part%20one.pdf

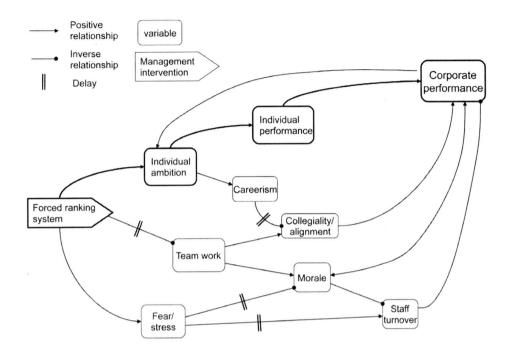

Figure 5: *Illustration of a structural model*

A leading proponent of systems thinking in the UK is John Seddon (Seddon, 2008). Seddon has been strongly influenced by the celebrated management theorist William Edwards Deming, especially his work on the Toyota Production System, invented by Taiichi Ohno (Deming, 1994). Deming insists that organisations should be managed as systems: "the greatest leverage for change is achieved when the organisation is understood as a system" (Seddon, 2008, p.68). Deming is highly critical of what he calls the "current management style", whose defining feature is its reactive "atheoretical" nature. Being based entirely on skill and experience rather than a theory of management, the present style "is the producer of waste, causing huge losses whose magnitudes cannot be evaluated" (Deming, 1994, p.22). Numerous examples of the deficiencies of the orthodox style are given, including our old friend forced ranking. Deming avers: "Ranking is a farce. Apparent performance is actually attributable to the systems that the individual works in" (*ibid.* p 25). Another relevant pearl concerns numerical goals:

> *A numerical goal accomplishes nothing... A numerical goal leads to distortion and faking, especially when the system is not capable to meet the goal (p.33)... Anybody can achieve almost any goal by: redefinition of terms, distortion and faking, running up costs* (Deming, 1994, p.43).

As an alternative to the prevailing style, Deming sets out his *System of Profound Knowledge* (*ibid*). It has four components, the first of which we have already encountered ("appreciation for a system") and the second we shall review shortly, "knowledge about variation". The third element (with resonances of EBM) is a "theory of knowledge", emphasising prediction based on theory and data, whilst the fourth encompasses "psychology", highlighting in particular the importance of intrinsic over extrinsic motivation. The former develops in people "self-esteem and confidence. They develop self-efficacy. Their work is meaningful, and they will make improvements in what they do" (Deming, 1994, p.111).

In his own work, Seddon dwells at length on the importance of measurement but, following Deming, he stresses that the organisation must first be understood as a system before relevant metrics can be identified and collected. The test of a good measure, he argues, is whether it helps us understand and improve performance; quite a different emphasis from the use of so-called 'key performance indicators' in a performance management regime! Like many other gurus invoked in these pages, Seddon is sceptical of codifying method or inscribing it in tools, citing a remark of Taiichi Ohno:

> *Mr. Ohno believed just-in-time was a manufacturing advantage for Toyota. And for many years he would not allow anything to be recorded about it. He claimed that it was because improvement is never ending, and by writing it down the process would become crystallised* (Seddon, 2008, p.68).

Important in a public sector context, Seddon makes a key distinction between service and manufacturing: "there is inherently much more variety of demand… you have to think of the system as one that brings (largely) intangible expertise together in response to the variety of customer demands" (Seddon, 2008, p.68). Service organisations therefore need to be designed for customers to "pull value" from the organisation, "to get exactly and only what they want in the most expedient fashion" (*ibid.*, p.69). Recalling Galbraith and the general thrust of sociotechnical thinking, this entails the necessity "to integrate decision-making with work (so the workers control the work) and use measures derived from the work" (p.70). Seddon makes another important distinction between two sorts of service demand: *value demand* (providing the service that people want) and *failure demand* (caused by service failures, e.g. missing a refuse bin collection).

Failure demand is endemic in the public sector and Seddon gives numerous examples. Reducing failure demand by doing things right in the first place is his primary lever for improvement: "when failure demand falls, customers experience better service and costs fall. At the same time capacity – the number of things you can do – increases" (p.72). Public services must therefore be designed against demand, by understanding what customers really want and involving front-line staff:

> When managers study demand in customer terms, they begin to grasp the expertise that call-centre workers will need to enable customers to get what they want. Engaging the workers in solving this problem ensures it becomes part of continuous improvement (p.74).

The need for managers to develop a deep understanding of the nature of variation is vital. Following Deming, Seddon distinguishes two sorts of variation in service performance: *common variation* (i.e. no two cases are ever the same, so spontaneous variation will always be present) and *special variation* (one-off or rare events, different from run-of-the-mill fluctuations). Deming refers to a phenomenon called 'tampering', defined as the "costly confusion between common causes and special causes [which] leads to the frustration of everyone, to greater variability and to higher costs, exactly contrary to what is needed" (Seddon, 2008, p.99).

Deming's famous 'funnel experiment' demonstrates the pernicious effect of such tampering and demonstrates the folly of managing by results if variation is not properly understood. The equipment needed is a funnel, a table marked with a target, and a marble. Your goal is to drop the marble on the target, using the funnel to aim; 50 attempts are allowed. Although the funnel is positioned directly above the target, the results scatter randomly around this central point. This is natural variation. Can we do better, asks Deming? Why not adjust the funnel after each drop to compensate for the last error, by moving it an equal distance away in the opposite direction; surely this will improve 'system performance'? But it does not; the micromanagement actually increases the scatter by 41%. Worse still, though Deming does not comment on this, the managerial intervention has itself cost time and effort. Deming goes on to show that any form of intervention will only make matters worse, introducing more variation and instability. And all because the metaphorical manager failed to appreciate the variation being observed was natural.

Throughout his book, Seddon is highly critical of the command-and-control management 'thought-style' of what is now the *ancien regime* of New Labour. Targets and inspection come in for particularly withering attack, as does the government's obsession with IT. Seddon enumerates the various fallacies underlying the "irrational belief in targets"; just a few examples will suffice to get the drift, see Table 6. Inspection is absolutely the wrong way to go:

> ...people should be their own inspector. Having trained against demand, people know what to do... in such designs, the worker is responsible for their own development. Training is much faster and more efficient (p.75).

Such a focus on prevention rather than inspection is, of course, a powerful challenge to "conventional beliefs about control". Like his guru, Seddon seeks intrinsic motivation, i.e. people actively wanting to do a good job and to improve the service they provide, with design thus built into the process. With relish, he quotes the aphorism of Frederick Herzberg (another management luminary) that "if you want people to do a good job, give them a good job to do". He is at pains to distance himself from false forms of empowerment, which he scathingly sees as "a preoccupation of command-and-control managers, who design systems that disempower people, notice the problem and send their people on empowerment programmes" (p.77) and then put them back into the same system!

Seddon briefly describes his own methodology, the Vanguard model. Central to this is the imperative to understand what the customer wants, with managers exhorted to "go to all the places where the organisation transacts with customers and study demand in their terms" (p.80). How well the system copes with demand is crucial, for which it is vital to study the 'flow of work', following 'pieces of work' through the system, rather than drawing elegant process maps. Identifying the 'system conditions' which produce 'waste' (i.e. unproductive or ineffective work) is critical. Later in the book, Moore's idea of 'public value', which we encountered above, is tentatively set out as an overarching philosophical principle to guide service reform. Seddon explicitly makes the link with design: "Moore argues for the integration of policy and administration – a powerful idea. In my language, it is to put design in the process" (p.163).

Belief	Seddon's debunking (from pp.100-104):
Targets make people accountable	Yes, they do and people behave accountably. But who should be held accountable for the fact that achieving targets actually makes services worse. The accountability bureaucracy serves the hierarchy… [it] interferes with the way services work.
It is impossible to run services without targets	Wrong again.. it is essential to run services without them – instead using measures derived from the work. Many managers are incredulous when first introduced to systems thinking… working without targets is such a challenge to their mental models.
The alternative is ambiguity and fudge	Wrong. The alternative is clarity and utility. Using measures derived from the work in the hands of people who do the work leads to better control and continuous improvement. Gaining knowledge and understanding is anything but ambiguity and fudge.

Table 6: The fallacies of targets

Borrowing from software engineering: user-centred design

> In the 1970s and 80s, the software industry embraced the idea of building software to a User Requirements Definition... This has informed the contemporary approach to product design... that of 'user-centred' design. This approach makes consideration of the needs of the user – the person who will ultimately use a product or service – primary when setting the goals and outcomes of the design process.

The above quotation has been taken from the Design Council's 'Transformation Design' methodology, referred to in the previous chapter (Burns *et al.*, 2006, p.10). It describes how the need for user-centred design was first acknowledged by the software development community, but has now spread well beyond this niche to influence product and indeed service design, including in the public services.

The Design Council's user-centred design approach is worth examining closely. The methodology begins by averring that "many of today's more complex problems arise because the latent needs and aspirations of end users are not being met by the current offer" (*ibid.*, p.18). It is recognised that end users are complex individuals: "their underlying needs are rarely evident or articulated at the outset, and are unlikely to be identified through traditional market research" (p.18). A user-centred approach is regarded as very different from a customer-centred one which focuses exclusively on meeting customer expectations; it "demands the ability to look at a problem from a perspective that may be fundamentally different from that of the business-owner or service-provider" (p.18). A user-centred design approach involves three core skills, paraphrased in Table 7 and taken from pages 18 and 19 of Burns *et al.* (2006):

Core skill	Elaboration
Looking from the point of view of the end user.	Designers use a range of qualitative research tools to understand a particular experience from the user's perspective. Observation helps uncover some of their more latent needs and desires. Immersing themselves in context helps designers to gain empathy and allows them to observe, analyse and synthesise simultaneously. These research methods do not aim to yield any quantitative or objective research 'truth', but rather to provide inspiration and actionable insights.

Making things visible.	Designers make problems and ideas visible, creating frameworks to make visual sense of complex information, and quickly sketching ideas to share work-in-progress with others. Making even intangible concepts visual creates a common platform for discussion, avoids misinterpretation and helps build a shared vision. Artefacts created can include concept sketches, representational diagrams, scenario storyboards, plans, visual frameworks and models or physical mock-ups.
Prototyping.	Designers like to 'suck it and see' by building mock-ups or prototypes before they commit resources to building the real thing. In business terms, this is a good risk management technique: commit a little and learn a lot; fail early to succeed sooner. This culture of trying things out quickly, getting feedback and then iterating the idea is a fast and low-cost way of moving a project forward. Websites can be represented with a paper prototype, products by making card mock-ups and services by staging interactions with props and role-play.

Table 7: Core skills of User-Centred Design

The report provides several case studies. Research on easing the burden of chronic disease provides the first illustration, specifically Type II diabetes. The work took place in the northern English city of Bolton and was aimed at helping individuals make adjustments to their lifestyle. The design team worked closely with one such sufferer, Angela, and involved an eclectic range of specialists: designers, health policy specialists, social scientists and doctors. Workshops with a wider group of diabetes patients and their carers were held. Importantly, Angela

> *…wasn't simply the subject of the research, but an active part of the design team. She helped develop ideas, participating in a number of prototypes and making suggestions for improvement: what we call a co-design approach"* (*ibid.*, p.13).

A number of simple innovations were produced, including a set of 'agenda cards' to help patients articulate their needs and requirements in clinical consultations. The cards were demonstrated to make communication more efficient, cutting down the amount of time getting to the heart of a problem from 10 minutes to 2 minutes, thereby freeing up time to spend on supporting the patient's needs:

> *Quick prototypes like these not only helped the team and the Bolton Diabetes Network see ways of reconfiguring an existing service around the user, but also gave them insight into how a very different health service*

might work: one where people and professionals collaborate to co-create new types of healthcare (ibid., p.13).

Another example is entitled "Transforming rural transport". It was based in Northumbria, a rural county where key services are widely dispersed and can be difficult for people, particularly the elderly, to reach. Working with a local innovation and design consultancy, the County Council set out to develop a design approach to rural transport issues. A spokesperson for the consultancy is quoted, reflecting glowingly on the experience of working together. This had proved:

> *...the value of taking a service innovation approach to rural transport... The projects have demonstrated how service innovation can bring a disparate team of stakeholders together and focus them on the service provided to the customer... As service designers we're interested in how service thinking can unlock complex problems by re-framing the issue from a service point of view – that is, focussing on access or mobility rather than transportation.*

Much has been written on User-Centred Design in software engineering. Although the central concern of the software developer is the design of a technical artefact, there is nonetheless much generic design wisdom to be gleaned. The writings of Don Norman have been particularly influential and the reader is warmly referred to his classic book, *The Design of Everyday Things* (Norman, 1998). Here we furnish one brief, though somewhat topical, example.

As we saw in Chapter 1, the last few years have seen a remarkable transformation in UK statutory children's services, with traditional paper records now universally supplanted by electronic ones. To embark on such a profound, technological change, you would imagine that the necessary technical design work had been carefully and diligently done. If nothing else, our natural predilection to print out electronic documents invites such a careful approach, especially when the files are lengthy and contain complex information and argumentation – rather like social care records! But our research on the ICS suggests the opposite, with policy seemingly driven by an article of faith, that "electronic is best" (White *et al.*, 2010). As noted above, we argued that the root cause of the difficulties of the ICS was the paucity of careful design work, with lack of user involvement being the primary failure, and we forcefully argued the case for user-centred design.

Good design for electronic documentation systems is particularly critical, given the intrinsic limitations of the digital medium, such as small screen size, the lack of depth and structure of the 2D display and other absent facilities, such as the ability to manipulate files physically, and so on. Research has shown that reading time is significantly longer than for paper, up to 30%, and there is evidence too that comprehension is impaired (Dillon, 2004). In his seminal book on the design of electronic documentation, Dillon (*ibid*) urges that several key principles should guide the design of electronic text.

> We still have a long way to go before we can come close to designing e-texts that compare favourably with paper for most routine uses. The process will be accelerated by good design, but conversely, it will be hampered by weak design… The human is the key; only by relating technologies to the needs and capabilities of the user can worthwhile systems be developed (Dillon, 2004, p.185).

One precept is paramount, namely the need to test the system "on users performing real tasks and redesigning accordingly" (p.186). Dillon also contends that an electronic system should "add value by offering facilities to perform activities that are impossible, difficult or time-consuming with paper designs" (p.186). I completely agree: design must be user-centred, aiming to give users something better than that which they have at present. It is significant that the research reviewed by Dillon involves the relatively simple situation of a reader with a single linear text, carrying out a proof-reading task that requires only superficial information processing. How much more crucial are his design strictures in the context of a complex documentation system comprising multiple linked records for every client, where deep understanding is essential.

But what has this to do with managers? I hear the muffled protest; this is surely a technical matter. But behind this technical failure lies a much more profound managerial failure. As I wrote in a polemical blog for the professional journal *Community Care* (Wastell, 2010):

> There are important messages in this for senior managers. When decisions were taken to move to electronic recording, were managers aware of the [research] evidence? Should not the ubiquity of "printing out" have prompted more critical interrogation of business cases set out in purely economic or policy arguments? The evidence-based approach in the field of management is steadily gaining ground in the public services. Its application in the present context might well have pre-empted expensive investments in technology, which actually compromise professional performance, and ushered in important new thinking at a much less consequential point.

Disquiet there was on the front line, but senior managers seem not to have been aware of it. If they were, why were no forceful steps taken to articulate concerns to central government? Why did no-one, with a few notable exceptions, speak out? I know of one case where a Director of Social Services was publicly singing the praises of ICS, yet his deputy was saying quite the opposite back-stage, and both at the same conference. Did 'pleasing the centre' rather than understanding their own organisation and representing its interests take priority? Or was the ICS seen as a technology project and, therefore, not their business? It is very hard to imagine that the needs of staff and the demands of the professional task were the dominant concerns rather than the implementation of policy diktats and hitting performance targets.

Homo Faber and the abundance of technique

There is no shortage of technique when it comes to design. More methods based on systems thinking exist, a cornucopia indeed. Flood & Jackson (1991) provide a handy overview of 8 distinctive approaches (with case studies) including SSM, VSM (see below) and Systems Dynamics as well as their own 'Total Systems Intervention'. The latter provides what could be called a 'meta-methodology', allowing the user to choose from a tool-box of systems techniques, according to the particular contingencies of the situation. 'Multiview' is another such multi-method framework (Avison & Wood-Harper, 1990), as is SPRINT, as we shall see in the next chapter. Software engineering is also replete with a rich variety of tools and methods. And doubtless further afield, across the range of engineering and design disciplines, more such technology may be found, readily adaptable to the needs of the enterprising, design-minded manager.

Attempting a comprehensive review is as impractical as it is undesirable. Technique, after all, is not the solution, as I have hinted at various junctures, and may indeed be the problem, a point to which I will return at length in the book's final section. But I do have some pet methods not yet mentioned and several of these are set out in Appendix 2, to which the un-sated reader is referred. From the systems stable, I provide an overview of Stafford Beer's Viable Systems Model (VSM), a conceptually challenging though esoteric perspective which can be used for both analysis and design, as the appendix illustrates.

And from software engineering, I briefly say some words about scenario-based design, followed by another software engineering approach, the 'agile methodology' known exotically as 'Scrum'. Scrum is popular in software development, but it can serve as a general project management framework (Pichler, 2010). The name (not an acronym) is said to derive from an holistic approach developed by Takeuchi & Nonaka (1986) for increasing speed and flexibility in commercial product development in which the whole process is performed by one cross-functional team.[60] Scrum is relevant here for several overlapping reasons. First, with its emphasis on self-organisation, learning and minimal structure, it exemplifies the sociotechnical approach in action. Second, it provides a model for the management of design projects and the work of design teams. Thirdly, because it is generic it can be applied to the design of work in a range of domains, especially for processes which are non-routine, to use Pava's term. How about social work, for instance? Of course, I am not suggesting that Scrum could be directly imported into social work, although there are some obvious points of similarity with the Erewhon "cell model". It is the comparison with Scrum as a heuristic which is important, i.e. by comparing the orthodox social work model with innovative approaches in other disciplines, aspects of its taken-for-granted character can be brought to the surface, challenged, and ideas for different ways of doing things could result. Thinking in this way is design thinking, par excellence. Could social work learn nothing from Scrum? Self-set deadlines, allowing a backlog of work but keeping track of it… Couldn't such principles be adapted and used in some form or other?

---

60 Takeuchi and Nonaka liken the "new product development game" to rugby, where the whole team "tries to go the distance as a unit, passing the ball back and forth", in contrast to the traditional model, wherein functional specialists "pass the baton" as in a relay race. The defining features of the "rugby approach" are: self-organising project teams, light management control, overlapping development phases and organisational learning.

CHAPTER 4

DESIGN IN ACTION

IT – commodity or competitive weapon?

> *No-one would dispute that IT has become the backbone of commerce. The point is, however, that the technology's potential for differentiating one company from the pack – its strategic potential – inexorably diminishes as it becomes accessible and affordable to all.*

So wrote Nick Carr in an article in the *Harvard Business Review (HBR)* in May 2003. Provocatively entitled 'IT doesn't matter', it created something a furore (Carr, 2003). Carr's argument was simple: that with the advent of generic software packages and standard hardware, IT had become a ubiquitous commodity and, like other "infrastructural technologies" (the railways and electricity), it could no longer confer on businesses a sustainable competitive advantage. A storm of protest was predictably evoked and the following issue of *HBR* contained a collection of letters extending over 17 pages, from various intellectual grandees. The response by Brown and Hagel[61] was typical: yes, they agreed, businesses may have overestimated the strategic value of IT and overspent accordingly, but they saw a dangerous sophistry in Carr's thesis, exacerbated by its all too memorable title. They argued that "it appears to endorse the notion that organisations should manage IT as a commodity input" (Brown & Hagel, 2003, p.2). Quite the contrary they averred: the real lesson to be learned is that IT "by itself rarely, if ever, confers strategic differentiation. Yet, IT is inherently strategic because of its indirect effects – it creates possibilities and options that did not exist before." (*ibid.*, p.2). As we saw in Chapter 1, quoting the same pundits, it is only those organisations that use technology as a means of "process innovation" that will gain advantage; simply using technology to automate the status quo will not do.

The imperative for using IT to innovate is not new. An important *HBR* article, also with a sensational title, had made the same argument somewhat

---

61   Chief Scientist of Xerox and management consultant respectively, regular *HBR* contributors.

forcefully over ten years previously. Authored by the aptly named Mike Hammer, its punchy title was 'Reengineering work: don't automate, obliterate' (Hammer, 1990). Hammer's argument was simple: "The heavy investments in information technology have delivered disappointing results largely because companies tend to use technology to mechanise old ways of doing business. They leave existing processes intact and use computers simply to speed them up" (Hammer, 1990, p.104):[62]

> *Speeding up those processes cannot address their fundamental performance deficiencies... [they] came of age before the advent of the computer... It is time to stop paving the cow paths. Instead of embedding outdated processes in silicon and software, we should obliterate them and start over. We should re-engineer our businesses: use the power of modern information technology to radically redesign our business processes in order to achieve dramatic improvements in their performance.*

Business Process Reengineering

With the publication of Hammer's piece, a new term entered the managerial lexicon, Business Process Reengineering (BPR). Although it has acquired some notoriety over the years, being seen as a euphemism for down-sizing or the replacement of human labour by machines, the original meaning had different connotations, with strong sociotechnical resonances. Hammer's principles for redesigning work distinctively revolved around the potential of IT to create larger, more complex jobs, reintegrating work which had become fragmented into functional silos. Although BPR can mean that fewer staff are needed, in its original formulation this typically involved machines taking over the only jobs for which they are ideally suited: those that involve repetition, routine and drudgery.

IT's capability to transcend time and space in the sharing of information provides this potential. Hammer gives the example of Mutual Benefit Life, an insurance company. Its old process was typically bureaucratic and labyrinthine: insurance applications would go through as many as 30 discrete steps, spanning 5 departments and involving up to 19 people. Typical turnarounds ranged from 5 to 25 days. A new approach was needed. It was realised "that shared databases and computer networks could make many different kinds of information available to a single person" (Hammer,

---

62 But actually, it's much worse than that, as we have seen with the ICS. Because computers are less flexible than paper, often requiring all sorts of ingenious but unproductive workarounds just to get the job done, you get a faster mess if you're lucky. As the pseudo-mathematical adage has it: OO + NT = EOO, i.e. Old Organisation + New Technology = Expensive Old Organisation!

1990, p.106). Existing job definitions and departmental boundaries were swept away and a new position was created called a case manager:

> Case managers have total responsibility for an application from the time it is received to the time a policy is issued. Unlike clerks, who performed a fixed task repeatedly under the watchful gaze of a supervisor, case managers work autonomously. No more handoffs of files and responsibility, no more shuffling of customer inquiries (ibid., p.106).

No crude Taylorism this, the epitome of STSD I would say: complex jobs and simple organisation. And the outcome? Applications were turned round in as little as four hours, with an average of between 2 and 5 days, and case managers were able to handle more than twice the volume of new applications.[63]

Writing at around the same time, another founding father of BPR should be mentioned. In collaboration with James Short, Thomas Davenport was pulling together a very similar manifesto. In a paper in the *Sloan Management Review*, Davenport and Short heralded the birth of a new management paradigm, which they initially dubbed the "New Industrial Engineering" (Davenport & Short, 1990). We have the same heady rhetoric. The paper begins by invoking Taylor who, at the beginning of the century, had "revolutionised the workplace… No subsequent concept or tool has rivalled the power of Taylor's mechanising vision" (Davenport & Short, 1990, p.11). Not until the advent of the New Industrial Engineering, that is, although that particular catchphrase has since sunk without trace (though the core ideas have endured). For Davenport and Short, the New Industrial Engineering represented the confluence of Business Process Redesign (the analysis and design of workflows) and Information Technology, or more specifically, its critical potential to enable radical process change. "How can business processes be transformed – rather than merely supported – by IT?" becomes the central question.

Rather than Hammer's homely mix of maxims and stories, which make up the rest of his HBR piece, Davenport and Short adopt a more scientific approach for the new industrial engineering, as would seem fitting for the direct heir of scientific management. The paper provides an overview of a 5-step methodology. The first step calls for the development of a "business vision"; this is seen as essential for a methodology that seeks

---

63 A rather similar case was widely reported in Manchester (UK) in the mid-1990s, that of National Vulcan (another insurance company). Comparable results were obtained, with identical methods, i.e. shifting to a case management approach. Some staff did lose their positions; the new work was more demanding but those who were able to adjust found their pay increased, along with a job that was more rewarding too. There are also obvious parallels with the Erewhon case in Chapter 1.

profound change, rather than piecemeal rationalisations. The need to set clear process objectives is a vital part of this; these could be efficiency gains, or indeed STSD-style improvements in the "Quality of Work Life" (*ibid.*, 14-15). Subsequent steps are to identify the processes to be redesigned, to understand and measure these, to identify IT levers (given its transformatory potential, IT must be considered in the early stages of redesign) and finally to develop a prototype of the new process. Davenport and Short end by emphasising that redesign is not a one-shot activity; continuous process improvement should be the overarching philosophy. In a subsequent book, Davenport sets out his espoused approach in much greater detail (Davenport, 1993). Again, there are strong sociotechnical resonances.

Returning to Hammer, although the *HBR* article had something of an impact within academic circles, it was the publication of the business 'blockbuster' *Reengineering the Corporation: A Manifesto for Business Revolution* which really put BPR on the practitioner's map (Hammer & Champy, 1993). In the second edition, Hammer and Champy define BPR as "the fundamental rethinking and redesign of business processes to achieve dramatic improvements in critical contemporary measures of performance, such as cost, quality, service and speed" (Hammer & Champy, 2001, p.35). Four terms are emphasised in this definition and, again, the hyperbole is striking: *fundamental* ("reengineering begins with no assumptions and no givens", p.35), *radical* ("getting to the root of things, not making superficial changes" p.36), *dramatic* ("reengineering should be brought in for heavy blasting, blowing up the old and replacing it with something new" p.36), and *processes*. This last term they acknowledge to be the "most important in our definition", but it gives managers the most difficulty. Most managers they claim:

> *...are not process-oriented; they are focused on tasks, jobs, on people, on structures... [they] lose sight of the overall objective, which is to get goods into the hands of the customer who ordered them. The individual tasks within this process are important but none of them matters one whit to customers if the overall process doesn't work, doesn't deliver the goods (ibid., p.38).*

Hammer and Champy go on to enumerate a set of BPR principles. These desiderata include: the need to combine several jobs into one, for workers to make decisions, for work to be performed where it most makes sense, to reduce checks and controls, and for case managers to provide a "single point of contact". Many of these principles are focused on eliminating "non-value-adding" activity. Simplicity should be the main aesthetic: multiple versions of the same process, each one "tuned to the requirements of different markets, situations or inputs" are to be preferred to complex "one-size fits all processes" (pp.58-9). IT is depicted as "playing a crucial role in BPR, but one that is easily miscast... throwing computers at any existing business problem does not cause it to be reengineered" (p.87). Hammer and Champy portray IT as a disruptive technology, one that enables profound change. They set out a range of exemplars, using the template in Table 8, of how the various potentialities of IT can revolutionise conventional assumptions about the organisation of work. Although sociotechnical writers such as Mumford have taken a more sceptical position (Mumford, 2003), I venture that, in terms of its original 'ideology', BPR is about as sociotechnical as you can get! Above all though, BPR is about innovation, not "paving cow-paths" (to use Hammer's metaphor), unless of course the cow-path is the best route!

Old rule (assumption)	Disruptive technology	New Rule
Managers make all decisions	Decision support tools	Decision-making is part of everyone's job
The best contact with a potential buyer is personal	Interactive video disk	The best contact is effective contact
Field personnel need offices	Wireless data communication and portable computers	Field personnel send and receive information wherever they are
You have to find out where things are	Automatic identification and tracking	Things tell you where they are

Table 8: Examples of IT as disruptive technology

BPR in the public sector

> *Compared to the public sector, I think life is easier in the private sector in that requirements and objectives are more clear cut, and what I see going on in the public sector is too many sets of requirements pulling in too many different ways. Whether the project is IT or not, it's trying to square too many agendas.[64]*

Although BPR in its initial incarnation was mainly associated with commercial organisations, interest soon began to develop in the public sector. I published a BPR methodology in 1994, for instance, in which one of the case studies was in the health service (Wastell, White & Kawalek, 1994). Writing in 2003, Mackintosh comments: "in recent years, business process approaches have become increasingly popular in the public sector in

---

64 Extracted from the interview with the Chief Information Office of a major UK financial services organisation mentioned in the previous chapter (Appendix 1).

general" (MacIntosh, 2003, p.327).[65] Mackintosh notes that the general take-up rate of BPR by organisations at that time had been estimated at between 50% and 70% and that many BPR projects had ended calamitously, with a typical failure rate of around 70%. Macintosh's own research compared two public sector projects with a private sector one. Two were "radical" initiatives (new structures with redefined job roles), one private and one public sector; both had been implemented rapidly and had produced significant improvements in performance. The other public sector project was, in contrast, incremental and had produced little corresponding benefit.

An earlier paper by McAdam & Donaghy (1999) is also noteworthy. It opens by commenting on the relative paucity of BPR research in the public sector, with the majority of studies focusing on key factors for successfully implementing BPR in non-public sector organisations. McAdam & Donaghy set out to examine whether the same "critical success factors" (CSF) found in this prior research also applied to the public sector. They noted that public sector organisations have a number of specific characteristics, which may have a bearing on the prospects for BPR. These include: rigid hierarchies, a collegial culture, the presence of multiple stakeholders for many processes, volatility of policy direction and the presence of overlapping initiatives. Their study found that, despite these features, "BPR was seen as having a large potential for improving processes within public sector organisations" (*ibid.*, p.48), and that many of the CSFs in the private sector were equally relevant to the success of BPR in the public domain. They note that the "professional politicized organisational climate" of the typical public body creates considerable scope for political manoeuvring, suggesting that the micro-political hazards are likely to be more problematic. Proper attention must hence be paid to many of the "soft issues" of people management if BPR is to flourish. They concluded by enumerating the factors deemed most important for successful BPR in the public domain including: top management support, commitment and understanding of BPR; communication and empowerment; the alleviation of downsizing fears; preparedness for organisational change and the need to enlist customer and stakeholder support.

As noted, one of the case studies in Wastell *et al.* (1994) was in the UK National Health Service and it is instructive to examine this in a little more detail, not least because the methodology deployed was a precursor of SPRINT and drew heavily on two of the systems approaches I reviewed in the previous chapter (STSD and SSM) as well as the work of Davenport

---

65 Of interest in terms of the academic 'fashion business', Mackintosh notes the "rise and fall" of research on BPR, by tracking the output of scholars such as myself. From a small handful of papers up to 1992, the graph then rises steeply, with between 200 and 300 papers being produced per annum until 1999, when the graph collapses just as precipitously.

and Hammer. The setting for the work was a major teaching hospital in the North West of England and the research took place in 1989. Major investments in IT systems had been made over the preceding years. This antecedent context is important.

One major initiative that had taken place was in the Outpatients Administration (OA) section. All outpatients' activity in the hospital (i.e. patients attending for consultations or reviews, as a result of referrals from family doctors) was centrally organised, making use of a common facility shared by all clinical specialties (a 'shared service' we'd call it in today's terminology). The appointments process had been of particular concern. The previous paper-based system had revolved around the appointment ledger. Upon receipt of a referral letter from the family doctor, clerical staff assessed the urgency of the case and made an appointment at the first suitable opportunity. A letter was then typed and sent to the patient. If the patient was unable to attend, they were asked to contact the OA department and a new appointment would be made. A major problem was the high rate of failed appointments, as many as 30% of patients simply did not attend (DNA). An expedient way of handling this had been to over-book the clinics, by writing additional names into the paper ledger below the official list of available appointment slots. It had been hoped that a computerised appointment system would 'improve efficiency' – the main changes being to make the appointments diary 'electronic' and to automate the printing of appointment letters.

Would these changes abate the DNA rate? Is this an example of BPR? The answer to both questions is, of course, a resounding no. The process is more or less the same as before, letters were still being sent (albeit marginally more quickly at the hospital end) and responded to in the same way. Recalling Pfeffer & Sutton (2006), where is the logic of the business case, i.e. the rigorous argument which runs from careful analysis through to the design of a solution? There had, apparently, been no investigation of why patients missed their appointments; how then could it be seriously hoped that the computerised system would help? Here was a paved cow-path if ever there were one, and because the new electronic ledgers would only allow the official number of slots to be booked, a worse process to boot, removing the over-booking workaround.

Subsequent to this central initiative, a grass-roots initiative took place in one of the clinical departments (Cardiology) of the same hospital (Wastell, White & Kawalek, 1994). OA was the main concern, as this was a source of many problems, not just missed appointments. Our sociotechnical analysis revealed the true complexity of the OA process; it involved the cooperative work of a diverse range of people: patients, doctors, nurses, secretaries, clerks, medical records staff, even porters who carted the medical records around the hospital. Specific attention focused on the identification and analysis of variances, i.e. recurrent problems that affected performance, especially from the patient's point of view. Many variances were found: e.g. the inability to identify patients on the hospital's central IT system, missing clinical notes when the letter to the GP was to be written, and so on. A detailed social analysis was also undertaken as we were aware that there were endemic personnel problems. A psychological analysis of each job involved in the process was performed using the Job Characteristics Model (Hackman & Oldham, 1976). One job, that of the Notes Clerk, was implicated in several key variances. Each clinical department in the hospital had such a clerk whose remit was to keep track of notes as they entered and left the department. The job was critical and required considerable informal knowledge as well as careful discipline, yet it was badly paid and suffered from high staff turnover. Poor performance of this job by unmotivated and inexperienced staff was the prime cause of one of the major variances afflicting the OA process, namely missing clinical notes.

Having completed our analysis, a new process design was elaborated which, following STSD precepts, attempted to optimise both technical (i.e. efficiency) and social (e.g. improved job satisfaction) objectives. It was proposed (in broad outline) that the hospital abolish its hitherto centralised OA bureaucracy, giving more authority to departments such as Cardiology to manage their own affairs. A number of specific IT-based measures were also suggested. It was proposed that Cardiology develop a local management information system to underpin the new organisational arrangements, which would provide a database of critical administrative and clinical information. A network of external electronic links was also proposed, for example to the hospital laboratory for speeding up the reporting of blood test results. More controversially, we recommended electronic links to community health centres so that family doctors could book appointments and receive reports directly. The business case for all these measures was clear. For appointments, we had established that many DNAs arose simply because the appointment times were inconvenient. There were other factors too, e.g. that the hospital's catchment area contained a high proportion of transient residents, such as students. Making appointments directly, while patients were present in health centres, would optimise the possibility of finding a mutually convenient time. On the social side, it was proposed that the Notes Clerk job be upgraded and training improved.

Many of these recommendations were accepted and implemented. Our proposals were made at a time when the hospital was actively considering the sort of decentralisation that we had proposed. As a result of this reorganisation, clinical departments were given more autonomy and the central support facilities were broken up. Local 'business managers' were appointed and more administration was devolved, with departments working more like independent business units. We assisted in the implementation of the new management arrangements in Cardiology and supervised the detailed design and implementation of a computer-based departmental information system, which was used as a template for other departments in the hospital. However, one crucial aspect of our prospectus was not implemented, the idea of direct appointments. It was deemed politically unacceptable, too open to queue jumping. There is an irony here. One of the more successful elements of the NHS's national IT programme mentioned in the previous chapter, the "Choose and Book" module, provides exactly this facility, though it has taken over 25 years before seeing the light of day!

Redesigning public services: A tale of two cities

At this point, I will present a longer case study of successful service redesign in the public sector. The case epitomises management as design, with IT used as the primary instrument of innovation within an implicit sociotechnical framework which stresses both improvements in service performance and in the quality of work-life. The case also provides a master-class in the management of (technological) change, brought out all the more cogently by comparison with the catastrophic failure of a similar initiative in another location.

Whether or not the problem of IT failure is more or less prevalent in the public sector, such calamities are certainly more visible, taking place in full public view. Perhaps the most celebrated such disaster in the UK came in 1992, when the recently implemented computer-assisted despatch system of the London Ambulance Service (LASCAD) crashed. LASCAD has since become notorious as an iconic example of information systems failure, spurring numerous research papers (e.g. Fitzgerald & Russo, 2005; Beynon-Davies, 1995; Wastell & Newman, 1996). The crash itself hit the newspaper headlines with lurid suggestions that 20–30 people had died as a result. The Chief Executive resigned and questions were asked in Parliament, leading to the instigation of a Public Inquiry. Intense media interest was aroused and further enquiries followed. In summary, the various investigations revealed a sorry state of affairs. Several immediate factors were implicated, although ultimately the root cause of failure was laid at the door of LAS's senior management. Although the LASCAD fiasco occurred some years ago,[66] the key issues remain as valid today as ever; sadly, they appear to be timeless. So, I shall dwell on this case and parallel developments in another city at some length, beginning with a summary of the highlights of the London fiasco.

Poor decision-making over the choice of supplier was one symptom of the managerial malaise. Despite the consultants Arthur Andersen recommending a working budget of £1.5 million and a cautious implementation time-scale, the successful bid, in an open tendering process, had come in at £937,000, nearly £700,000 cheaper than the next tender. Part of the reason for this low price was the quotation of only £35,000 for software development from the software partner (SO) in the successful consortium. The previous IT experience of SO for emergency services had been limited to administrative systems and the software had perforce to be developed from scratch. SO were persistently late in delivering software and the package had manifest technical deficiencies. Despite these clear warning signs, no action was taken by LAS management. No formal quality assurance processes were in operation and it appeared that the consortium had been largely left to get on with it themselves.

Also problematic at the time was the parlous state of industrial relations in LAS, where a climate of distrust and 'them and us' antagonism reigned between management and staff. A core feature of LASCAD was its capability for locating and allocating ambulances to handle incidents, an explicit attempt to automate the despatching task. It is unsurprising that it was seen by control room staff as a reflection of management's desire to reduce discretion and to eliminate outdated working practices. There had also been very limited consultation with ambulance crews in the design work and a gap of several months arose between training and implementation. During implementation there had also been evidence of deliberate sabotage, with staff entering incorrect data, for instance, a classic 'counter-implementation' tactic.

Having exhumed the bones of the LASCAD fiasco, let us turn to our main case study, a similar initiative at roughly the same time in another metropolitan district: the Greater Manchester Ambulance Service (GMAS). At the time, GMAS's emergency ambulance service was provided by a fleet of around 65 highly-equipped vehicles with paramedical support, based at a number of dispersed ambulance stations. The movements of the ambulances were coordinated by a control centre in central Manchester. At the time, GMAS was undertaking a similar computerisation project to the LAS one. It involved a product known as ALERT which had been procured

---

66   Lest there is anxiety that the story is relatively old, I invoke still older wisdom, of Confucius: "If by keeping the old warm one can provide understanding of the new, one is fit to be a teacher".

from a local software house and was based on tried and tested software used by other emergency services.

Of note was the computer project's direct alignment with the business strategy of GMAS. GMAS had recently applied for 'Trust status', endowing greater managerial and commercial independence in the 'internal market' conditions instigated in NPM's early ascendancy under the Thatcher regime. Computer-based information systems were seen as essential. Quoting from the Trust application:

> ...[they] enable planned initiatives in the pursuit of improved service delivery. In the short term, this information will ensure that management can, where necessary, re-deploy resources to become more effective and cost efficient. In the long term, the information will provide an accurate, comprehensive and detailed database which will be available when the Trust is entering into negotiations with purchasers.

A brief history of the GMAS computer project

From interviews with key staff and from my personal involvement with GMAS over 18 months, a short history of the project will now be reconstructed, highlighting critical aspects of the way the change process was handled.[67] We take up the story in the summer of 1993, with the appointment of an experienced middle manager (PC) from within the service. PC possessed a strong combination of technical and managerial skills and worked full-time on the project. Implementation was set for the Spring of 1994. From the outset, PC took a firm hold on the technical side of the work, engaging in extensive and thorough negotiation with the software providers. Although ALERT was a proven product, considerable customisation was required in order to ensure that the system exactly satisfied GMAS's requirements and was consonant with their working practices. 'Getting it right' was seen as the top priority in project planning rather than hitting deadlines. On the user side, the importance of keeping control room staff well informed and up to date with progress was recognised; a newsletter was created and regular meetings were held to inform staff of progress and to allow anxieties to be voiced. Where possible, staff were involved the development of the system and many features were included of direct help to them, e.g. a database of key unofficial landmarks (such as public houses).

Live implementation of ALERT occurred in June 1994. Stress levels were beginning to rise in anticipation of the transition to computer-based

---

67   The narrative is digested from the full research report published in Wastell & Newman (1996).

operation. The manager of the control centre commented as follows on the testing phase conducted immediately prior to full implementation:

> *There was a great deal of apprehension at first... A lot of people didn't want the system, they feared it would make their job harder. Now they all want it... they didn't want it switched off at the end of the trial.*

PC handled this critical period with considerable élan. A comprehensive training programme was executed, building up from basic training in keyboard skills to role-playing exercises with simulated incidents. Staff were provided with well-designed, individually customised, user manuals. The successful execution of a series of live trials was used to build up confidence in the system and to test it under real operational conditions. The quality of the training, the care taken in tailoring the design of the system and the thoroughness of the testing programme helped to ensure that the switch-over to computerised operation was a complete success.

Prior to computerisation, ambulance command and control had involved two basic stages, beginning with receipt of a "999" telephone call. Call-takers took down details of each call on a paper form, the "Call Receipt Record" (CRR), which was then handed to an ambulance despatcher depending on the incident's location. There were four such despatchers, each responsible for a quadrant of the GMAS area. Having decided which vehicle to deploy, the despatcher contacted the appropriate ambulance station and the vehicle was mobilised. Communication between despatchers and ambulances was mediated via a combination of the telephone and a radio link. Ambulance crews used a small panel of buttons in the cab to transmit status signals back to the control room, indicating the time at which the ambulance left its base, the time of arrival on scene, etc. This information was vital and, prior to computerisation, the despatcher was required to transcribe it manually onto the CRR and also onto a 'plotting chart', an A3-sized grid recording the changing disposition of each despatcher's ambulances.

In essence, the computer system had replaced this paper-based process with a shared database: call-takers now typed the requisite information directly into the database and jobs were automatically routed to the appropriate despatcher, appearing in a job queue on the despatcher's display. ALERT indicated the ambulance stations closest to the incident and provided a number of other useful information displays, e.g. an electronic version of the plotting chart. Although ALERT had not changed the basic structure of the command-and-control process, it had improved it in a number of areas, e.g. assisting in establishing the definitive location of incidents by providing an on-line 'street-finder' and a thesaurus of well-known landmarks. The integration of the radio link (i.e., the automatic recording of status messages) provided a major advantage as this laborious activity had sapped a significant amount of time and attention.

Over the implementation period, a number of changes were also made to the physical arrangement of the control room. Its austere decor was given a face-lift and the layout of the room was changed, in order to concentrate the despatchers at one end of the room with the call-takers at the other. Before the change, control staff worked in two teams, each a mix of call-takers and despatchers. While the new configuration at first sight appeared to be detrimental in breaking up the teams, there was a strong rationale for the re-organisation, namely that it brought the whole group of despatchers into close proximity, which facilitated cooperation and coordination for incidents close to quadrant boundaries.

Evaluation

A comprehensive evaluation of the impact of ALERT was carried out, which was my primary responsibility on the project. Two periods were compared: pre- and post-implementation. Baseline measurements were taken in January/February 1994 and post-implementation data was collected in October/November 1994. By this time, ALERT had been running smoothly for several months and was well bedded-in. The evaluation took a sociotechnical approach; both staff welfare and performance were treated with equal importance. In particular, the alleviation of stress had been an explicit design objective. Ambulance command-and-control is stressful enough, as can be imagined, so aiming to reduce rather than add to this, was an important goal. To assess this, a real-time psychophysiological evaluation was carried out focusing on the relationship between work demands and stress levels for despatchers during operational conditions. Two cardiovascular parameters were measured (heart rate and blood pressure) using a device purchased from a high street chemist, which was simply slipped onto the left index finger with minimal intrusion. Despatchers were also asked to indicate their 'subjective state' at the same time, i.e. how anxious and fatigued they felt using a simple rating scale.

Then, as now, national targets and indicators were used to appraise the performance of ambulance services, e.g. an ambulance should be on scene, for instance, within 8 minutes for 50% of incidents. There was clear evidence of an improvement in performance with ALERT, with the hit rate increasing from 55.4% to 64.4%. This improvement is particularly impressive as the number of emergency incidents had increased by 15% between April and October. Underpinning the improvement was a small but significant reduction in incident response time of around 1.5 minutes. Although seemingly small, it is possible to translate this, albeit tentatively, into a meaningful outcome for one important class of emergency, that of cardiac arrest, where the relationship between emergency care and survival has been extensively researched. Nichol *et al.* (1996) combines the findings of 36 major research studies, quoting an improvement in the probability of survival of 0.7% for each minute reduction in response time.[68] Although theoretical, with 2530 cases per annum this translates into 35 to 40 lives saved.

Regarding stress in the control room, let us begin by noting that the despatcher's job is a very demanding one. In essence, despatching involves two inter-linked tasks. The primary task involves identifying the location of an incident, prioritising its importance and finding the most appropriate ambulance to despatch. Linked to this is the complementary task of ensuring that there are no gaps in cover, i.e., local areas where all ambulances are active on jobs with none available for new emergencies. This secondary task can involve moving ambulances from one location to another, "like pieces on a chess board" as one despatcher put it. The essence of the despatcher's job is to balance these two tasks, knowing that life or death can depend on getting it right. Moreover, there is little spare capacity: at peak times as many as 80% of ambulances may be occupied on jobs. The combination of cognitive complexity, an uncertain dynamic environment, low spare capacity and high risk, adds up to a cocktail of acute stress. Comparing high and low levels of workload, it was found that whereas blood pressure increased with workload for both paper and computer-based operation, the rate of increase was approximately 50% less steep for ALERT. This represents dramatic evidence that ALERT was helping operators to cope with escalating task demands with less stress. Similar results were found for subjectively recorded anxiety levels.

A short post-implementation questionnaire was used to elicit users' opinions about the impact of ALERT. Overall, control staff reported that ALERT had significantly enhanced their level of job satisfaction. There was also a majority feeling that ALERT had improved their ability to cope with the stresses of control-room work, that it was easy to use and helped them do their job better. Only 8% said they would prefer to return to the paper system, with the overwhelming majority (83%) indicating that ALERT had led to significant overall benefits.

Comparisons with LAS: management lessons

In contrast to many IT initiatives, the GMAS project appeared to have been a success – all the more striking when compared with the failure in London.

---

68   See Epilogue – subsequent research in GMAS suggests this is a reasonable estimate.

In our original paper we systematically contrasted the two cases in order to identify the critical factors in the Manchester project that were responsible for its success, highlighting key differences with London in a number of areas (Wastell & Newman, 1996).

Undoubtedly the appalling state of industrial relations in the LAS case had been a general toxic factor. By contrast, in Manchester good relations between staff and management prevailed, characterised by trust, constructive cooperation and open communication. User involvement had also represented an area of obvious difference, with GMAS management having seen ownership as critical and taken care to involve end-users in system development. The attention given to staff training and communication had also led users to feel involved in the process and to feel some attachment to the system. Management commitment had been another area of critical difference. In the London case, management involvement had been lamentably weak, with project management virtually non-existent. In GMAS, by comparison, we have a model example of decisive leadership. An experienced manager had been assigned full-time to the project, an effective man-manager who worked with close attention to detail on the human side of the implementation process as well as the technical aspects.

Technologically, there were also critical differences between the two projects. The LAS system, for instance, had involved significantly more software development work, with an unproven supplier. Hence, the technical risks were much higher than the GMAS case where the decision had been made to opt for tried and tested software, albeit requiring extensive customisation. There were also crucial differences in design philosophy. LASCAD had followed what we called a "machine-centred approach", aimed at reducing the human role through automation (Wastell & Newman, 1996). In GMAS, however, the design philosophy had embraced a "tool paradigm" (p.296); there had been no question of the computer system usurping the human role. Through helpful information displays and the removal of unskilled secondary work, ALERT's role had been to support operators in their primary task of despatching ambulances; it had not encroached on the problem-solving kernel of their job. Suggestions of candidate ambulances were for information only; decision-making had remained solely the prerogative of the operator.

Epilogue

Several after-events of our 'tale of two cities' are noteworthy. First, in London a remarkable turnaround was achieved. In 1996, a new despatching system was successfully implemented, enabling LAS to improve its performance substantially and indeed to win the British Computer Society award for Excellence in IS Management in 1997 (Fitzgerald & Russo, 2005). The key factors behind this transformation were: the adoption of an in-house development approach supported by a formal project management methodology; thorough testing with warm-up projects; the involvement of users and the setting of realistic timescales. Peace was also made between management and the unions. Most importantly of all, there was "still desire to change but not using IT as a battering ram for process change" (Fitzgerald & Russo, 2005, p.255).

Back in Manchester, there were less momentous developments, but nonetheless salient ones. An ethnographic investigation was subsequently undertaken by David Martin, who had earlier carried out the study of Blighty (Chapter 1). This focused on the complexities of the despatching task, highlighting the presence of multiple contingencies. Although the nearest ambulance was often the correct one, the research demonstrated that each dispatching decision had to be seen in the context of previous decisions. Relevant considerations were: Are the crew due a meal-break? When does the crew's shift end? When will a new crew's shift begin? Has the crew just dealt with one or more harrowing incidents? Other factors included: does the ambulance have the right equipment for the incident; are there road works, traffic problems etc. on a particular route? The research concluded that: "Simple automation is not the solution; discretion is key and a good relationship between control centre and crews. It should be clear that it would be negligent to simply select the system's suggestion for dispatch without attending to these many and varied matters" (Martin, Bowers & Wastell, 1997).

There were developments too regarding another of my themes – evidence-based management. An important aspect of subsequent IS development in GMAS was the collection of hard data to improve service design, as prefigured in the quote from the Trust application. This involved crews entering clinical data regarding incidents, interventions made, outcomes and so on. This clinical audit system showed, for instance, that there were parts of the city which were not well served in terms of response time. A possible solution to this was to use stand-by locations, i.e. to move ambulances from ambulance stations to strategic positions, such as lay-bys, where they could more quickly attend to incidents in such 'black spots'. Experiments were tried, although there was resistance from crews, who disliked being parked up in remote spots without the obvious amenities of the ambulance station.

The reasons behind the increase in emergency calls were also examined from a systems thinking perspective. A range of factors were implicated, including the growing prevalence of mobile phones, meaning the tendency for more calls relating to the same incident when it occurred in public.

There had also been a reduction in general hospital services for patient transport over the period in question, which had led some individuals to call an emergency ambulance when it was not required. This had suggested the idea of prioritised despatching, i.e. giving despatchers the authority to make decisions as to whether an emergency ambulance was required or not. This was difficult to implement at the time for statutory reasons, as the ambulance service was required to respond to all calls, but it is an idea which has been widely taken up since, as has the stand-by concept.

The clinical data furnished some particularly important 'business intelligence', especially regarding the relationship between response time and clinical outcome for cardiac arrest, as well as shedding light on the critical importance of a second variable, the presence (or not) of an individual on the scene who could provide cardiovascular pulmonary resuscitation (bystander CPR). The data showed that survival rates fell from 19% alive at hospital in the 1-4 minute response category to 12% alive in the 9-12 minutes category, suggesting a decline of around 0.9% per minute lost, which compares well with the aforementioned figure from the research of Nichol *et al.* (1996). Bystander CPR also showed a profound effect, echoing results in more rigorous research studies of the efficacy of emergency medicine. This finding prompted a second line of intervention to improve the emergency service, this time in the community. Following pioneering work in North America, it suggested the need for greater public training in CPR and for the wider installation of resuscitation equipment in public places, as has now occurred on a national level (though not as a direct consequence of the GMAS work).

SPRINT: a design and innovation methodology[69]

At this point, I will take the reader back to the end of Chapter 2 and the SPRINT methodology developed at Salford. It will be recalled that SPRINT is a BPR methodology, specifically designed for the public services, and that it built on the prior work described earlier in this chapter. SPRINT is an eclectic methodology, more a tool-box of techniques and best practices than a coherently designed, integrated system. Architecturally, it is post-modern not modern, a bazaar not a cathedral! The goal was to bring together what appeared to be a useful set of tools and disciplines within a loose overarching framework, with the aim of enhancing the quality of design and innovation by managers, business analysts, IT practitioners and other professionals in the public services. SPRINT has been described as more of a curriculum than a methodology, or even just an "attitude of mind" as one experienced SPRINT practitioner memorably put it.

---

69   Much of the material for this section is based on Kawalek & Wastell (2005)

General precepts – best practice for design

I have written before of the dangers of fetishising techniques and of over-prescription (Wastell, 1996), which are linked themes of this book. SPRINT does have structure, but following sociotechnical principles this was deliberately kept to the critical minimum: "Structure not stricture", as another colleague once quipped. The practitioner looking for a step-by-step manual will be disappointed. SPRINT was designed to ensure practitioners always have to take the responsibility for working out what has to be done to adapt SPRINT to the contingencies of the situation: it is most definitely not a magic bullet! Before discussing the more practical aspects of the methodology, the main philosophical principles underpinning SPRINT will be delineated, indicating connections with other concepts and techniques (such as STSD and SSM) which have influenced or fed into it, and to the evidence-base which justifies its various elements. Note that I have generally used the present tense in this exposition, but the reader should bear in mind that these principles were very largely developed and codified over ten years ago. This also explains why many of the references cited are somewhat 'long in the tooth'!

Radical innovation: "don't pave the cow-paths"

SPRINT emphasises the need to be innovative with technology, taking its inspiration from the work of the BPR pioneers. Although IT is seen as an innovative tool, the emphasis is firmly on the business process; it may well be that only a process redesign is required, with no new role for technology. In Erewhon, for instance, the critical change was the adoption of a different form of work organisation, based on the work-group concept. For the outpatients example, a wide-area IT network could have been installed, to provide on-line access to the appointment books, but actually the telephone could simply have been used, without any such expensive infrastructural investment. Why not have the clerical staff in the health centre ring and arrange the appointments? Why not indeed! Whilst design is the exercise of creative imagination, and boundless in scope, SPRINT acknowledges that implementation is the art of the possible. Whilst it is important to encourage and exhort radical ideas, in practice the pragmatics of implementation may oblige an incremental approach and the realisation of more modest aims. Following the example of SSM, the important point is not to fetter imagination by implementation constraints, but to save these for later.

Breadth of Vision and Depth of Understanding

Again taking inspiration from SSM, SPRINT recognises that many managerial problems are unstructured and that a range of different points of view are relevant and must be triangulated to develop a full understanding of the problem situation and provide a secure foundation for design and intervention. SPRINT thus stresses the importance of seeking out and examining all stakeholder perspectives in order to appreciate the complexity of the problem and the different views that people hold. The need to develop a rigorous, evidence-based understanding of the realities of everyday practice and organisational life is a *sine qua non*. I need say no more in justification of this than to refer to the various atrocity stories already told in this book when this research is omitted. It is critical to know what goes on now, why things are the way they are and what the important contextual factors are. Ethnographic methods (i.e. detailed, immersive investigation) are recommended to achieve this depth of understanding (Martin, Wastell & Bowers, 1998).

Learning Organisation and Knowledge Management

BPR projects are regarded in SPRINT as opportunities for organisational innovation; learning and knowledge management are seen as the key to successful change. SPRINT projects should be seen as 'transitional spaces', i.e., supportive learning environments in which users are encouraged to reflect critically on current processes and experiment with new process designs (Wastell, 1999). To support the management of knowledge within and across change projects, SPRINT emphasised the use of intranet technology (a novel idea at the time) to share and disseminate knowledge, recommending that a website be created for each SPRINT project, to provide a shared repository for the project's documentation.

An Emphasis upon Innovation through Participation

Another theme of the book is the recognition that much innovative thinking comes from front-line practitioners and team managers, i.e. from the denizens of the "lower levels" of the organisational pyramid (Borins, 1998). SPRINT aims at nurturing a culture of innovation at all levels; as users become skilled with SPRINT, it is hoped they will become more confident to develop ideas independently and eager to implement them in their organisation. A participative approach is, therefore, indispensable to the effectiveness of SPRINT as a means of generating and implanting innovation, directly reflecting the influence of sociotechnical theory and user-centred design.

Designed-in Strategic Alignment

While SPRINT places considerable emphasis on the achievement of recognisable business benefits, it eschews top-down approaches to achieving business alignment. Street level bureaucracy (Lipski, 1980) shows that, whatever the aspiration of senior strategists, "facts are created on the ground". Critics of the "rational paradigm" of business strategy (Ciborra, 1997; Hackney & Little, 1999) also stress the emergent, practice-based nature of the strategy process. Alignment is thus seen as an integral part of the on-going process of change, not as something in advance of, and separate from, the design work itself. SPRINT does not recognise the concept of the IT project; "there are only business projects with IT elements".[70] In Ciborra's terminology (*ibid*), alignment is something that should be "taken care of" throughout the design process. SPRINT exhorts change participants to address themselves to business goals at all stages in a BPR project, from goal identification in the analysis phase to the establishment of rigorous mechanisms to track and manage the achievement of business benefits (Serafeimidis & Smithson, 2000) following implementation.

An Improvisational Change Model

Whilst BPR is associated with the idea of large-scale, rapid change, the demands this places on the organisation are potentially huge in terms of human and technical resources, and the risk of resistance is high (especially in a public sector organisation with strong collective traditions). SPRINT rejects the idea of change as a discrete, convulsive event imposed on the organisation. Instead, the approach draws in part from the improvisational change model of Orlikowski & Hofman (1997). SPRINT argues that change should not be determined by a top-down plan, but rather guided by a set of business objectives and enacted through a series of incremental steps emphasising continuous reflection and adaptation to changing circumstances. Each step should be seen as a learning experiment in which the new process is implemented, evaluated and refined, in an ethos of excitement, even of fun (Davenport & Short, 1990; Pfeffer & Sutton, 2006). It goes without saying that a participative approach is key, with users leading the prototyping process and colleagues involved in giving feedback. A plan is required, but only as a coordinating device and as a means for managing progress; the plan does not drive the change.

Flexibility and Extensibility

As noted, a danger with methodologies is that they can become an end in themselves, with users slavishly following the method's catechisms rather than thinking for themselves (Wastell, 1996). To guard against this, SPRINT was designed deliberately with a minimum of procedural structure; in essence, it comprises a toolbox of recommended techniques within a

---

70   See the interview with the CIO of Acme Financial Services, Appendix 1.

loose, general framework of tasks and phases. Users should be familiar with SPRINT's structure and appreciate its ethos, but they are encouraged to interpret and adapt the methodology according to the particular circumstances of the project they are undertaking. For instance, if they think that some new tool or method is ideally suited to solving a particular problem, they are encouraged to adopt it and bring it into their local version of the framework, and to share this experience with others in the wider SPRINT community.

Evaluation and benefits management

Evaluation is also an integral part of SPRINT. The need is stressed to define clear business goals at the outset of projects and to measure achievements against these goals. In today's terms, projects must be devoted to the creation of public value and measured accordingly; this is a *sine qua non* (see Chapter 2). Two forms of evaluation are distinguished:[71] *formative* (feedback during the design process, integral to the design work) and *summative* (after completion, to appraise the degree to which the project was successful). Recognising that such benefits may take time to materialise, summative measures of (public) value should be collected over a period of time. SPRINT underlines the need to measure real outcomes (not simple inputs or outputs), and the process of implementation itself should also be measured. Such implementation metrics are necessary in order to tell the full story of any project, without which interpretation of outcomes is impossible.[72] In following a process-outcome approach,[73] SPRINT also stresses the need to address the full range of hard and soft benefits (e.g. reduced workplace stress) and the use of qualitative as well as quantitative measures. Innovation in methods is encouraged, a good example being the use of blood pressure to measure stress as in the GMAS case above.

---

71   To a degree, the distinction between formative and summative is not a hard and fast one when design work is seen as an open-ended process of continuous improvement.

72   In a SPRINT working paper, I described an actual intervention, namely the implementation of a street drinking ban, aimed at curbing alcohol-related violence in a town centre. The intervention was apparently successful in terms of police crime data. But key questions still remain. How was the enforcement implemented and were there subtle changes in the way incidents were treated and recorded, was the problem solved or merely displaced? In particular, process data on the way the ban was policed (number of confiscations, etc.) is critical, especially had the intervention failed.

73   Such a process-outcome orientation is sometimes referred to as a 'theory of change' approach. This originates in the USA and, in an adapted form, has been applied to evaluate complex policy interventions in the UK (Sullivan, Barnes & Matka, 2002).

Further principles

In general, SPRINT should be seen as an attempt to operationalise many of the concepts, themes and principles expounded more discursively in this book. Other key general principles include its advocacy of evidence-based practice and the need to embrace complexity with systems thinking. Regarding the former, as noted above, effective design should always be informed by the best evidence. As well as gathering detailed local intelligence (qualitative and quantitative), SPRINT encourages its users to look externally, at published research as well as studying other organisations facing similar issues (benchmarking). The need to build capacity is also a core principle. "Give a man a fish and you feed him for a day, teach him to fish and you feed him for life"; so goes the old adage, and this is SPRINT philosophy too. Its aim is to build capacity for change, design and innovation; to leave users at the end of a project or intervention more able to do it for themselves.

An overview of SPRINT

This section provides a practical overview of SPRINT, focusing on its key phases. Detailed information about its structure, tasks and phases can be gained elsewhere (there are various websites[74]) and only a very high-level description will be set out here. Before proceeding, note that SPRINT has been through a number of incarnations. The first version covered the complete design life cycle, comprising three primary phases: of analysis (understand process context), design (business process redesign) and implementation (intervention). Such separation of stages should be seen as conceptual; in practice there will always be considerable iteration and cycling backwards and forwards between activities. Design ideas, for instance, will inevitably start to emerge during analysis and are often present at the outset, driving the whole initiative. Analysis and design are particularly difficult to separate. Although SPRINT distinguishes a specific 'design stage', when models and blueprints are the focus of attention, generally when I speak of design and design work, I mean the entire life-cycle of innovation, from inception to conclusion.

Figure 6 provides a bird's eye view of version 1 of SPRINT, with three distinct phases. Version 2, in contrast, stopped at the end of Phase 2. It was developed at the zenith of electronic government in the UK around 2002 and was entitled "Enable IT with SPRINT: a BPR methodology for delivering e-government solutions".[75] This version of SPRINT stopped

---

74   For version 1, see www.wastell.org/SPRINT1/ Other websites are referenced below.

75   www.wastell.org/SPRINT3/

with the production of a business case, as it was envisaged that a project would be launched at this juncture which would adopt whatever project management methodology was in place in the organisation (with the widely used PRINCE 2 being the most likely option). It seemed redundant or even counter-productive to attempt to replicate such functionality, especially if the project management methodology was the mandated way of proceeding. Having said this, SPRINT is a continuous improvement process and it was envisaged that some residual interest would remain throughout project management to ensure that the cycle of ongoing adaptation and learning would continue beyond formal project completion.

The most recent version of SPRINT reinstated explicit support for change management, although the level of prescriptive detail is much less than for the earlier two phases.[76] It also introduced a baseline phase 0 (entitled 'Initiating a Project') which formalised the various preparatory activities required at the outset of a SPRINT project: setting up a steering group, establishing the BPR project team and identifying the scope of project (its 'terms of reference'). Due to the instability of these before and after phases (0 and 3), I shall focus here on phases 1 and 2 only, which are about analysis and design, as these two heavily interdependent activities form the heart of SPRINT and have remained more or less unchanged since its inception.

First some words on the formal composition and governance of a SPRINT project. At the outset, SPRINT nominally recommends that two groups be established, a Steering Group and the Change Team, although how formal this needs to be will depend on the size of the project and other local circumstances. The former group is strategic, set in place to provide the mandate for change and to make key decisions regarding resources and design alternatives. It should include: the departmental director for all operational areas impacted by the project, the BPR project manager and Lead Consultant, and senior representatives from Human Resources (HR) and ICT services. Leadership at such a senior level is critical, as we have seen; given the potentially radical nature of the change process, it is vital that such commitment be made from all those departments that will be directly affected. Detailed design activities are carried out by the Change Team. It was recommended that this group comprise a Senior User at deputy director level, to play the role of Project Manager; a Lead BPR Consultant and supporting consultants; and HR and ICT experts. Staff groups whose work would be directly affected by the initiative should be represented on the Team by one or more Practice Representatives, i.e. user involvement is built into the SPRINT process.

---

76   See www.wastell.org/SPRINT4/ for details.

Phase 1: Understanding Process Context

As noted, version 1 of SPRINT comprised three main phases (see Figure 6). Each phase is defined in terms of a set of aims and there is a set of tasks within each phase intended to help the realisation of these aims. Although the impression may be gained of a tightly defined structure, this is emphatically not the case, as I have stated. The division into phases and tasks is merely to provide a loose organisational framework to allow the work to be structured and divided up amongst the Change Team. There is no requirement, for instance, for tasks to be performed in strict sequence and there are no dogmatic injunctions on the use of particular techniques.

Phase 1 is essentially one of analysis. The general aims are: 1) to understand the business context of the project by considering all relevant perspectives and to analyse the effectiveness and efficiency of current processes in this broader context; 2) to generate preliminary ideas for process improvements (technical and organisational); and 3) to help develop the business vision on which the detailed proposals in Phase 2 will be founded. The emphasis on understanding the business context is crucial. This forces the Change Team to stand back from the original remit, which may focus too narrowly on a particular process or processes. 'Zooming out' in this way will assist in identifying and understanding the real business goals that should be being addressed, leading towards the identification of more relevant, and indeed radical, reengineering opportunities.

Of the various tasks carried out in Phase 1, two require brief further comment. The construction of formal process models is a key feature of SPRINT. To this end, a simple modelling method known as Role Activity Diagramming (RAD) was proposed as the technique of choice. RAD makes use of a small number of relatively straightforward constructs (primarily Roles, Activities and Interactions). Emphatically, teams are exhorted not to become engrossed in modelling for its own sake; the goal is to generate and test understanding and to facilitate communication. Although RADs are recommended for routine processes, any method may be used, including narrative descriptions. Critical Goal Analysis (CGA) is another useful technique. This task constitutes the crux of Phase 1 – focusing all strands of inquiry on two pivotal questions: What are the business goals relevant to the process context? and How well are they supported by the current processes and support systems? For each business goal, the following key issues must be addressed: What is the goal? Who are the primary stakeholders? How does it align with or divert from the strategic aims of the organisation? How well is the goal currently achieved and how should it be measured (i.e., what metrics could be used)? SPRINT recommends the use of a Goal Network Diagram to depict the set of goals and their interrelationships. Structural modelling is also encouraged, as described in the previous chapter.

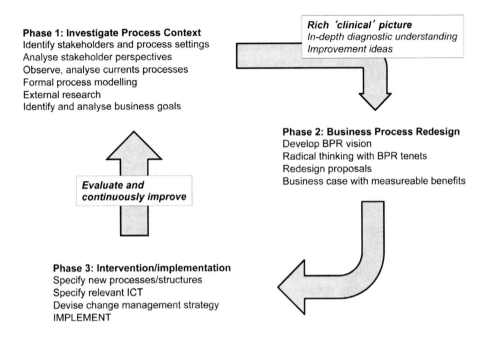

Figure 6: *The Three Phases of SPRINT*

In Figure 6, I have described the output of Phase 1 using a medical metaphor[77] as a rich 'clinical' picture, thus likening the organisation to a patient suffering some malaise, for which a treatment intervention is being sought, once the requisite diagnostic investigations have been carried out. The metaphor was suggested by Edgar Schein's depiction of management consultants as "helping professionals".

Phase 2: Radical Process Redesign

The analytical work of Phase 1 constitutes essential preparation for the second phase of SPRINT, the aim of which is to devise a set of process reengineering proposals, embracing the potential of ICT to underpin new processes aimed at dramatic improvements in the organisation's performance. The first task in Phase 2 is to develop a business vision in terms of key goals and 'critical success factors' for achieving the goals. It is vital to assess the importance of each goal and the effectiveness of current process support.

---

77   See http://andewal.com/archive/process_consultation.pdf

Having established a clear business context, the next task requires the Change Team to reflect, in a radical way, on reengineering opportunities. Although innovative thinking cannot be reduced to technique, SPRINT suggests it can be stimulated in a number of ways: via literature research, benchmarking, studying best practice, as well as brain-storming based on the investigative work of Phase 1. SPRINT also proposes a set of "re-visioning heuristics" drawing on Hammer's early work to aid in the search for new ideas. In his 1990 paper, Hammer had expounded a set of injunctions which provide a useful discipline for thinking about how processes can be reengineered. The first is to organise work (i.e. to design jobs) around outcomes not tasks. The second is to have those who use the output of the process, perform the process. Further principles include the following: to treat geographically dispersed resources as though they were centralised; to link parallel activities instead of integrating their results; to put the decision point where the work is performed, building control into the process; and finally, to capture information once and at source. The case management approach described in the opening section of this chapter operationalises and exemplifies many of these useful precepts.

The end point of Phase 2 is one or more proposals that embody new process designs, using whatever notation is appropriate. Crucially, each proposal must be supported by a detailed business case, including the specification of a set of metrics to aid in the delivery of real business benefits and to establish an on-going feedback loop to facilitate continuous process improvement. Once a decision has been made to proceed with one or more of these options, the project would move into implementation in phase three (version 1). It was envisaged that the original Change Team would become much larger at this point in order to carry out the detailed work required to implement the proposals. Implementation was recognised to be a long, arduous process, requiring strong user leadership. An incremental implementation plan was recommended to provide an overall organisational framework and to translate process designs into new working structures and procedures. Training must be addressed and technical requirements for new ICT elaborated, following whatever software development method was deemed appropriate (in-house development, packages, etc.). Crucially, a positive attitude towards evaluation needed to be instilled at this stage.

Case Studies

SPRINT has been deployed on numerous projects across many local government authorities in the UK. Four of these, all from Salford, are described below in order to illustrate the difficult pressures and the varying outcomes that develop around the pursuit of organisational change.

The Decision-Making Project

Profound changes in local governance in the UK formed the background to the first project. At the behest of national imperatives, local government in the early days of New Labour (from 1997 onwards) engaged in a process of democratic renewal, wherein the decision-making process became the subject of fundamental change (Wilson & Game, 1998). The traditional method of decision-making involved a set of committees, chaired and staffed by elected representatives, with a committee devoted to each area of the Council's work (Housing, Social Services, etc.). The most common model replacing this was that of cabinet-style government, which involved the constitution of a small, central body of 'Lead Members' (the Cabinet), each with decision-making power for a given operational area; in effect, they resembled ministers in the national system of government.

In early 1999, a conventional ICT project had been instigated to address issues of IT support for the administrators who would service the new structure. This came to focus on office automation and text research facilities, solely for the use of the administrative staff. Concerns developed that this was too narrow, that it had failed to address the broader issues regarding the enhancement of local democracy embodied in Salford's Information Society vision. What was needed was a wider and deeper study that would coalesce a more radical vision of change, and the decision was made for members of the then nascent BPR team to deploy SPRINT. The project served an important role in testing the embryonic methodology and developing it into a finished product.

Interviews with key stakeholders (e.g., elected members, council officers, community representatives) were carried out, supplemented by a detailed ethnographic observation of the administrative process supporting the committee decision-making system, still operating at that time. Essentially, the support process was paper-based, involving the circulation of agenda packages in advance of committee meetings. These packages included an agenda, the minutes of the previous meeting and a set of detailed reports relevant to the agenda items. A Role Activity Diagram for the support processes was constructed and a Critical Goal Analysis was carried out. This prompted a highly productive discourse among stakeholders about how well the existing process operated and its relationship with the goals of the organisation. This was important, as it forced stakeholders to confront the fact that the existing support mechanisms were seriously deficient. For instance, effective decision-making was impeded by the fact that large volumes of documentation would be delivered to Council members just a few days before a committee meeting. How were they expected to read it all in such a short time? How were they expected to identify the parts relevant to their constituents? Equally, the need to involve the community in the decision-making process was severely inhibited by lack of ready access to documentation. It was clear that here was a process severely out of alignment.

Phase 2 led to the formulation of a design proposal with the potential for profound change to the decision-making process and the roles of the committee support staff within it. Hammer's heuristics played a helpful part in formulating the new design. The injunction to organise around outcomes put the emphasis firmly on improving the quality of information, with the aim of enhancing decision-making, participation and communication. "Having the users of the process perform the process" directly suggested a range of ideas, including the provision of an 'agenda management tool' which would allow senior officials themselves to add items and reports directly to an evolving electronic agenda (rather than this being handled by the administrators). This would enable elected members to access information as soon as it became available. The final design centred on the creation of a comprehensive information repository (CIR) for the Council and a transformed role for the committee support staff as 'knowledge managers'. All documents (e.g., reports, agendas, minutes) would in the future be stored in the CIR directly by their authors. They would be indexed rigorously in terms of the policy issues they addressed and the areas of Salford to which they related. The committee support staff would no longer simply act as paper pushers but would take responsibility for ensuring that documentation was correctly classified; they would also monitor the quality of reports and actively seek out additional research material to be placed in the repository.

In effect, a knowledge management (KM) system was envisaged that focused clearly on enhancing the quality of local policy-making. Documents would be circulated to elected members electronically, thus reaching them more quickly. Members also would be able to register their interests (e.g., policy areas as well as localities) and information would be proactively supplied to them based upon this profile. Retrieval would no longer depend upon the committee support staff; elected members could search for electronically held documents using the indexes provided for them. Thus, from its humble origins the use of SPRINT had enlarged the scope of the project to embrace the whole process of decision-making. The project was considered a success by many of those involved and, crucially, by all the key sponsors. Nonetheless, implementation proceeded slowly and it was sometime before a version of the CIR was fully operational, named SOLAR (Salford Online Archive and Retrieval). A review of the project found that although some benefits had been derived, in many ways the project had not achieved its hoped-for potential. In particular, the work of the administrators had not fundamentally changed. They had not embraced the KM role, but had recreated their former role, albeit in the changed context of an electronic information repository. Authors of documents were also not able to enter reports directly, but had to send them to the administrators prior to publication on the CIR.

Births, Deaths and Marriages

A further engagement for SPRINT followed in the Registry for births, deaths and marriages (BDM). One SPRINT consultant took primary responsibility for the project, working closely with two managers of the service (one a senior manager). The BDM service in Salford was located in a large, converted Victorian house some distance from the Council's main offices. The majority of transactions involved requests for appointments and for copies of certificates and family histories. Staff reported problems with overstretch at peak times. Queues would build at the service counters and on the telephone lines. Despite this, targets were generally being met, although the targets themselves were not always ambitious (i.e., visitors should be seen within 30 minutes).

The main discussions revolved around ideas from central government for service developments, including the potential for partnerships within the public sector (e.g. hospitals) and beyond to the private sector (e.g. local wedding or funeral services). One important set of ideas for modernisation was particularly influential, based on the general concept that services could be organised around life events, such as births, deaths and marriages. Organising services around such events offered the prospect of minimising the number of discrete interactions between citizens and public agencies. But beyond a general airing of these ideas, debate faltered, becoming focused on the use of the corporate call centre (see below, then in its first flush of development) to provide basic information and appointment making services. Although of some value, such changes were incremental. Whilst it was acknowledged that the SPRINT project had prepared the ground for more profound reorganisation, the timescale and means for achieving such changes were not defined.

Social Services

Responding to anxieties that SPRINT was falling short as an enabler of radical change, an effort was made to reinvigorate the participative element by introducing a new concept, that of the 'e-envoy.' Although SPRINT is avowedly participative in nature, in practice staff were often unable to give the focused commitment needed, due to the demands of their normal work activity (the 'day job'). E-envoys were volunteers from an operational area who came to work on the BPR Team full-time for the life of the project. Their mission was to think creatively about change possibilities and to promote these ideas amongst their colleagues. Members of staff were asked to apply for such posts prior to the commencement of the BPR study and, as part of this application process, they were asked to include a statement describing their feelings and ideas about e-government and service innovation.

The advertisement of an e-envoy position in Social Services brought forward two applicants, both qualified social workers. Both were appointed for a period of five months and rapidly became adept at using SPRINT. They soon found their way to generating some noteworthy innovations, potentially the most radical of all the cases reported here. One such proposal was to restructure the whole service around self-contained practices (analogous to local medical practices); another was to develop a web-based information service, which would be responsible for the sourcing and maintenance of care information (e.g. residential vacancies). Whilst these ideas aligned with the overriding goals of the social care function, to provide high quality care to members of society, they were manifestly challenging to the *status quo*. As the project progressed, these ideas lost none of their radicalism but were joined by a number of less profound, incremental proposals. Ultimately, it was only these less radical ideas that were implemented, with the bolder ideas of self-contained practices and web-based sourcing placed on hold. As the project had developed, the e-envoys had faced the problem of selling their radicalism back to their colleagues in Social Services but had been unable to build sufficient political support.

The Salford Contact Centre

The final Salford study to be reported represents in many ways SPRINT's finest hour, certainly in terms of the scale of change if not its radicalism. In Chapter 2, I alluded to the involvement of the SPRINT team in the establishment of Salford's Contact Centre and the subsequent creation of Salford Direct as an independent customer services directorate. Over the following years, the Contact Centre enjoyed a sustained period of organic growth. In early 2006, I interviewed Martin Vickers, then head of Customer Services, and John Tanner, the Operations Manager. The present narrative has been constructed from that interview supplemented by material from the Council's website.

At the time of the interview, 15 services were housed in the Contact Centre, which had 110 staff, and the service had recently celebrated its millionth caller. Salford's website proclaimed a radical change from the "bad old days", when the phone would ring "in an office full of people busy doing other things and it was an inconvenience for officers to have to pick it up". A culture of "customer service professionalism" had now been developed: "There are now swift call response times. The aim is to answer 70% of incoming calls within 30 seconds and our monthly customer surveys show satisfaction rates to be consistently above 90%".

The Contact Centre had been built piece-by-piece, adding one service at a time. In every case, customer services had taken over both the 'front office functionality' and the staff from the prior directorate. Housing services had been a big step forwards, with 45 new 'seats' (i.e. Contact Centre jobs) accruing. JT remarked:

> There was an inspection [of Housing] in May 2003, and the result was basically nil star. We were told to take in the front line people. Staff were given the option to stay where they were or come to us, and we got the highest level volunteers, the best people, to come over and we delivered it.

Notably, SPRINT had been used to evaluate critically each new acquisition, in particular to identify areas where significant service improvements could be made. The website emphasised that:

> ...every new service is subject to a business process reengineering programme... we are not looking just to replicate old services, but to carry out new processes with benefits for the customer. BPR helps the city council to go for a win-win, combining better front-end services with more efficient back-office processes.

Free school meals (available for children in households with an income below a certain level) was cited in the interview as a good example where dramatic service improvements had occurred. In the past, it had been necessary for applicants to take proof of eligibility to one of the council offices and several visits might have been involved before the paperwork was in order. Because all citizen-related information was then integrated on Citizen (Salford's home-grown CRM system, see Chapter 2) the checking was automatic. The caller rings and "as soon as eligibility has been approved an email is sent off straight away and the pupil will get it the next day" (MV).

MV provided another example:

> We're dealing with vulnerable people, and we need to maximise the contact in terms of opportunities. We've had lots of health promotion successes – flu jabs is the best example. The take-up was 30%. Now we know all the over 65s, so when the caller rings up about, say rent arrears, a box pops saying "Mr Vickers is over 65". The take-up is now 70%. And because

> *we have direct access to the appointment books of the health centres, an appointment can be made, there and then. We're the only authority in the county doing that...*

Citizen, by providing an integrated database covering all services, was at the heart of things. Described by MV, as the best "customer database" of any organisation in the City, it enabled seamless sharing of information across council services and with other agencies. MV highlighted its 'value for money': "it was originally built by 2 people and now it's managed by 5. XYX [a neighbouring authority] had paid £1.5 for their CRM". Such sharing of information may not seem so radical, but it had required something of a buccaneering approach and was an area where Salford was in the vanguard at the time. The issue of consent had been critical. JT explained:

> *Consent arises at the first contact. After authenticating the caller, a box pops up, asking if we can share information to improve the services to them. Pretty much everyone agrees to this. We've spoken to 280 councils about what we're doing, and we're still the only one doing it. Local government people tend to get hung up about issues like data protection, they use it as a reason for not doing things. It's still very silo-based. We don't have a silo here; we're a corporate service.*

An important principle in the growth of customer services had been the requirement for staff to volunteer out of their old organisational unit. JT explained:

> *They have to feel it is right for them, and we have to feel they are right for us. I spend a lot of time just taking staff round the Contact Centre and explaining to them what we do and how we do it. Those that get excited by the vision will volunteer – we sometimes have to turn people away.*

The work culture in the Contact Centre was highlighted by MV, especially its multi-skilled nature, with staff covering a range of services, and its collegiality:

> *We call it the "family business". We were recently assessed for Investor in People and in the feedback the assessor said "you're right, this is a family business". 5 years ago everyone had the one skill, now they've got 8 business areas. There's great potential for career development and job satisfaction. Our turnover is not the traditional call centre turnover; they often move on to better positions in the organisation because they've got a broader range of skills. We really work hard with our staff – we really do empower people.*

Although there had been dramatic gains, the approach taken had a distinctively piecemeal, pragmatic character. The presence of a like-minded, 'can do' philosophy in IT Services had been key:

> *When we launched it, it wasn't that clever – we try to learn in real time. Too many people are looking for sophisticated solutions, but then the piece of work is too big, the change process is too large. We just do the first bit, then see where we are and what we can do, one stage at a time. If we'd written a detailed business case, we'd still be stuck at the start. It's about seizing the opportunities when they come along… We're very flexible here. The IT people don't insist on dotting i's and crossing t's. If we say we need something by Friday, they'll do their best to get it done (MV).*

This spirit of pragmatism extended up to senior manager level. The Contact Centre was located in the Directorate of Corporate Services; MV commented as follows on the philosophy of the Director: "I think we often underestimate his role in protecting us – his motto is JDI[78] and he really means it". JDI may well have been the methodology which really mattered, but SPRINT had been vital too in building capacity for change, which it will be recalled is its overarching rationale. In the interview, MV remarked:

> *In many ways we're the validation of BPR. SPRINT brought formality and control. We were lucky in having some good people, but we needed the discipline of SPRINT. It gave us a structure for doing service design. We're going to re-BPR tax and benefits, but it's part of the day job now. We'll be doing it ourselves. We won't need BPR analysts… Once you've been BPRed, you've been BPRed for life.*

Reengineer or repent: two call centre horror stories

In this lucky-bag of cases, we have witnessed the deployment of SPRINT with a mixed record of success, not always a resounding triumph, but equally there are no disasters to report. To put this record in context, I shall conclude by recounting two brief cases where there was an indirect connection with the SPRINT programme, and where spectacular failure was evident. Significantly, this could have been pre-empted had SPRINT's core precepts been heeded, above all the need to base design on careful, critical analysis.

For the first of these cautionary tales, I will return to Social Services in Salford, to a small SPRINT project which took place subsequently to the e-envoy episode. The aim had been to investigate the case for integrating 'front office' functions into the Contact Centre. A metrics investigation of

---

78   'Just Do It'; JFDI was the actual motto!

telephone calls to local offices had found that over 50% of callers needed to speak to either a social worker or a district nurse; less than 40% were of a routine administrative nature, involving either appointments or simple advice or information. On the basis of this evidence, the Report unequivocally recommended retention of the *status quo*.

> *...a single point of contact would not improve access to the services in question, and removing the telephone answering function from the professionals would have a detrimental effect. The evidence collected demonstrates that a good service is provided, and that this is largely dependent on the physical co-location of the staff who answer the calls with the social workers and district nurses...*

Some years later, the BPR team received a visit from a neighbouring authority, who were contemplating setting up a corporate call centre, and there was specific interest in moving social services into that centre. Although the results of the Salford investigation were shared with their visitors, the authority in question pressed on with their strategy to move the 'front door' of social services into their call centre, which was located on a remote industrial estate. By coincidence, the authority in question was one of the ethnographic sites in our ICS research, which revealed the deleterious effect of that earlier decision. In an interview, one manager commented:

> *Prior to the contact centre, we used to have a customer care person sitting in the room with the social workers. That, in my opinion, was a much better system than the contact centre... the customer care person had access to the social workers, who they could also direct a lot of questions to.*

When asked about the rationale for the centralising of referrals, the manager replied cryptically: "You'd have to ask higher management that". Another social worker commented:

> *...the office is now really quiet, phones used to be ringing all the time. Workers can get on with work, but it's not so great for families who want to make contact. It's not really having the desired impact on making service more accessible, but there's no way the local authority can backtrack now the Contact Centre is set up. Even if a service user comes into the reception the reception worker can't call upstairs for the social worker, the reception worker has to call the Contact Centre.*

Subsequently the contact centre was closed and its staff redeployed, generating an immediate saving of £500k per annum, according to press reports.

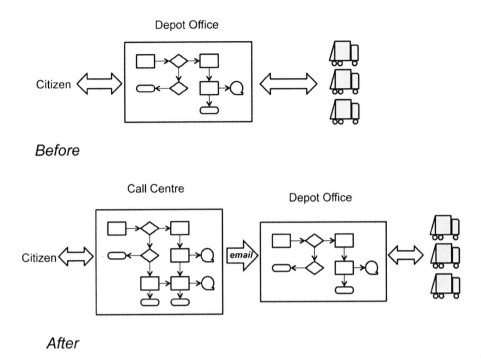

Before

After

Figure 7: *Reengineer or repent!*

The final exhibit also comes from another authority. The Salford BPR team received a request in 2004 for some assistance in carrying out a SPRINT project in their Environmental Services department, and some preliminary help was given. As a result of a top level policy decision, uninformed by research, the authority in question went ahead willy-nilly with their Call Centre, and Figure 7 graphically shows the result. The upper part of the figure shows the process involved in handling a customer call prior to the call centre; generally these calls represented 'failure demand', e.g. a refuse bin has not been collected. Calls at this time went straight to the waste service's administrative office, located in the same yard as the refuse wagons used as their operational base. The staff knew the crews well, were in direct touch with the service and handled all the rostering and schedules. With the implementation of the Call Centre, such direct contact was impossible; all incoming calls were routed to it. An entire level of complexity had been added, as the diagram shows. No need for any detail to know that this process is worse, much worse. The Call Centre staff added no value; their job was merely to record information in the CRM system. When action was required they communicated via email with the administrative staff in the waste collection service (outward telephone calls were not allowed!).

The implementation of the Contact Centre, driven by policy diktat, had ingeniously produced a much less responsive service, at very significant additional cost.

Reflections on innovation at Salford: a curate's egg

The various case studies of SPRINT's application in Salford present a fascinating 'natural experiment' on the nature of organisational change, at a time when the processes of local government modernisation were in full spate. A rather mixed pattern emerges: radical change in ITSD and Customer Services, but incremental advance and frustrated ambition elsewhere, of relative failure to realise the potentially radical nature of e-government. In the Decision-making project, the outcome was partially successful, but the most innovative ideas were left on the shelf. Ostensibly supported by the senior manager and his staff, all agreed that radical innovation could improve the performance of the service, but the familiarity of the *status quo ante* proved hard to dislodge. In the case of births, deaths and marriages, we see a similar pattern. Although ownership again resided with the manager of the BDM function and there was a radical agenda, ultimately the SPRINT project did no more than prepare the groundwork for this new vision. The third case adds a further twist. Here, users were fully in charge of the design work and a radical vision emerged. However, conservatism again won out. The e-envoys struggled to sell their proposals to their colleagues; that they were insiders mattered little when significant realignment of established structures was entailed.

Writing at the time, I argued that the three cases exemplified just how difficult it was to meet the challenge of "remaking government for the information age" (Kawalek & Wastell, 2005). Whilst government rhetoric called for radical solutions to be the norm, with new technology the catalyst, a different outcome had been encountered: projects that started with high ambition but then slipped backwards to appreciably more modest results. It is not as though the radical possibilities were unappreciated, but each time it was the more conservative options that prevailed. In reviewing the overall progress of Salford's e-Government programme (based on interviews with service directors) I concluded that in 2003 this was typical for the Council as a whole. e-Government had very largely been translated into changes at the organisational interface, namely the creation of new access channels, mediated by the Internet and the Contact Centre:[79]

---

79 Salford was not alone in this, indeed I suspect they reflected the norm. I clearly recall that the term "e-veneering" was a popular satirical trope in the local government community at the time.

> *There is little sense that e-government is really seen as anything new or radical; it has seemingly been translated into… internet access to services. The service providers have a lot to gain from this defence, as they can escape the rigorous scrutiny that fundamental re-engineering might entail* (Wastell, 2002).

What stands out from the Salford experience is the variety of outcomes that may be expected from change projects, even when those projects are carried out by the same change-agents in a single location. Cule and Robey (2004) argue that change in organisations is propelled by rational individuals attempting to modify the way things are, but their efforts take place in contexts populated by other actors whose purposes may be incompatible. The vector of change reflects the on-going negotiation and dialectical resolution of these conflicting interests. In a similar vein, Bacharach *et al.* (1996) depict organisations as complex political landscapes, with multiple interweaving "logics of action";[80] conflicts and tensions between these logics are inevitable, with dissonance reduced through local "micro-political" accommodations. The clash of two general logics can be seen in our various vignettes: the logic of radical change and the logic of reaction, with the latter tending to win out.

But such a conclusion is little more than a dressed-up statement of the obvious, that the ultimate outcome of any change initiative reflects the indeterminate playing out of a complex political force-field, with more powerful and incumbent interests tending to prevail. Arguably a more interesting view is that of Martin (1992) who maintains that organisations are not homogenous cultural entities, but comprise different subcultures, characterised by distinctive professional identities or local features of different business units[81]. Martin identifies three broad categories of subculture, according to the dominant attitude of staff towards top management: *enhancing subcultures* (characterised by exaggerated support for the centre), *counter-cultures* (characterised by scepticism and dissent) and *orthogonal subcultures* (defined by occupational group or demographic features, such as race or gender). Such subcultural features will inevitably modulate change efforts: Ravishankar *et al.* (2009), for instance, show how the enhancing subculture of one business unit led to the smooth adoption of a centralised IT initiative, whereas a countercultural business unit, true to form, largely rejected it (Ravishankar, Pan & Leidner, 2009). Such deviance

---

80   Defined as "a general cognitive framework that guides behavior" (p.477).

81   The nature of the work itself will influence the culture. The level of risk and regulation in children's social care, for instance, is likely to engender a culture of conservatism and compliance, whereas in other services, a more entrepreneurial spirit is likely to flourish, especially where a militant citizenry is pushing for service improvements.

may seem deviant, but countercultures also generate innovation, as we saw at Salford; let them thrive, in the interests of all!

A further point concerns technology transfer, which is of considerable practical import. From a policy point of view, the question naturally arises as to whether SPRINT can be 'exported'. An important difference between the public sector and its commercial counterpart is the ethic of cooperation between organisations, of sharing innovation to enhance 'public value' (Hartley *et al*, 2008). Much public funding is provided accordingly, such as the Pathfinder grant which Salford won to disseminate SPRINT. To what extent has this promoted the external diffusion of SPRINT? This should provide a good test of the policy assumption that innovation can be readily shared. At first sight, the signs are good. A user group was set up in 2005, which has now held 5 annual conferences. Over 1000 people have been trained, in over 150 different organisations, mainly local government. But the critical question is, has SPRINT become embedded in those organisations in the same way as it took root in Salford? Here the results are salutary. A recent user group survey has revealed very limited impact: only 13% of respondents indicated it had had "significant impact on my practice" and even fewer reported that it was "used on most change projects" (7%). These results further underline the point made at the end of Chapter 2, that SPRINT's efflorescence in Salford is inseparable from the singular historical circumstances of its development there. A unique constellation of factors were in alignment at that time; it cannot simply be transplanted to replicate the same capability. That innovation is not a portable commodity has profound implications for both policy and practice.[82]

Small is beautiful

> *All really important innovations normally start from tiny minorities of people who do use their creative freedom. Yet, it seems, large-scale organisation is here to stay. The fundamental task is to achieve smallness within a large organisation....In any organisation, there must be a certain clarity and orderliness. Yet, orderliness is static and lifeless; so there must also be plenty of elbow-room for breaking through the established order, to do the thing never anticipated by the guardians of orderliness. Therefore any organisation has to strive continuously for the orderliness of order and the disorderliness of creative freedom* (Schumacher, 1993, pp.203-4).

So wrote Schumacher nearly half a century ago. In looking at the mixed fortunes of SPRINT in Salford, we see Schumacher's dilemma writ

---

82 For a fuller development of implications for theories of technology transfer and innovation, the interested reader is referred to McMaster & Wastell (2005) and Wastell *et al.* (2007).

large, of how to engender the spirit of innovation in large, cumbersome bureaucracies. In some areas of the organisation, creative freedom flourished; elsewhere initiatives quickly petered out, stifled by the imperative for order, for maintaining the *status quo*. It is worth asking what might have been done to engender a wider spirit of change. Perhaps for radical change to prosper, an unorthodox change strategy is needed if it is to challenge the existing settlement of interests. In this pursuit, my SPRINT co-author Peter Kawalek turned his attention to the history of discontinuous change in business (Kawalek, 2007) and I will now trace out the ideas he developed.

Drawing on Christensen's research on product innovation, Kawalek suggested an alternate change strategy to the classical linear model, which he dubbed the Bubble Strategy. This involves building new satellite service operations and allowing them to run alongside (and potentially take over) the older structures (Christensen, 1997). Christensen's argument pivoted on the need to create such new and separate entities serving new goals; if the change is a threat to the prevailing organisational interests, then its future cannot be entrusted to these interests. For change to flourish, it is essential to create a structure outwith the "normal cultural framework of the organisation", an entrepreneurial 'skunk-works' (Kawalek, 2007). Such an entity is liberated from wrestling with the political *status quo*, enjoying a "free space of reduced complexity and enhanced autonomy"; smallness within the large.

For Kawalek, the Salford Contact Centre epitomises innovation via the Bubble Strategy. Its leader had notable entrepreneurial ability, robustly rebuffing external interference. Kawalek highlighted the creation of 'Salford Direct' as a new brand, reinforced by a dress code of dark suits, magenta ties and carnations worn on days when important visitors were expected. He also notes the distinctive ethos of the "family business" and the fostering of a "new culture of the customer services professional", reinforced by the interview process ensuring that only believers joined. Kawalek goes on to articulate a set of general prescriptions for the Bubble Strategy: the need to create and resource the new structure; the need for incentives to "take functionality from other, more traditional parts of the organisation"; the definition of the role of the manager of the bubble as that of "corporate entrepreneur"; the need for a distinctive brand, and so on (Kawalek, 2007). There is certainly interest in these ideas and perhaps some version of the Bubble Strategy may work, although it is clearly problematic as a universal prescription. Both Salford Direct and Advance do seem to exemplify the bubble method, but the extent to which this was designed-in or emergent is debatable and it was certainly a product in both cases of rather unique local contingencies. Would the same results have been obtained had the Bubble Strategy been enacted top-down?

Another set of potentially useful ideas comes again from Pava (Pava, 1986). He distinguishes two key dimensions of change: complexity and conflict. In situations of low complexity and low conflict, he argues that the conventional top-down, "master planning" methods will work best, but they are much less well-suited to other configurations. The combination of high complexity (i.e. messy situations where a great number of intertwined or unstable factors exist) and high conflict between vested interests is particularly challenging. Here he suggests the need for a "non-synoptic" systems approach, which he dubs "normative incrementalism". Its essence is to keep things open and liquid. A broad, deliberately vague theme should be articulated, hinting at the general direction of change and providing a kind of liturgy. To implement the theme, local projects should be instigated. Bottom-up initiative is mandated, with different groups left to decide the exact nature of what they will do. This combination of ambiguity and responsibility creates a bind: "No alternative exists but to force the theme and action to inform each other… Slowly a reservoir of shared experience accumulates, and the theme is appreciated in hindsight as something more than a disembodied slogan" (p.621). Pava provides a relatively detailed case study in the field of industrial relations and there are also some affinities between his approach and Kawalek's Bubble Strategy.

Perforce, only very provisional ideas have been adumbrated in this section. In general terms, the way forward will depend on some combination of Schumacher's principles of subsidiarity and the middle axiom, of providing a degree of local autonomy, but aligned around a normative framework. It is important though, as Schumacher emphasises, to avoid simplistic either-or thinking based on false antinomies, such as standardisation versus flexibility, or centralisation versus decentralisation. Orderliness and creative disorder are not exclusive categories, with more of one meaning less of the other: "whenever one encounters such opposites, it is worth looking into the depth of the problem for something more than compromise. Maybe what we really need is not either-or but the-one-and-the-other-at-the-same-time" (*ibid* p.203). Why not think of autonomy and conformity as independent dimensions and, instead of trying to decide the optimum balance point, why not set each dimension separately? We have no trouble with this for our TV sets, one dimension for contrast and one for brightness! The concept of organisational ambidexterity (aligned and efficient yet simultaneously adaptive to changes in the environment) represents an attempt to combine such seeming opposites and there is evidence that firms higher in this complex quality perform better than others (Gibson & Birkinshaw, 2004).

CHAPTER 5

Implications for Education, Research and Policy

Having proselytised the cause of design, in this final chapter I will reflect on how professionals can best be educated in the disciplines of design at the individual level, and how capacity for design and innovation can be built within the organisation as whole. I will then explore some general implications of the design perspective for management education and research, deriving from both the redefinition of design as the primary task of management and the need to cultivate evidence-based practice. I will then develop the general implications of the design perspective for policy reform at a national level. Finally, I will return for a last critical look at technomagic, warning of its enduring thrall, again purveying design as the elixir vitae.

Learning design and building organisational capacity

> *Education is an admirable thing, but it is well to remember from time to time that nothing worth knowing can be taught* (Oscar Wilde).

If design is the remedy, then how can we best develop this capacity in organisations and in the daily practice of managers? This is the subject of this section, which has been heavily influenced by Don Schön's ideas propounded in his book *Educating the Reflective Practitioner* (1987). First let us consider what is meant by 'practice'. In a colourful metaphor, Schön likens everyday professional practice to the "swampy low-ground" of "messy, indeterminate situations", a world where problems do not arrive pre-structured and where theory only gets you so far (Schön, 1987). Because of their preoccupation with theory, he laments (like Simon) that the professional schools, such as Law and Business, are not the places to go to learn the practice they purport to teach. But fortunately such schools do not represent the only form of education for practice; "deviant traditions" exist including apprenticeships in industry, music conservatories and the studios of the visual and plastic arts. In such places, "we find people learning to design, perform and produce by engaging in design, performance and production… . Emphasis is placed on learning by doing" (p.16). Drawing on John Dewey, Schön stresses that students learn by performing that which they seek to master, under the tutelage of senior practitioners who initiate them into the traditions of the practice:

> *He has to see on his own behalf and in his own way the relations between means and methods employed and results achieved. Nobody else can see for him, and he can't see just by being told* (Dewey, 1974, p.151).

The essence of "professional artistry" is knowing what to do when faced by "the unique, uncertain and conflicted situations of practice" (p.22). Such knowledge is typically tacit and cannot be algorithmically prescribed. To become skilful in any "swampy domain" is to learn "to appreciate, directly and without intermediate reasoning" (p.23). Schön defines a professional practice as "a community of practitioners who share a calling and conventions of action that include distinctive media, languages and tools" (p.32). They operate typically within particular kinds of institutional settings, be it the school, the hospital or the business, and their "practices are structured in terms of particular kinds of units of activity – cases, patient visits, or lessons" (p.32). Schön goes on to ask how the practice is learned, taking the architectural design studio as his prototype: "architects are fundamentally concerned with designing… and designing, broadly conceived is the process fundamental to the exercise of artistry in all professions" (p.41). Learning a practice involves initiation into its traditions, conventions, terminology and technology, learning in the company of others. Apprenticeship is one model, but Schön notes that most workplaces are not set up for the demanding task of initiation and education; pressures for performance are high, mistakes costly, and so on. What is needed is a practicum:

> *A practicum is a setting designed for the task of learning a practice. In a context that approximates a practice world, students learn by doing… They learn by undertaking projects that simulate or simplify practice; or they take on real-world projects under close supervision. The practicum is a virtual world, relatively free of the pressures, distractions and risks of the real one (ibid., p.37).*

In the practicum, novices learn to recognise competent practice, they learn the "practice of the practicum", its tools, methods, possibilities, and develop an emerging image of how they can best learn what they want to learn. Much of the rest of Schön's book is taken up with observations on the nature of learning in the architectural studio, and other practicums such as the musical master class. Of his experiences in the architectural design studio, he writes in a subsequent article of the conditions and processes inherent in learning any professional practice:

> *I have observed that students must begin designing before they know what it means to do so. They quickly discover that their instructors cannot tell them what designing is, or that they cannot learn what their instructors mean until they have plunged into designing. Hence, in the early stages of the design studio, confusion and mystery reign. Yet in a few years or even months, some students begin to produce what they and their instructors regard as progress toward competent design. Coach and student finish each other's sentences and speak elliptically in ways that mystify the uninitiated.* (Schön, 1988, p.42).

The only way of teaching design is by doing it and a practicum must be the way forward in terms of developing the 'design attitude' in the public services. Our experiences with SPRINT training show the limits of the teaching model, as revealed by the user group survey mentioned above. Provisional thinking for a SPRINT practicum is set out in Appendix 3, which also describes how Schön's concept of reflective practice has been embedded in the SPRINT accreditation system.

The aim of the practicum should go beyond the development of individual expertise: the larger purpose is to build organisational capacity, as illustrated by a vignette cited in the Design Council's transformation design methodology. It involved the food company Kraft, which was experiencing major problems with its supply chain, with too much managerial time consumed fighting logistical fires. An innovation project was set up, supported by a design consultancy. The outcome was a new way of palletising products and a streamlined process to get products to stores. The results showed a 162% increase in sales and a 50% reduction in distribution time. But the real gain was not efficiency. The philosophy of the design consultancy was to "leave behind the tools of their process" so clients could do it for themselves: "For Kraft, the supply chain redesign project has led not only to increases in revenue, but a new culture of innovation" (Burns *et al.*, p.15).

Implications for Management Education and Research

> *The university has abandoned its historical mission to teach students to learn… We are training students to be unreflective technicians and magicians. Those of us in the social sciences and applied human sciences are most to blame for this tragedy. We are the magicians who provide the information and techniques, whose sole purpose is to adjust students as future technicians to the technological milieu, giving them the deadly impression that they are free individuals* (Stivers, 2001, p.209).

As noted, management education in general and the Business School in particular, stand at a point of crisis, in terms of both teaching and research. From Simon through to more recent writings (Boland & Collopy, 2004; Dunne & Martin, 2006), there is a strong sense that management education has lost its way. Simon saw this as a crisis for professional education across all the disciplines and Schön, too, takes a similar view. Their diagnosis is much the same: the privileging of basic science over applied science, with the technical skills of day-to-day practice at the bottom of the heap. Business schools teach a mixture of pure theory (economics, psychology, etc.), some applied theory (operations research, IT), but typically there is no systematic practicum in which the practice of management can be learned.

This "faulty epistemology of practice" places the business school in an invidious position; that which students most need to learn, it is ill-equipped to teach. And what is taught has itself been critiqued: "the problem is rooted in the training of managers as decision-makers and in the vocabulary of choice that is imbedded in our increasingly monoclonal MBA programs" (Boland & Collopy, 2004, p.7). Starkey & Tempest (2009) go further than mere concerns over relevance. Parodying the traditional business school as an institution "to create masters and mistresses of the universe" (*ibid.*, p.578), they go on to identify the carnage on Wall Street and the world's other major business centres as a direct consequence.[83] As an alternative, Starkey and Tempest make the case for a design approach to management education, looking to the arts and humanities for "lessons to guide us through our current difficult times". They extol the "narrative imagination" as a 'core competency' for managers, as well as Dewey's concept of 'dramatic rehearsal'.[84] Jazz is also lauded: "Education in jazz mode is not about individuals competing to outperform each other, but about learning how best to work together" (p.584). Congenial ideas indeed, but it is not easy to see how such idealism is to be put into practice. My project is more prosaic; there is a practical discipline to design, which I have attempted to set out.

The importance of design in an educational context is its integrative nature. Designers solve problems by synthesising ideas in a collaborative milieu; design thus naturally brings together the various specialisations that make up the fragmented business curriculum, not only showing their practical relevance, but binding them into an integrated whole. As Senge observed, "Design is, by its nature, an integrative science because design requires making something work in practice… the essence of design is seeing how the parts fit together to perform as a whole" (Senge, 1990, p.342).

---

83 As a specific symptom, they point to the proliferation of Enron case studies "extolling the company and its management practices as the paragon of the new economy" (p.582); such unthinking and egregious lionisation is all rather embarrassing in retrospect!

84 Defined as experimentation in "in finding out what the various lines of possible action are like by tentative rehearsals in thought" (*ibid.*, p.582).

Figure 8 shows a notional generic design life-cycle (loosely applicable for service, process or product) proceeding from analysis and design, through development, to implementation and evaluation. The various building blocks of a typical business curriculum are also shown, with arrows indicating potential lines of input into the various stages of design. Bearing on the opening phases of analysis and design are: business strategy (deciding what to do), operations management (thinking about efficiency), marketing (the voice of the customer), knowledge of IT (the potential for innovation), research methods (carrying out empirical investigation, quantitative or qualitative), HR (understanding staff, current competences and capacity for change), and finance/accounting (evaluation of cost/benefits and return on investment). And so on and so forth.

Fundamental reform of professional education will be difficult. Schön concludes his book with an account of his attempt to implement a practicum at the Massachusetts Institute of Technology, based on an integrative curriculum. Although a new spirit of cohesiveness and excitement developed, this proved difficult to sustain, due to the burdens of sitting in on one another's courses and running the small-group teaching that was a feature of the practicum. Over the three-year period that the experiment ran, the faculty members did construct a new integrative curriculum, but in the end this "meant more to them than to the students [and] showed a very strong tendency to drive out the students' reflection" (Schön, 1987). In a subsequent article, he drew a pessimistic conclusion:

> *In the university-based professional schools, prevailing models of professional knowledge and classroom teaching are bound to be hostile to the creation of a reflective practicum like the architectural design studio, where overriding importance is attached to the process of coaching by learning by doing* (Schön, 1988, p.6).

The design movement in management education is still at the fledgling stage. Being realistic, it is clear that a profound shift will be needed in both the mindset of the Academy and in the sublunary world of Practice. Whilst Martin is "totally" convinced the business world will be receptive to "MBAs as designers", he also notes they will "hate that name" and say "they don't want designers" (Dunne & Martin, 2006, p.516). Staff will also resist the change: "some professors will decide they don't want these ideas at all – all they want to do is teach the building blocks" (Dunne & Martin, 2006, p.516). Starkey and Tempest concur: "To move in this direction will not be easy, not least because it will be opposed by powerful interest groups. It will require strong leadership to develop the intellectual case for such changes" (Starkey & Tempest, 2009, p.583). But it will require much more than this; it will mean, speaking euphemistically, the development of entirely new 'capabilities'. That will be the real challenge.

Reforming the whole of management education is a tall order. But crises, as I noted above, are the symptoms of the need for paradigm change and we may well be at the cusp of a natural evolutionary shift across the 'institutional field'. Incremental changes can certainly be sought, nudging management education in a new direction. Rethinking our use of case studies would be a good place to start. Associated with the Harvard Business School, the case method is much hyped as "a powerful interactive learning tool that brings the complex and dynamic realities of business analysis and decision-making into the class room" (Starkey & Tempest, 2009, p.582). A rather strong claim, to my mind, and one that is easily debunked. Starkey and Tempest express strong reservations about the "totemic status they have attracted in business school education". In a telling analysis of "best-selling cases", they report that the research base for many is slight and skewed in the extreme: 58% of the quotations contained therein came from senior managers, 28% from other managers, only 1% came from employees and customers. They regard this bias as downright dangerous, setting "a poor example for students, who might well be persuaded that interviewing the CEO is a sufficient method for researching an organisation" (p.582). Worse still, students may understandably carry away the idea that only the view from the top matters in their subsequent practice! I fully concur that richer cases are needed, reflecting a range of 'stakeholder perspectives', but even so there are important epistemological limits to the written case. Documentation, however rich, is intrinsically limited as a representation of reality; business cases will always be pre-structured, pre-defined, closed systems. Practical action is not possible, which is ultimately the only way of gaining real understanding.

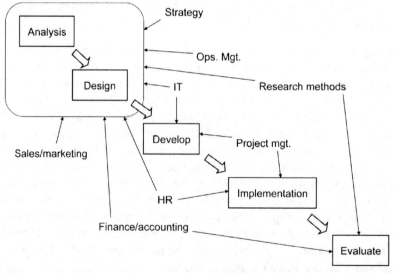

Figure 8: *The design life-cycle and the business curriculum*

A further option is to develop the one practicum that is a feature of most business school programmes, namely the dissertation project. In many schools, I suspect, this is motivated on largely academic grounds – part of the honours degree requirement to carry out a piece of scientific research. Typically, a narrowly defined 'research question' is pursued, involving literature survey, data collection and analysis, following a single research method. I have no objection to such an exercise, but I would ask one thing, that it is not seen as a purely academic exercise but should be related directly to management practice. Should not managers be first and foremost good researchers? Taylor knew that, although he would not have said it in such terms. Senge makes the same point too via his concept of "manager as researcher" (Senge, 1990, p.299), and the whole notion of EBM is predicated on this axiom. To make well-informed decisions is the very essence of management, and how else can such decisions be made but on the basis of research? Ideally, the dissertation project should be a practical design project, but by this I do not mean an atheoretical exercise. Quite the opposite: it should be an opportunity to bring together as much as possible of the theoretical knowledge acquired in the formal teaching. It should also involve a range of research methods; eclecticism of theory and of method should be encouraged and rewarded. Critical reflection will be vital on the value of the theoretical ideas used; indeed, a degree of irreverence should be encouraged.

There are implications too of the design perspective for management research. Again, the same criticism of lack of relevance to practice has been made; for business research there is a "utility gap" (van Aken, 2005). Rigour is vital in all academic research, but "for professional schools, one may want to add a second criterion, relevance" (*ibid.*, p.19). Van Aken distinguishes between two forms of research: Mode 1, knowledge for the sake of knowledge, aimed at explanation and description; and Mode 2, which is multidisciplinary and aimed at solving problems.[85] Van Aken argues for the recasting of management research in the mould of *Design Science* (mode 2), rather than conventional explanatory science. The aim of design science, he argues, is the production of field-tested and grounded technological rules, i.e. chunks of "general knowledge linking an intervention or artefact with an expected outcome in a certain field of application" (p.22). Importantly, such rules should not be used as instructions, but as *design exemplars*, to be invoked because of their relevance to resolving a problem. Practitioners then "have to translate this general rule to their specific problem by designing a specific variant of it" (p.27). The question must always be "why does this

---

85 The distinction between these two forms of knowledge recalls Aristotle's distinction between Sophia (science, understood as the search for universal truths) and Phronesis (practical wisdom, the application of knowledge in concrete situations to bring about desirable aims). Van Aken is thus making the case for what could be called a 'phronetic turn' in management research, a case which Flyvberg makes for social science in general (Flyvberg, 2007).

intervention in this context produce this outcome?".[86] The rationale of mode 2 research is thus to furnish a body of knowledge informing design, which must be applied critically and sensitively to important features of the local context.

At this point, we see how design science, evidence-based practice and managing-as-designing naturally come together, making common cause. The *raison d'être* of design science is to produce exactly the kind of knowledge that EBM in design mode is seeking, i.e. Mode 2 knowledge "that the professionals of a discipline can use to design solutions for their field problems" (van Aken, 2005, p.20). Putting this knowledge into practice requires both the design attitude and the time and space for design work to proceed. This process of design can operate at the micro level, when an individual practitioner redesigns finite elements of her own practice, or on the larger scale when an organisation sets out to make major changes in its systems and processes. The point is the same: design creates the context, the time, space and attitude for evidence-based practice informed by design science to take effect.

Teaching Evidence-Based Management (EBM)

How then may EBM inculcated? Encouraging managers to think of themselves as designers takes us a considerable way forward; the natural attitude of the designer is intellectual curiosity, i.e. research-mindedness. But EBM itself can be fostered through the educational process; indeed, this is where it should begin. What is the point of an educational system that does not produce evidence-based practitioners; surely, that should be the paramount goal of any professional school. Sadly this seems not to be the case. Rousseau and McCarthy comment that it is not only managers who are resistant to EBM: "management educators make limited use of the vast behavioural evidence relevant to effective organisational practice" (Rousseau & McCarthy, 2007, p.84).

Drawing on the more successful experience of evidence-based education in other fields (primarily medicine[87] and education), they set out a series of principles for teaching EBM. Principle 1 (The need to focus on evidence

---

86 Explicated thus, Mode 2 research has clear affinities with the so-called "What works?" research paradigm, recently prominent in policy and practice research in the UK, in various social fields such as criminology (Davies, Nutley & Smith, 2000). Van Aken actually gives the example of CCTV cameras; their installation on its own will not always deter crime; it is also vital (for instance) that the cameras be visible, that there be conspicuous notices drawing attention to their presence, and so on..

87 It is interesting that EBM made an early appearance in health care (Kovner, Elton & Billings, 2000) and has arguably made most inroads in that domain, presumably reflecting a general cultural bias in favour of evidence-based practice in health care.

where there is a strong knowledge-base), we have already encountered in Chapter 2. Principle 2 (Develop decision awareness) encapsulates the idea of 'critical reflection': "through the development of critical thinking… learners become aware that any decision may be an opportunity to apply evidence" (*ibid.*, p.87).[88] Principle 3 (Diagnose underlying factors related to decisions) involves the development of a sensitivity to underlying causes rather reminiscent of systems thinking. Students should be encouraged to pose questions such as 'why did this happen?', thus stimulating fact-gathering and critical enquiry.[89] The injunction of Principle 4 is also familiar, namely the need to adapt knowledge to the particular contingencies of situations, to be sensitive to complexity and to avoid the blind application of rules. Principle 5 calls for the development of evidence-based decision supports, such as checklists or protocols. This is where methodologies such as SPRINT fit in, as guides to effective practice.[90] Finally, Principle 6 calls for educators to prepare people to update their research knowledge over time: self-evidently, "evidence-based practice does not stop on graduation day" (*ibid.*, p.89).

Rousseau and McCarthy move on to reflect on some of the key challenges in promulgating EBM. First and foremost is the problem of access to research evidence. In management, there is a general paucity of authoritative summaries where people can read and appreciate up-to-date research evidence: "the existing mass of management research needs to be distilled into easily accessible, updateable repositories" (*ibid.*, p.91). This will be culturally problematic, given the existing reward structures in management research, as reflected in the editorial policies of the research journals:

> *Management scholars are rewarded often for new ideas, as opposed to assembling cumulative evidence regarding ideas other scholars might have already entertained. Even the Academy of Management Review pursues*

---

88   They acknowledge that this may be more problematic for management compared to other domains such as surgery, where recognition of such decision points is inherently more clear cut: "Day-to-day actions that managers take involve a host of discretionary behaviours, some habitual others more deliberate [compounded by] the unstructured, non-discrete, ambient nature of many organisational problems" (p.87). Such difficulties make it all the more important to develop decision awareness and this must therefore be a priority for teaching EBM.

89   Business cases can be helpful here, but fundamental reform of their application is needed. Rousseau and McCarthy contend that current pedagogy tends to use cases as templates for action. This risks "creating confident amateurs who believe they can become experts by emulating a case's ostensibly successful manager" (p.88) . Instead, they recommend that learners be posed critical management questions and invited to search for the best available evidence relevant to the case and apply this again in a self-critical vein.

90   Rousseau and McCarthy are at pains to stress that such supports are "merely tools, unlikely in themselves to bring about effective management practice", and that they are not written in stone "but require updating over time and should act to guide but not limit enquiry" (p.89).

> *the editorial policy of rejecting papers unless they develop new theory.*
> *Providing systematic evidence of what we can know with confidence is a*
> *recipe for rejection (ibid., p.91).*

The Web can provide part of the solution, enabling such repositories to develop outside of the conventional publishing system, as has been the case in medicine and education (*ibid*). Further impediments are to be found in the traditional business curriculum which they describe as fragmented, overly theoretical and remote from practice. There is also "a dearth of good examples regarding how real managers use research evidence or systematically gather data" (*ibid.*, p.92), in other words we need business cases that lionise EBM, rather than heroic or charismatic leadership. Rousseau and McCarthy also acknowledge the lack of opportunities to practice management within the curriculum; there is no equivalent of the teaching hospital. They suggest that this could be alleviated after graduation by providing opportunities for managers to come together to share experiences, "to meet together to discuss what worked and what did not, as an on-going part of the job" (*ibid.*, p.93).

EBM is not without its critics. Learmonth and Harding (2006) contend that EBM is an instrument of managerialism, that managers will always have disproportionate access to evidence and the power to bend it to their will. They are concerned that EBM exaggerates the certainties of knowledge and embodies a narrow definition of valid research practice; furthermore, that EBM privileges the abstract knowledge of the researcher over the "lived space" of the practitioner. I share these anxieties but take a more sanguine view. Whereas EBM could be seen to serve the interests of managers, research is available to all, especially if public repositories are created, and could indeed be used to resist managerial power. In the case of the ICS, had practitioners been aware of the research on IS design, this would have enabled a more effective critique to be mounted against its imposition; and indeed it was our research evidence which finally turned the tables. Whilst EBM may exaggerate the certitudes of knowledge, this is already a feature of *vade mecum* knowledge as encapsulated in text books. Those directly involved in research are more aware of its open-ended provisional character than the authors of many text books, and are therefore better-placed to reflect this in research summaries for practitioners. A robust health warning would need to be a required feature of any such summary, complete with evidence and discussion of variation in results. Dogmatism regarding research methods is also far from insuperable. I would go along with Learmonth and Harding in calling for "radical heterogeneity" in terms of research questions and methods, including the need to address organisational power relations and to pursue research that reflects the interests of all groups, again as we have exemplified in our work on the ICS.

Implications for Reform: Policy by Design

Thus far, I have focused primarily on design and innovation within the organisation. Much of the impetus for change in the public services comes from central government initiatives and, in this section, I will consider the wider ramifications of the design perspective for policy development and implementation at a national level. I shall set out the case in favour of a different approach to the top-down model which appears to have been the dominant one, at least over the New Labour years (1997 – 2010). Seddon denounces this as 'deliverology', referring to the setting up of the Prime Minister's Delivery Unit (PMDU) in 2001, headed by Sir Michael Barber. Seddon sees Barber as the wicked high priest of command-and-control; for the PMDU, all "change had to be driven by the centre" (Seddon, 2008, p.120). In chapter 8, Seddon forensically deconstructs the hubristic claims made by Barber that targets were working when in fact public satisfaction with government services was declining. Moreover, when Barber's evidence of success is held up to rigorous scrutiny it is found wanting, such as his much-vaunted literacy strategy. Seddon couches his verdict on deliverology in entertainingly robust terms:

> Barber describes deliverology as 'world class tools and processes'. I think of it as Mickey Mouse command and control. That is being generous to Barber and unfair to the mouse. Deliverology's method amounts to determining change on the basis of opinion and driving activity down with no knowledge of the impact on the way the system will perform. It is tampering on a massive scale, ploughing onwards with nothing more than a set of plausible ideas, ignoring their lack of success and showing persistence in the face of contradictory evidence (p.117-8).

Barber's method is "to create a bureaucracy for measuring and reporting that then deludes people into assuming improvements are real" (p.120). We are back to the world of magical thinking! In less lurid terms, the Chief Executive of a London Borough also excoriated deliverology in an interview for this book: "People have been very good at developing policy, I'm talking Whitehall, but they are very bad at helping any of the connections to delivery. They haven't been very good at thinking about what people need to do to deliver this policy; they kind of assume that somehow or other, it will happen".

Something is clearly rotten in the state of policy-making. In this section, I will begin by recounting two policy mishaps, the first from the UK and the second from the US (in the field of educational reform), before I set out the case for a different approach to the development of public policy, informed by design thinking.

Magic in the Risk Society: the Vetting and Barring debacle

> *Madame Sosotris, famous clairvoyante,*
> *With a wicked pack of cards. Here, said she,*
> *Is your card, the drowned Phoenician sailor*
> (T.S. Eliot, *The Wasteland*).

Those of us in the UK will remember the Soham murders only too well, but I will begin with a brief recapitulation of the case. In August 2002, two ten-year-old girls, Holly Wells and Jessica Chapman, were drawn into the home of Ian Huntley, in the village of Soham (Cambridgeshire). We do not know why, but they may have thought his girlfriend, Maxine Carr (a teaching assistant in Holly and Jessica's class at primary school) was inside, but she was not and the children were brutally killed. The reasons for the murder have never been established, though sexual motives were implied at the trial. That Huntley was a caretaker at Soham Village College (located adjacently to the victims' school) caused much public disquiet; it appeared he had been investigated in another part of the country for sexual offences involving girls under the age of consent, but this information had not emerged during the police vetting check carried out as part of Huntley's appointment as caretaker.

In December 2003, a public enquiry was instigated – led by Sir Michael Bichard – to investigate the apparent failings of record keeping, vetting practices and information sharing that had occurred, and to make policy recommendations accordingly. Central to Bichard's recommendations was the setting up of a single, central body, with exclusive responsibility for administering the registration of all those wishing to work with children or vulnerable adults. Police and other agencies would supply this body with information, and registration would be mandatory. A Steering Group was set up, of much the same character as we saw for the ICS, to fashion what became known as the Vetting and Barring Scheme (VBS). This would be operated by an Independent Safeguarding Authority (ISA) which, crucially, would have the power to bar as well as vet:

> *The Scheme aims to protect children and vulnerable adults by ensuring that people who are judged to present a risk of harm are not allowed to work with them. In the past, barring decisions have been taken by Ministers and civil servants. They are now made by an independent body of experts, the Independent Safeguarding Authority, and follow a clear and structured judgement process, which is about assessing the risk of future harm based on the information that is known about the individual* (Home Office, 2010, p.6).

Announcing the Scheme in April 2008, Sir Roger Singleton (ISA's Chairman) is quoted in a BBC report as saying: "The Independent Safeguarding Authority will provide a ground-breaking vetting and barring service... allow[ing] us to ensure an improved level of safeguarding as well the development of better information sharing systems." Despite such worthy aims, the inception of the Scheme in October 2009 was greeted with dismay on many sides given its scale and range. Over 11 million people would be covered and it seemed that relatively minor contact with children in a voluntary capacity would require registration.[91] Soft data (e.g. evidence of drug misuse reported to social services[92]) as well as hard data (criminal convictions) would also be gathered. School leaders in particular were concerned that the Scheme was overly bureaucratic and disproportionate and that it would deter volunteers. Such representations led to the VBS being scaled back, although the adjustments were relatively minor with 9 million individuals still caught in the net. The key date of November 2010 was set, by which time anyone working in a 'regulated activity' must be registered. Criticism rumbled on though throughout 2010. Civil liberties groups protested and the Royal College of Nursing also called for a judicial review. In June 2010, shortly after coming to power, the Home Secretary of the new Coalition Government, Teresa May, announced that the Scheme would be put on hold and reviewed, describing it as draconian: "You were assumed to be guilty until you were proven innocent".

In campaigning against the Scheme, I wrote a pamphlet with Sue White[93] lambasting its systemic deficiencies. We put forward the hypothetical case of a 16-year-old youth, with a fractured family background, who becomes involved in a fracas with another boy in a taxi queue after a night on the town. The police are called and he is cautioned; because the other boy was 15, a violent assault against a 'minor' is now on his record. Over the next few years, there are other minor non-violent crimes (shoplifting) as our protagonist struggles with drug misuse, but in his early twenties, he settles down determined to make something of himself. He volunteers to work in a third sector young person's service, aiming to train to be a social worker, and is vetted. The ISA case-worker reviews his application; they do not meet him but evaluate his electronic record in the database, following their "clear and structured judgment process". What else could be decided other

---

91 For example, parents helping with lifts to school sports events, where this was organised by the school. Anyone seeking formal employment would also have to pay a significant fee.

92 Even press reports of dubious behaviour could be recorded and taken into account by ISA staff.

93 Professor of Social Work, Birmingham University. The pamphlet was entitled: Catching Sex Offenders: Vigilance is the Best Safeguard. In: *Why We Should Scrap the Vetting Database*, Manifesto Club Report, pp.13-19.

than "minded to bar", especially in an agency set up to extirpate risk. The wicked card is dealt; all are informed, the applicant and the agency, and although there are further formalities, including the provision to contest the decision, the damage has been done... ironically to the very sort of young, vulnerable person the Scheme was designed to protect!

Aside from destroying 'public value' on all sides, will the Scheme actually work in protecting children? We were highly sceptical. Most salient of all, it is hard to see how it would have protected Holly and Jessica. Yes, it would have excluded Huntley from the caretaker's job, but this was at another school; his connection with the children came via his girlfriend, and even the Scheme's intrusive tentacles would stretch short of checking partners. It might not have stopped Huntley, though it might have hindered him; it certainly would not have stopped Humbert Humbert, the ogre of Nabokov's infamous novel. Though his hideous plan was ultimately superfluous, H. H. ponders monstrously on his marriage to Lolita's mother:

> *I did not plan to marry Charlotte in order to eliminate her in some vulgar, gruesome and dangerous manner... Other visions of venery presented themselves to me swaying and smiling. I saw myself administering a powerful sleeping potion to both mother and daughter so as to fondle the latter through the night with perfect impunity* (Nabokov, *Lolita*, pp.70-71).

Other absurdities derived from the definition of activities it regulated; car park attendants and kitchen staff in the Health Service would be covered, but not a self-employed violin instructor working with a child alone in their own home. We drew particular attention to the publication of a 'myth-buster' web-page by central government, intended to defuse adverse media critique. Such criticisms were described as 'myths', an example being: "A measure like this will not truly increase the safety of children" quoted from the *Independent* newspaper. These were systematically refuted by the marshalling of so-called 'facts'; in this case, "the VBS will make it much harder for anyone known to pose a risk to gain access to children through paid or unpaid work". This is in no sense a fact. How can it be until the Scheme becomes an evaluated reality? We described such self-styled facts as an exercise in magical thinking, that wishing something necessarily makes it true. Such magical thinking is typical of the language used throughout to describe the Scheme, exemplified above; there is no doubt that it will produce the desired effect!

The Scheme's apparent ignorance of the nature and circumstances of child abuse and particularly sexual abuse was particularly concerning. We noted how the Internet had exponentially increased the number of adults to whom children were exposed all outwith the gaze of the VBS. If one were a predatory paedophile, one could make contact through Facebook, My Space and similar chat-rooms with any number of children and young people. Add to this the vast numbers of workers from overseas in our public services whose history cannot be traced. And on, and on – the complications multiply as the myths of the Scheme meet the facts of the real world. Putting all this together, we argued that such inconsistencies betrayed the real motives of the Scheme as less about protecting children than protecting government and employers from the lynch-mob of public outrage in anticipation of future adverse events.

Reform as learning

In San Diego in 1998, an ambitious programme of educational reform was launched focusing on the teaching and learning of literacy skills. It was led by Anthony Alvarado, recruited on the basis of his national renown as the architect of school reform in a highly disadvantaged district of New York City. Under his stewardship, the district had risen from near the bottom of 32 districts to second from the top, and had become widely heralded as proof that low-performing urban districts can succeed. Alvarado set the direction of policy in San Diego, appointing and leading a cadre of 'instructional leaders' who were to carry through his reforms. However, two years later, the programme was in a shambles. Alvarado's "relentless insistence on change" had alienated teachers, parents, community members and the local press. His 'Balanced Literacy Program'[94] had become seen as a rigid, one-size-fits-all-remedy, an intrusion on teacher autonomy. In 2002 he was fired. A fascinating contrast of the same reform working well in one locus but backfiring spectacularly in another.

Hubbard, Mehan & Stein (2006) set out to explicate these very different outcomes, asking why a reform that began with so much promise and celebrated leadership miscarried so profoundly. Lipsky's concept of the Street Level Bureaucrat (SLB) is central to their detailed ethnographic analysis. Lipsky, a US political scientist writing in the 1970s when there were serious cuts in public services, drew attention to the practical fact that front-line workers (policemen, social workers, etc.) have considerable discretion in carrying out their work and their everyday practices might thus depart from what is expected of them by managers and politicians. In their mundane encounters, they effectively decide what policy is:

---

94   The Balanced Literacy Program is a highly structured programme which assists children by first assessing their level of comprehension and then providing texts and instructional supports appropriate to that level.

> *The decisions of street-level bureaucrats, the routines they establish and the devices they invent to cope with uncertainties and work pressures effectively become the public policies they carry out* (Lipski, 1980, p.xii).

Hubbard *et al.* attribute the difficulties in San Diego as the failure of top-down reform, which they characterise "as a linear process in which policy is formulated by elite decision-makers" which then follows a one-directional "arrow of change" with reform put into practice by "passive and compliant implementers" (2006, p.13). This was the 'theory in action' of Alvarado and it had failed. In contrast, Hubbard *et al.* propose another model of reform as a "co-constructed" process (p.13), in which participants are treated as "active agents who make policy in their everyday actions". As active agents, they have the power to carry out directives, to resist or even actively subvert policy: "In all these cases – passive resistance, active subversion, faithful rendering of top-down mandates – we treat the agency of participants as an act of co-construction" (p.14).

Alvarado had succeeded in New York though. However, there were important differences, apart from the size and demographic profile of the two locations. The key difference lay in the design of the literacy programme. In New York, it had evolved over a period of five years, with teachers able to tailor it to meet specific local needs. A group of international experts had been recruited to help develop the system; roll-out had been relatively slow and adjustments made on the basis of feedback from principals and teachers. Although there had been absolute insistence on the adoption of the programme, there was also considerable flexibility in the manner in which schools were accountable for its enactment. In contrast, the San Diego package had not been "organically developed but had been presented to educators more or less as a finished product to be implemented" (p.52).[95] The rapid pace of the reform is memorably described as "learning to fly the plane while flying it" (p.2): "San Diego educators were asked to suspend doubt and to implement the program based solely on assurances that it would work" (p.56). Alvarado had come to San Diego with the firm conviction:

> *that reform from the very start should be expected to penetrate all schools and classrooms across the district. Staggered implementation or demonstration schools were counterproductive, he argued, because such reforms often failed to take hold and spread* (p.42).

Given the problems encountered by Alvarado's centralised, top-down approach, driven by 'technical rationality', a new approach was adopted

---

95 A manual had even been produced precisely specifying the presentations (copies of transparencies, scripts of what to say etc.) which members of Alvarado's reform team were required to follow in presenting the model at conferences and workshops.

following his departure. School principals participated from the earliest stages in planning and were encouraged to tailor the reform to their own school's needs. There were also cautious moves towards decentralisation, including an increase in financial discretion at the school level. The pace of reform was characterised by "a slower-paced, more incremental, locally sensitive approach... shorn of its moral urgency" (p.232).

Reforming reform

In their conclusions, Hubbard *et al.* characterise the essential nature of public policy as: "contingent, co-constructed and mutually adaptive –*implementation dominates outcome,* that is local choices about how to put a policy into practice are of greater importance than policy design features such as technology, funding or governance". They argue that reform, especially ambitious reform, needs to be seen as a process of learning. To enact the Balanced Literacy framework effectively, teachers needed to understand its theory of how students learn to read and write, and how the framework supports this. Principals above all needed to understand the new framework to be able to explain it to their staff, interacting one-on-one, figuring what was working and what was not, and setting new goals tailored to teacher's individual needs.

Hubbard *et al.* conclude with a set of recommendations for effective policy reform, based on its fundamental reformulation as a learning process, recognising that the more ambitious the reform, the greater the learning challenges. Reform must always be adapted to local circumstances: what works in one location won't necessarily work in another. Above all, it is critical to pay close attention to the "conditions which gave rise to the reform in the first place". They go on to urge an incremental approach, aimed at building capacity: "A negotiated collaborative reform may take longer, but it stands a greater chance of being accepted and institutionalized by key constituents and thus is more likely to be sustained" (p.253). It is vital to foster trust, as an essential feature of successful reform: "the absence of trust can doom even the most thoughtful and carefully planned reform" (p.254). Regarding reform as learning means it must be seen as a two-way process; "upwards learning" for those in leadership positions from the front line is just as important as the flow of policy downwards.

I am much in sympathy with this credo. When we looked at the wreckage of NPM in Chapter 2, we saw the massive failure of the top-down, dogma-driven approach to reform. ICS is a case in point and the VBS a more recent example. Hubbard's work highlights the disconnection between the policy aspirations of reformers and actual street-level outcomes, and the critical need to engage local managers and front-line professionals. But it is less clear how to do this from their work beyond broad exhortations and general philosophical principles. A new approach is needed to policy development and implementation. Hubbard *et al.* talk of learning; I would speak of design.

In the astral zones where 'policy elites' devise reform, the importance of understanding the need for design is critical, and ignorance of it is the cause of much mischief. Metaphors are important, they shape our view of the world, but they can be dangerous traps. The idea that policy is 'delivered' is altogether the wrong metaphor, and wholly pernicious, pandering to the conceit of an all-powerful centre. Implementation is not a passive conduit; yes, the policy document can be sent through the post or the electronic equivalent, but putting it into operation is a matter of *design* not of delivery. In practical terms, moving from delivery to design requires the opening up of 'creative space' at the local level, the freedom (and responsibility) to experiment and to tailor bespoke solutions that reflect local contingencies, preferences and modes of working. More *laissez-faire*, less *dirigisme*! This very much resonates with Eason's beef against the 'push strategy' of NPfIT, which we looked at briefly in Chapter 3. Also mentioned in that chapter was the Munro Review of Child Protection. Munro's Interim Report articulates clearly the way to go. The report extols the virtues of good design and cites several examples of what can be achieved when the shackles are loosed of the 'electronic iron cage', giving mangers the freedom to develop 'work systems' based on local conditions and methods of work. Let us hope it is the harbinger of a more liberal regime in the times ahead:

> To start to encourage change the review has been working with the Government on how to give local systems greater flexibility to keep their focus on helping children. Cumbria, Westminster, Knowsley, Gateshead and Hackney want to make locally driven changes to the assessment processes that seek to give greater autonomy to frontline social workers. Specifically, the changes proposed would focus on allowing more flexible timescales so that social workers can exercise their professional judgment more effectively to improve outcomes for vulnerable children (p.69).[96]

Managers should see themselves as designers, but more fundamental still, a design attitude is needed in the development of policy itself. Policy should be designed not developed, and designed well to boot, following the sorts of core disciplines we looked at in Chapters 3 and 4. A genuinely evidence-based approach should be adopted, with critical and balanced appraisal of relevant research, actively guarding against confirmation bias

---

96   Munro, E. *The Munro Review of Child Protection Interim Report: The Child's Journey.*
     Published February 2011. See http://www.education.gov.uk/munroreview/downloads/
     Munrointerimreport.pdf

by seeking out evidence which challenges core assumptions. In-depth empirical engagement by policy makers is crucial, listening to professionals and citizens, not relying on superficial, intrinsically skewed consultation exercises. In the case of the ICS, one might ask rhetorically how much time civil servants actually spent in social work offices; a little ethnography goes a long way!

Beyond technomagic – reprise

> Our worship of technology and irrational belief in its omnipotence prevent us from seeing the obvious: the technological system can accomplish none of its mythological goals. It can guarantee us neither happiness and health, nor success and survival. Instead, the technological system is the greatest threat to their realisation (Stivers, 2001, p.206).

In this final section I return to the characterisation of technology as magic, paradoxically equating the epitome of rationality with its very opposite. I follow Ellul in adopting a broad definition of technology as: "the totality of methods rationally arrived at and having absolute efficiency in every field of human activity" (Ellul, 1964, p. xxv), i.e. a systemic method to achieve a desired end. Technology is thus synonymous with technique, which is the definition implicit throughout my writings.[97] Although all operations involve a degree of technique (even the simplest ones such as fruit-gathering by primitive peoples – *ibid.*, p.20), the emergence of 'Technique with a capital T' in modern times has given rise to what Ellul calls *technical civilisation*. This is characterised by the replacement of natural and spontaneous effort with the systematic search for "best means in every field…it is the aggregate of these means that produces technical civilisation" (*ibid.*, p.21). In the technological society, "technique has taken over all of man's activities… it ceases to be external to man and becomes his very substance" (*ibid.*, p.6). The modern state represents the culmination of such technical civilisation: as kinship and community decline, increasingly isolated individuals more and more look to the State for help and protection. The modern state is technical and "asks nothing better than to intervene" (Ellul, 1964, p.228):

---

97 Although the use of the word technology invokes the idea of the machine, Ellul stresses it is much more than that, as we can see from his definition. Although "technique certainly began with the machine…technique has now become almost completely independent of the machine. .. It is the machine which is dependent on technique. Technique integrates the machine into society. It constructs the kind of world the machine needs and introduces order where the incoherent banging of machinery heaped up ruins" (Ellul, 1964, pp.4-5).

> *We look to technology to solve all our problems… Technology is much more immediate to us than nature, for in modern societies our physical environment is one of plastic, glass, steel and concrete… technology mediates all our relationships. Human techniques tend to supplant morality, manners and social institutions. Bureaucracy, advertising, public relations, psychological technique… are only some of the most obvious examples* (Stivers, 2001, p.23).

So much for technology, what then of magic? Ellul makes an important distinction between two forms of technique: the concrete, material techniques of *Homo faber* (man the maker) and magical techniques. These two streams of technique have existed from the beginning, but there is a crucial difference. Some technologies (such as machines) do work instrumentally by material causality, others work by magic: "In the material domain, the result can readily be seen. That one form of axe is superior to another is a judgement not beyond the normal man. But with magical practices the same certainty of evidence does not exist" (p.27). Stivers gives several examples of such modern magical practices. Psychotherapy is one. It is often effective, but not in the material sense of conventional medical treatments. Unlike drugs for instance, its specific technical 'ingredients' have been shown to matter less than general factors which are common to the therapeutic situation, such as the strength of the 'therapist-client alliance', the faith of both therapist and client in the particular technique being used, and the intrinsic skill of the therapist (Messer & Wampold, 2002). Not conforming to the 'medical model', Stivers concludes that therapy "is a psychological technique, a form of magic that operates as a kind of placebo" (p.168).

Technological society is thus characterised by an all-pervasive faith in technique, which is increasingly magical. In the field of management, this is especially powerful. Boland and Collopy were slightly wide of the mark. It is not the decision attitude which is wrong in management, it is the technical attitude which is the real malaise, i.e. that there is a technological fix for every problem. But what is the evidence for the efficacy of such technics? Stivers puts Strategic Planning in the dock as his test case, citing Mintzberg's exhaustive research showing it to be a failure.[98] Other examples are provided, leading Stivers to conclude that much "management

---

98   Much hyped in the 1970s and 1980s, the essence of this technique is the setting of formal strategic objectives for organisations based on prognostications of success, followed by detailed planning and implementation. Mintzberg argues that its failure derives from several fallacies: that thought can be separated from action (divorced from action, planning becomes a vague conceptual fantasy), that strategy creation depends only on quantified data, and that the future can be predicted. Together these fallacies produce the magic illusion that "Because our planning process is logical, the outcomes we predict are inevitable… reality must conform to human logic" (*ibid.*, p183)

technique is as unsuccessful as therapy is successful" (*ibid.*, p.192), and that when it works it succeeds for the same reasons, as a form of placebo effect, working on the same "positive thinking" as psychotherapy. Self-fulfilling prophecy is the key: votaries aspire to organisational success and, when success is seen, for whatever reason (like the rain that eventually falls) this is always attributed to the technique: "they do not produce their intended outcome, but because they are always used to some extent, they appear to be efficacious" (p.197). Stivers concludes:

> *Management technique involves magical practices… [it] is faddish; theories have a brief shelf life, and old theories are constantly being re-packaged with new buzzwords and clichés. Obviously they don't work – they don't control uncertainty and predict the future. So why are we so susceptible to each new preposterous technique? Management technique promotes itself as a kind of technology; it clothes itself in the aura of technology. So if this management technique does not work, the next one to come along will* (p.199).

But technique on its own does nothing. The ICS, the VBS, the fantasy of 'transferable technology', the computerisation of the outpatients' ledgers are all examples, large and small, of magical thinking, of wish fulfilment. The antidote to magical thinking, as I have argued, is the robust empiricism of design. Doing design well involves hard work, concern for detail, critical engagement and rigorous argument leading from interventions to effects. Children can be made safer, ambulances despatched faster, vulnerable people protected, the rate of missed appointments reduced. These are not magical effects.

Managers must therefore engage fully in design, or at least understand how good design work should be done so they can manage it effectively. At a senior level, top executives need to be able 'to recognise it when they see it' and this book provides criteria whereby they can distinguish between the good and the bad, so that the right questions can be asked. Has any ethnography been done? Have front-line staff been involved? Have old processes been critically interrogated? And so on. If the answer to any of the questions is no, then the tocsin should ring. Without knowing something of the nature of design work, how can senior managers build capacity for design and innovation in their organisations?

Design is the missing link, but must itself be done non-magically, not reduced to a magical practice. Although methodology is important, it is merely technique again and cannot substitute for the all important ingredient – first class people. Fred Taylor knew this, as did many other key figures in this narrative.[99] Whilst methodology can function as a "transitional object"[100], in itself it can achieve nothing (Wastell, 1999). As MW at Salford astutely observed, "Methodology is useful, it gives structure, but getting people to think innovatively is something else. Methodologies are no substitute for creative thought". We have seen the folly of emphasising technique over people, process over practice, in the ICS debacle. Software engineering went through a similar period a number of years ago, when rigid processes were introduced, the so-called structured methodologies. The effort failed and gave way to the development of alternative approaches, such as the agile methods (see Appendix 2), which gave full space for the virtuosity and creativity of individuals, imposing only a minimum of structure. Social work is learning now what software engineering learned over a decade ago.

Magical thinking remains a powerful and pervasive force. Going back to the VBS gives us a final example, of technomagic carried to new levels. Examine again the quotation on page 156: "The Scheme aims to protect children…". The phrase "risk of future harm" implies the ability to predict. It is one thing to exclude an individual from a job on the basis of their past record; certainly, had Huntley's unsavoury history been known, he would rightly have been appraised as unsuitable for the school job. It is quite another to predict the future, as the Scheme purports, using the language of risk.[101] This is magic pure and simple. The phrase "risk of harm" occurs repeatedly throughout the document from which the quotation was taken, 22 times in all, and yet nowhere is the phrase defined. What harm? What risk? The Scheme depends critically on this concept as if it were a calculable probability: it provides "a clear and structured judgement process, which

---

99 In the field of software engineering, Fred Brooks provides another example. Brooks cites research evidence on the performance of experienced programmers: "the ratios between the best and worst averaged about 10:1 on productivity" (Brooks, 1982, p.30). He went on to coin Brooks law: "Adding manpower to a late software project makes it later", as we saw to spectacular effect in Blighty. Or as Tom Peters put it: "I've never seen a project being worked on by 500 engineers that couldn't be done better by 50" (Peters, 2005, p.59). The remedy is not to put more people on the project, but to identify and remove the weaker individuals, making the team smaller *and* increasing its effectiveness.

100 The transitional object (TO) is a key idea in educational theory, deriving from studies of play and learning in children (Wastell, 1999). The child's teddy bear is the classic example. It serves to help the child separate from its mother by acting as a surrogate protective figure; supported by the TO, the child develops self-confidence and ultimately makes the transition to independence. Generically, the TO concept thus refers to some 'entity' that enables intellectual and emotional development by providing a temporary source of support allowing the learner to let go of a former, dependent relationship. This dependency could involve a person, an idea, a theory or a technique.

101 The VBS exemplifies many salient features of Beck's Risk Society: *manufactured uncertainty* (the production of risk by the effort to control it), bureaucracy as a form of *organised irresponsibility*, and the application of "scientific models of hazard assessment" (Beck, 1998 p.17) to control risks which are fundamentally incalculable.

is about assessing the risk of future harm". To see the absurdity of such a claim, let us compare it with a situation where such an actuarial approach is possible, the use of diagnostic testing in medicine.

Appendix 4 provides an illustrative example, the faecal blood test to screen for bowel cancer. The contrast is striking. This is a test whose efficacy has been materially appraised in terms of objectively defined and measurable properties. Like the sharpness of an axe, credible non-magical claims can be made regarding its performance. Whereas the ability of the test to detect cancer is not strong (its sensitivity), its ability to identify accurately individuals not at risk (its specificity) is relatively high (91%). The distinction between sensitivity and specificity is crucial; for a screening test like this, it is specificity which is important: the purpose is to provide reassurance to those without the disease with a minimum of unnecessary distress (and expense) from false alarms. When a positive result is returned, this will be the occasion for a second stage of more rigorous investigation. Whether 91% is satisfactory is not the point; the point is that the figures allow rational decisions to be made about the value of the test.

Turning to the VBS, its black magic should now be self-evident. There is no data whatsoever to appraise its efficacy. At the very least, one would have expected some piloting; its reliability[102] could certainly have been appraised by submitting a sample of cases twice, checking for agreement. Empirical evidence that the "clear and structured judgement process" produced consistent results would be reassuring and important to demonstrate. But no evaluation was even attempted. Worse still, especially for such a consequential scheme, the need for such an evaluation seems not even to have occurred to policy-makers, and one doubts that the nuances of sensitivity and specificity ever troubled the consciences of its votaries; a magical belief in its efficacy was quite enough. Another system being designed without a glimmer of systemic thinking.[103] Evidence-based policy? The very idea!

---

102 The degree of agreement among different assessors evaluating the same case is referred to as "inter-rater reliability" and is an elementary feature of good research practice in social science.

103 Even when metrics are available, they are seldom used by government bodies to understand the behaviour of the system being measured. An example may be found in Broadhurst et al, where we show how the priority accorded to initial assessments compared to child protection investigations falls off as the volume of referrals increases. This is perfectly rational behaviour, what one would expect of a system working well. Without this systemic view, appraising performance in terms of completion rates of Assessments is meaningless, yet this is what the Government does. The data also demonstrate the nonsense of standard timescales given the manifest variation in service demands.

Carrying out an analogous evaluation to that of the clinical screening test would, of course, be difficult, if not impossible, although I doubt this was the reason. Let us pursue this though, as there are important points to make regarding magic, design and policy. The equivalent of the cancer would be the occurrence of a case of serious harm to a vulnerable person. But unlike cancer, serious harm can only be known once it has happened. And we are then in the position of looking backwards, not forwards, for evidence after the event. Looking back, something will always be found which would seem to provide advance knowledge of impending catastrophe. But to be sure that this evidence is the decisive factor, we need to know how often it was present in other cases but did not lead to calamity.[104] Designing on the basis of retrospective correlation is a recipe for disaster, intrinsically linked with magical thinking, but unfortunately in the domain of child protection it is the norm. Laming's reforms are one example. For another, we need look no further than Ofsted's recent "evaluation" of Serious Case Reviews for 2009-2010, also mentioned in Appendix 4 (Ofsted, 2010). Tragically, 194 children were involved, of whom 90 died. As well as reviewing the reviews, the Report attempts to look for common factors from which "lessons might be learned":

> *A consistent finding from the reviews was that there had been a failure to implement and ensure good practice, rather than an absence of the required framework and procedures for delivering services. Most of the serious case reviews identified sources of information that could have contributed to a better understanding of the children and their families. They also highlighted concerns about the effectiveness of assessments and shortcomings in multi-agency working* (p.5).

Leaving aside Ofsted's egregious failure to quantify their "evidence", the reasoning is as seductive as it is treacherous. Unless it can be shown that there was a distinctive difference in the features they invoke, that assessments, information gathering and multi-agency collaboration were conspicuously worse in the serious cases, how can it possibly be claimed that these were critical causal features. There is more than a strong whiff of magical thinking here: that there are rituals to be followed (the "required framework") and that it is the failure to follow these which leads to tragedy.

Make kitsch the enemy

> *Design thinking and systems thinking are one and the same. In great design, form and function come together seamlessly. Every part contributes*

---

104 The problems with this form of reasoning are explored in more depth in Appendix 4, highlighting in particular the crucial difference between post-hoc and a priori conditional probabilities, and the perils of conflating them.

to the whole in a way that seems inevitable. So too in a great system. Hence I've coined the term beautiful system (Peters, 2005, p.54).

Peters is right, there is a delight in the well-designed artefact, whether it is high-tech or mundane. He is also right that aesthetics is more than a simple question of appearances. Norman gives the example of a friend, trapped in a set of swinging doors in a Boston hotel (Norman, 1998). Designed for visual appeal, with no visible pillars or hinges, his friend was pushing against the hinge: "Pretty doors. Elegant. Probably won a design prize", the friend comments ruefully. Bad design abounds throughout everyday life, especially where technology is concerned: "the same technology that simplifies life by providing more functions also complicates life by making the device harder to learn, harder to use. This is the paradox of technology" (Norman, 1998, p.31). But he goes on to argue that complex technology does not have to be difficult, if designed well from the user perspective.

In thinking about good and bad design, the idea of kitsch is helpful. Although, the term was originally used in connection with art, to distinguish between mass-produced imitations and original works of great quality, nowadays we use it to refer to anything second-rate and tasteless, the tacky stuff of gift shops and the like. But kitsch is not confined to the gift shop; it is ubiquitous. Launer (2008) talks for instance about medical kitsch, using the example of a recent UK government scheme to offer cognitive-behavioural therapy (CBT) to large numbers of people with depression by practitioners given minimal training. Launer notes the CBT scheme's popularity with politicians as a cheap, quick fix, and the public benefit it thereby confers in reducing unemployment and social security bills (Launer, 2008). Launer characterises kitsch as "the mindless confusion of what is banal, glossy, easy to produce and cheap, with what is complex, subtle, painstaking and unique" (p.111). The idea that a short course of treatment given by practitioners with very limited training can yield long-term transformation of people's lives is pure kitsch. It is difficult to resist though, in giving us what we want in a simple prescription; who could be against it? In medicine, Launer advocates the evidence-based cause ("good, painstaking science") as the antidote to its "plausible slogans".

Lugg (1998, pp.2-3) speaks of kitsch as a powerful political construction:

> *...designed to colonise the receiver's consciousness. As such Kitsch is the beautiful lie. It reassures and comforts the receiver... through readily understood symbolism. But Kitsch neither challenges nor subverts the larger social order. Kitsch must pacify, not provoke the general public. The political status quo must be legitimated and upheld as morally superior.*

We all too easily associate political kitsch with communist regimes: May Day parades, simplistic slogans, sentimental images of happy workers in a workers' paradise, political party posters evoking idyllic folkloric scenes (Božilović, 2007). But kitsch is everywhere once you get the nose for it. The VBS is pure kitsch, providing meaningless reassurance that all will be well, avoiding confrontation with unpalatable truths, that some children do die in appalling circumstances, and perhaps there is little that we can do about it. Its publicity, like so much other official documentation of the day, is even more obviously kitsch: glossy and sloganistic, chock-a-block with syrupy images of smiling, contented folk, kept safe from harm by the benign State. Propaganda is another name for it! When I compare contemporary policy documents with those of yore, the tawdriness is striking. I have a copy of Barbara Castle's *In Place of Strife* in front of me as I write this:[105] carefully argued, nuanced and caveated, conscious of the limits of state power, showing proper respect for evidence; I will not say more.

Kitsch is ubiquitous, like a rash. In a letter to local authority leaders in 2010, Eric Pickles[106] urged the case for "local innovation" to cope with reductions in government funding. In emphasising innovation, the letter would seem to make the case for design, but it goes on "that must mean sharing departments, officers and back office services between different local authorities". In doing so, the exhortation for innovation produces its exact opposite; such prescription of 'off-the-peg' solutions is profoundly anti-design. Yes, shared services can work, certainly on a local level within a single authority, as we saw with Salford. But equally, the approach may fail badly, as we observed in several other authorities. There is, in fact, an evidence-base regarding shared services, though it is seldom consulted. Writing from a Australian perspective, Dollery & Akimov (2008, p.97) conclude that the available empirical evidence:

> *...is suggestive rather than persuasive. It appears clear that shared local service models by themselves will never represent a panacea for the deep financial problems confronting a large number of contemporary Australian local councils. However, the judicious use of shared service models for carefully selected local government service functions can make a modest contribution to cost savings and improved local service provision. But shared service arrangements should nonetheless be implemented on the understanding that they represent only one of several policy instruments.*

---

105 Barbara Castle was Secretary of State at the UK Department of Employment and Productivity in the second Labour government of Harold Wilson (1966-1970). The white paper, In Place of Strife, contained proposals to limit the power of the trade unions, particularly the ability to call "wildcat" strikes, as well as positive ideas for the promotion of industrial democracy. The legislation threatened to cause a major split in the Labour movement and was dropped.

106 Secretary of State for Communities and Local Government. Letter dated: 20/10/10.

The systems of the public sector should inspire admiration and delight, but so often they don't, and we have witnessed more than enough design calamities in these pages. But design can be done better, and I have attempted to adumbrate how this might be achieved. Above all, a change of managerial mindset is needed; managers at all levels need to see themselves as designers, abjuring the magical and the meretricious. In the austere times ahead, the design attitude will become ever more pertinent as managers in the public services, and the 'public value' they add, are apt to come under increasing scrutiny. Let designing be the 'day job', be it radical innovation, continuous improvement, or the mundane fine-tuning of existing designs, keeping form and function in alignment. As Farson stirringly declaims:

> *The broad ranging discipline of design adds to the stature of the manager as a true professional. The insecurity that comes from taking on the most complex role in society makes managers vulnerable to simplistic bromides. To fulfil the high calling of leadership, managers must move away from dependence on the welter of quick fix techniques heaped upon them by most management books and articles*(p.3).[107]

Although the two can be conflated, innovation and design are different notions, with the latter being the wider concept, as I made clear in Chapter 2. Its general meaning is the creation of form, the translation of conceptual specifications into concrete working systems. Innovative or not, what matters from the design perspective is fitness-for-function, that systems do what is required and do it well, with the minimum of unintended, adverse effects. To a degree, designing can be helped by following certain disciplines, which I have set out in the middle chapters of this book, but it is a matter of ingenuity too, of bricolage and resourcefulness. It is the design attitude which ultimately counts.

Finally, kitsch cannot be mentioned without invoking Milan Kundera, the Czech writer. For Sabina, the painter-protagonist in *The Unbearable Lightness of Being*, "kitsch was her image of home, all peace, quiet and harmony, and ruled by a loving mother and a wise father… The less her life was like that sweetest of dreams, the more sensitive she was to its magic". Sabina thus proclaims kitsch as the enemy of her creativity, and managers should do likewise:

> *Precisely by deflecting the creative and the uncertain, kitsch advances the repetitive, the secure and the comfortable, supplying the reassurance that what is to come will resemble what has gone before, that the hazards of innovation and uncertainty are far away, and that one is safe and secure in the routines of an unadventurous genre* (Binkley, 2000, pp.135-6).

---

107 Again quoting from his pamphlet *Management by Design* (p.3), see Chapter 2 of this book.

APPENDIX 1

A CONVERSATION WITH A CIO ON ALIGNMENT

In 2005, I interviewed the Chief Information Officer (PG) of Acme, a major UK financial services company regarding his role, priorities and views in relation to the alignment of IT and business strategy. Acme is made up of several insurance businesses (life and pensions, general insurance, motor and household) and two banks, a standard high street bank and a separate internet bank. The size of the IT department was 660 staff at the time, with an annual budget of just over £100 million.

Regarding 'short term alignment', PG was generally confident. This was achieved by the simple device of not having IT projects as such.

> *There is no such thing as an IT project. We don't believe in the concept. We have business projects, and those projects have IT components within them. An IT project by itself is pretty much a meaningless concept. What matters is the value we get out of a project and very rarely do we get value out of IT per se, we get it from the combination of IT implementation, process change and all the rest of it that ultimately delivers some value, and that might be cost reduction, some improvement on the revenue side or whatever it might be.*

The only pure IT projects were those of an infrastructural nature and winning the argument for investment in these could be problematic:

> *The areas where we struggle are around how to prioritise a clear business-delivering project against an "ought-to-do" IT project, like some investment in disaster recovery, or re-cabling this building. Those projects can sometimes be hard to get funding for, because there's usually no clear return on investment.*

There were tensions between the long and short term, that IT projects tend to unfold over much longer periods than the annual business cycle, and the short-term reporting of results. PG's comments bring to life the distinction between short and long term alignment alluded to in Chapter 3 (Reich & Benbasat, 2000):

> *There's a short/long term tension. A chief executive tends to live or die by the corporate results, but most IT investments tend to deliver benefits in a 2 to 5 year time line. The areas where I don't think we're as aligned as we could be are some of the more strategic things. In the financial services business there's a lot of stuff you need to do now for benefit in two or three years' time. Take something like a CRM [Customer Relationship Management] system, that's a long drawn out process. We in IT can see some big opportunities in return for some big investment, but we don't necessarily have the sponsorship to make those investments right now. I can think of three or four in that space. People tend to agree in principle that we ought to do these things but then when it comes to the practical level of finding the cash to actually do it, you tend to struggle. The price that we risk paying is that in 2 or 3 years' time, the business will say, where is our shiny new CRM system. And the answer will be that you don't have one because you didn't make the right investments and decisions 3 years ago.*

Demonstrating the delivery of benefits to the business is an important aspect of IT alignment. But this can be technically and intellectually problematic. PG reflects on the problems of attributing causality, given the spatio-temporal distance between the IT investment and the materialisation of benefits:

> *The problem you've got is, when the project delivers and it's a real success, that's fine but the benefit is then in the customer's profit and loss. But the chief executive sees we're spending 50 million quid a year on development. Now, how do I explain that that £50 million is good value for the business. It's very hard, it's sprayed around all these projects everywhere and I have no mechanism that allows me to say that by spending all this money on IT, the business is this much better off. I don't have the ability to track the benefits that come off IT, and yet we all know that most of these things we're doing are wholly and completely dependent on the IT components of them. There's a problem there and its around demonstrating value.*

> *What you can't do is take the benefit and say x% of that benefit is attributable to IT, y% to the business process, or whatever. I'm coming to it from the angle of "if we didn't do this we wouldn't have that". So you turn it on its head as it were. I can't put benefits numbers against IT investment, but I can build a kind of sequence that says investment here, this will benefit there... that's roughly it.*

Finally, the CIO moved on to talk about innovation, particularly the tensions between this and alignment, also discussed briefly in Chapter 3.

Innovation is key and IT is a critical part of this, but IT people are preoccupied with keeping the lights on… if our systems were down for 36 hours, we'd be out of business. This is something that all IT departments struggle with. The danger is that you get into a situation where do what you're asked to do. Because you're under severe cost pressure, all your available resources are focused on keeping the show on the road and you end up struggling to divert as much resource as you'd like to the proactive elements. I suspect that a lot of IT directors, and I include myself in this, spend a lot of effort building that sort of stuff by stealth. You continually find yourself in the position of trying to shine your crystal ball and make a few punts in the hope that'll position you well for when the requirement finally surfaces.

To finish, magical thinking makes an appearance. The CIO also affirms that the real locus of innovation is the front line, an important thread in the book's argument. He notably puts middle managers and management consultants in their place:

…the driver is the CEO… his vision is key. Without the emotional engagement of senior executives nothing will happen, but all too often they just hand over to the project managers and expect it all to happen by magic…

Middle management is the problem – front line professionals have their vocation, they show worth through professional competence; all middle managers have is their precious position in the hierarchy… they want to hold on to this status, their little empires. Let me let you into a secret: management consultants never innovate – they just do the job they're asked to do. You ask them for a strategy and they give you one – the people with the bright ideas are on the front line.

APPENDIX 2

Methodological Potpourri

This section contains an overview of several further design methods, which the reader may be interested in. The first is from the systems field, namely Stafford Beer's Viable Systems Model, an esoteric though conceptually challenging perspective on organisational design. Then from software engineering, I briefly describe scenario-based design, followed by an 'agile' methodology for software development, known as Scrum.

The Viable Systems Model

No account of systems thinking would be complete without some mention of the Viable System Model (VSM), developed from cybernetic theory by Stafford Beer. The rationale and principal features of VSM are set out by Beer in several rather idiosyncratic books, including Beer (1979). This chapter does not aim to provide a tutorial on VSM, just an outline of its main ideas, based on Kawalek & Wastell (1999).

By 'viable system', Beer refers to a system which is capable of maintaining a separate existence, of surviving on its own (1979, p.113). Organisations are seen by Beer as systems, i.e. goal directed entities made up of interacting parts, operating in an environment of some kind; the central issue is: what form of internal 'architecture' is required if these systems are to be viable? Beer's answer to this question is built upon a fundamental concept in cybernetic thinking, namely the Law of Requisite Variety (Ashby, 1956). Crudely-speaking, this law stipulates that the 'variety' of a 'control system' must equal or exceed the variety of that which is being regulated (variety is defined as the number of possible 'states' a system can be in).

Beer thus sees organisations as structures for handling variety. For an organisation to survive in a particular environment it must be attuned to the variety of its surroundings. If the environment becomes more complex, the organisation must adapt itself in order to manage this variety and to preserve its viability. Such adaptation is not a simple process. Beer's concepts of 'variety attenuation' and 'variety amplification' provide the two adaptive mechanisms whereby organisations seek to manage their variety and that of their environment. Variety attenuation describes the process of reducing the variety of the relationship between the organisation and its environment (e.g. a children's social care agency restricts its services to only those children at very high levels of risk). Variety amplification describes the reverse, e.g. a hospital sets up a new diabetic clinic thereby increasing its variety from the perspective of the local population.

The concepts of operational system and meta-system are fundamental to the architecture of the VSM. All viable systems comprise these two elements: an operational system which performs productive work and a meta-system which is the means of regulating the operational system. These concepts are recursive in that the combined structure of 'operational system/meta-system' at one organisational level together constitute the operational system at another 'higher' level in the hierarchy (e.g. project teams organised in departments, departments nested in enterprises). VSM proposes a distinctive view of control in organisations which emphasises the need for self-organisation and localised management, whilst maintaining the integrity of the whole.

Conceptually, Beer sees organisational systems as structures with five component sub-systems. System One (the operational system) comprises a collection of entities, each carrying out an area of operational activity. System Two is concerned with coordination. It is the element which 'dampens' the instability caused by conflict between parts of System One and its sole function is anti-oscillatory. For example, a procedure manual might constitute a System Two where it provides a framework for cooperation between production teams. System Three is concerned with management. Its role is to steer the organisation towards its current objectives. It interprets the policy decisions of higher management and manages the operations of System One on a resources-results basis, facilitated by the 'resource bargain', an agreement stipulating that, in return for certain resources, System One will achieve certain goals. System Three can also gain additional information about System One through the sporadic use of an audit.

System Four is concerned with intelligence. It enables the organisation to learn and adapt. It is an intelligence-gathering and reporting function that seeks useful information about the environment, scanning for opportunities, threats, etc. Finally, System Five sets policy. An important part of this role is to arbitrate between Systems Three and Four, as conflict can arise between the imperatives to maintain the *status quo* and for change. System Five should also be open to the other elements of the viable system. A special kind of signal is the 'algedonic' signal which reaches directly from System One to System Five. In a well-functioning organisation the signal will simply say that all is well, but it can also quickly alert System Five to a sudden crisis (e.g. the failure of a new product).

It is important to stress that the VSM is entirely conceptual. It is a way of thinking about organisations and the conditions for viability. Whatever real-world structure we are looking at, all the conceptual elements must be present and working in smooth harmony if the organisation is to adapt and survive.

VSM in action: a case study

VSM is certainly of interest theoretically, as a way of thinking about the design of organisations. It is also useful as a diagnostic tool for probing and critiquing the design of actual organisations, attempting to pin-point areas where the current settlement is dysfunctional. With Peter Kawalek, I applied it in the late 1990s as a consulting tool first in a major IT organisation and subsequently in a UK manufacturing organisation, known by the pseudonym Heather Manufacturing Systems (HMS).

The subject of the latter analysis was the Sales Department. Following a long period of stability, in which 80% of sales had been to a single UK customer, the company had diversified itself into new markets across the whole of Europe. The Sales team had led this expansion; they had shown themselves to be innovative and entrepreneurial and, over a short period, 75% of orders now came from abroad. Despite this, Sales faced ever more ambitious targets and they decided they needed their own Sales Information System, being dissatisfied with the services they were receiving from the centralised IS function. Work began in 1997 on the project, dubbed the Whole Europe Information System for Sales (WEISS). It was developed by the sales staff themselves using Lotus Notes. The case for such a local development rested on the assumption that Sales had a high degree of local autonomy. However, although strategically aligned for Sales, WEISS seemed to be causing problems in the wider organisation. In particular, delivery time problems were on the increase, as a result of Sales staff quoting unrealistic estimates. Customers were becoming frustrated and there were signs that market share was being affected.

VSM was used in our analysis, which involved mapping real world teams and departments onto the conceptual structure of the model. In simple terms, our analysis served to challenge the assumption of Sales' autonomy. In fact, they were closely and critically involved in a range of dependent interactions with other parts of the organisation, especially with Production. Both in the processing of new orders and the production of new parts, they had significant influence over scheduling decisions, though this was often informal and could be highly disruptive (for instance, when sales engineers went straight to the factory floor intervening directly in production decisions in the interests of favoured clients). Our main conclusion was on the need to formalise collaboration between Sales and Production. Accordingly, we recommended that a successful information strategy would have to recognise this: "the need to share information about scheduling between the Sales, Production and Engineering teams should be a prime concern". We recommended that the WEISS project be developed to "come under the ownership of more teams than just Sales and hence address IS issues from a broader standpoint".

Scenario-based design

In reading software engineering texts, it is striking how often the word 'system' is used to refer not so much to the design of the system, but of the technical artefact within the overall 'sociotechnical system', i.e. the computer software. The work I shall briefly describe here is quite typical in this respect. But much of what is said could be applied to the design of systems in the broadest sense as used in this book, directly or with minor adaptation. In this section, I shall provide a brief overview of a software engineering approach, known as scenario-based design, popularised by John Carroll. I shall draw on a book he edited which is a collection of chapters by various authors (Carroll, 1995).

Carroll begins by arguing that computers no longer belong to the esoteric realm of engineering but are "ubiquitous cultural artefacts that are embedded in nearly everything we do"(p.1). Their design is therefore everybody's business: "they must smoothly augment human activities, meet people's expectations, and enhance the quality of life by guiding users to satisfying work experiences...." (p.2). Carroll argues that new vocabularies are needed for discussing design in terms of user needs ("use-oriented design representations") which are accessible to all and which should drive the design process. Scenarios afford such a flexible and democratic medium. Scenarios can be simple narratives, or storyboards of annotated cartoon panels, video mock-ups, or physical simulations. The defining property of a scenario is:

> ...that it projects a concrete description of activity that the user engages in when performing a specific task, a description sufficiently detailed so that design implications can be inferred and reasoned about. Using scenarios in system development helps keep the future use of the envisioned system in view as the system is designed and implemented (pp.3-4).

The chapter by Thomas Erickson of Apple is of particular interest. Drawing on Schön (1987), he begins by characterising design as a "messy, indeterminate situation": problems must be set, a team must be built, with users involved in a collaborative social process. A degree of "design evangelism" is also critical if the design is to be transferred into sites of application and the buy-in of all secured. Above all design is "a process of communication among various audiences", and design artefacts must support this protracted "conversation with the situation in which designers embody their ideas in some representational medium, reflect on them, and then modify them" (Carroll, 1995, p.39). Erikson titrates the design 'life-cycle' into three phases: exploration, refinement and transition. During exploration, all is characterised by confusion and unease and the imperative is to crystallise a design proposal, a blueprint for the system.

Two scenario-building tools are proposed as helpful in this critical first phase: stories and prototypes. I will focus here on the former and the part they play in design work. For Erickson, design begins by "talking to users and listening to the stories they tell":

> *The stories people tell say a lot about what they do and how they do it. Stories reveal what people like about their work, what they hate about it, what works well, what sorts of things are the real problems. As one hears more and more stories, themes gradually emerge... Story gathering is also an excellent way of promoting team building... [it] sensitizes everyone to the usage domain (p.45).*

Stories provide a natural way of engaging users. A "good metric for stories" is how much they:

> *...nod or laugh when they listen... When they hear a good story, listeners say, "Oh yeah, something like that happened to me", and tell their own versions of the story. People who believe they have nothing to say about how technology shapes their lives are quite happy to tell stories that – to an attentive designer – may be far more revealing than a cautiously ventured generality (Carroll, 1995, p.48).*

Listening to such accounts, the astute designer begins to develop her own "design stories", scenarios which "attempt to capture some of the recurring characteristics in stories" (p.46). Erickson gives the example of the "Guilt Pile", whose gist goes as follows: You receive something you ought to read but it's not vitally important, so you toss it into a pile of documents, which sits in the corner of your office. You feel good; things feel under control. But time passes and the pile grows higher and higher. You begin to feel uncomfortable. You sort through it, discarding articles that no longer seem interesting. The winnowed pile is put back in its place. You feel good – things are under control again!

Erickson likes this design story because it not only explains how people use piles but *why* they use piles. It provides the design rationale behind piles. And when it comes to designing the system itself, stories show their efficacy yet again: "when describing the design for an electronic analogue of piles, it is much easier to convince listeners of the design's value by telling them the guilt pile story, than by just describing piles [technically] as 'self-revealing containers that support casual organisation and lightweight browsing'" (p.49). The pile metaphor actually sounds like a very useful design idea for developing an electronic system for supporting the informal management of a set of documents (and a prototype was apparently built in Apple). Indeed, it sounds like something which would have been rather more useful to social workers than the ICS. Which, of course, is the moral of this story, and of its story-in-a-story!

Agile Software Development with Scrum

I shall briefly describe the main lineaments of Scrum here, leaving the interested reader to explore further from sources such as Pichler (2010). As noted in the main narrative, Scrum is popular in software development, although it can serve as a general project management framework. It is known as an 'agile method' for reasons which will become clear.

Scrum's 'process skeleton' contains various practices and predefined roles. The main roles are: the ScrumMaster, who facilitates the development work (akin to the conventional project manager role); the Product Owner, who represents the stakeholders and the business; the Team, a cross-functional group of between 5 and 9 people who do the actual analysis, design, implementation, testing, etc. Product development itself is organised into Sprints, typically a 7 to 30 day period, with the length being decided by the team. The Product Owner writes customer-oriented requirements (typically user stories), prioritises them and places them in the Product Backlog. Each Sprint has a focused target representing a significant increment in product content, based on the product backlog. At the outset of each Sprint, there is a planning meeting, in which the Product Owner leads the Team in defining the work priorities and the team then determines how much of this they can commit to complete. The Sprint is 'time-boxed', i.e. it must end on time, and any uncompleted requirements are simply returned to the product backlog.

The essence of Scrum is our old friend, the self-organising team, which is encouraged by the co-location of all team members. The ScrumMaster is not in charge, as the team is self-organising, but acts as a buffer between the team and any distracting influences, resolving any external issues affecting progress. A key principle of Scrum is its embracing of variety; it recognises that customers can change their minds and that unpredicted challenges can arise. Such variations are not readily handled by conventional highly-planned project management approaches. The emphasis in Scrum is on maximising the team's ability to deliver quickly and to respond to emerging requirements.

Scrum roles fall into two distinct groups: pigs and chickens, with these comical names deriving from an old joke involving a pig and a chicken opening a restaurant. The chicken suggests the idea; the pig responds, "Good idea, what do you want to call it?" The chicken proposes "Ham and Eggs". "I don't think so," replies the pig, "I'd be committed, but you'd only be involved." So the 'pigs' are committed to the development work, they are the ones with 'their bacon on the line', while everyone else is a 'chicken'. Chickens, for instance, are only directly involved in the process during the Sprint reviews and are not allowed to interfere with work in progress.

Each day during the Sprint, a project status meeting occurs, called the 'daily scrum', or 'daily stand-up'. All are welcome, but only 'pigs' may speak. At the end of a Sprint cycle, two meetings are held: the 'Sprint Review Meeting', at which the completed work is presented to stakeholders, and the 'Sprint Retrospective', at which all team members reflect on the past Sprint, asking what went well and what could be improved going forward. As well as the product backlog, important Scrum artefacts include the burn-down chart, which gives a simple view of the Sprint progress and is updated every day.

APPENDIX 3

SPRINT ACCREDITATION AND THE PRACTICUM

At the time of writing, over 1,000 people have received initial SPRINT training, duly receiving their certificates, and feedback from delegates at the end of the training sessions has been generally good. But as we saw from the survey, the long-term impact on their practice had been much less than hoped. The following quotations from interviewed attendees get to the heart of the problem:

> The SPRINT course was excellent. Our line manager booked us on the course and although we would love to put our new found knowledge together, we don't know where to start or how we go about getting a mandate or budget.

> After the training we felt we didn't know how to apply what we had learnt to the work we needed to carry out. You get hit by this and that and then you end up dropping it. What we needed was for another experienced practitioner to come on site and show us how to get moving.

> I was really impressed by the opportunities the SPRINT training course provided – however it has been hard to implement back at the office. This is mainly because my manager sent me on the course, but she should have booked herself on it.

There are two related points to note here. The first is the need to embed the theory of SPRINT in the everyday practice of professionals, the second is the need to engage higher levels of management to ensure that the benefits of training are translated into practical action. Current developments with SPRINT have attempted to address these issues. An accreditation system has been introduced, founded on Schön's principles of reflective practice, and we are currently attempting to set up a SPRINT practicum, again inspired by Schön.

For Schön, professional competence consists of 3 core elements. The first is autonomy: the ability to act independently and responsibly. The other two elements derive from his well-known distinction between reflection-in-action (spontaneously adapting practice to the contingencies of the work in hand) and reflection-on-action (examining critically how one's practice could be improved). Most of the time reflection-in-action works, but not always – the familiar routine produces an unexpected result, stimulating the 'reflective practitioner' to stop and think, looking back at the unexpected outcome and its "assumptional structure".[108] Schön uses the improvisational nature of jazz music to exemplify the former; through reflection-in-action, listening to one another and to themselves, musicians "feel where the music is going" (p. 30), smoothly integrating individual contributions into the ongoing performance. But when a surprise occurs (e.g. a unique array of symptoms for the physician or an unexpected consumer reaction for the market researcher), then the skilled practitioner rethinks her routines:

> *...in ways that go beyond available rules, facts, theories or operations... restructuring her strategies of action, theories of phenomena, or ways of framing the problem. She invents on-the-spot experiments to put her new understanding to the test (p.35).*

Following Schön, SPRINT accreditation has been designed to be:

- Practice-based (grounded on experience not theoretical knowledge)

- Flexible (accommodating a range of profiles of experience)

- Simple (completion is not onerous, around 3 days' work)

- Personally useful (completion should stimulate critical insights and personal learning)

- Communally useful (knowledge so-garnered should be disseminated to the whole SPRINT community).

Applicants are requested to submit a portfolio of work, providing brief details of project(s) they have done, supplemented by a short Personal Reflection on the candidate's use of SPRINT, commenting on its strengths and weaknesses and general areas where it could be enhanced. The rest of the submission comprises 'Reflections on key disciplines', which takes further the concept of reflective practice. SPRINT embraces a range of core disciplines and techniques, as we have seen: process modelling, systems thinking, etc. Candidates select three topics, writing a reflective mini-

---

108 The distinction is similar to that made by Chris Argyris between two types of learning: single loop learning (the detection and correction of errors in performance "without questioning or altering the underlying values of the system") and double loop learning, when "mismatches are corrected by first altering the governing values of the system (the preferred states that individuals strive to satisfice when they are acting) then the actions" (Argyris, 1999, p.68).

report for each, addressing benefits, problems, criticisms and suggested improvements. An example is shown in Table 9, a reflection on ethnography.

> *Ethnography is for me the most interesting part of SPRINT. Originally I was dubious, but I realised that spending time in a setting gives opportunities to observe interactions and communication methods that I would otherwise never know about. For example, I was never told about the reliance of social workers on the duty team eavesdropping on one another's phone conversations and subsequent ability to interrupt with vital, recent information. This was not because the information was deliberately kept from me, but because the people concerned did these things without thinking or realising they were doing them.*
>
> *Ethnography highlights the difference between the theory and the practice – between how a procedure manual may instruct and what actually happens, between the way managers may think a job is done and the way staff have found works best for them. It can identify differences in the way different people carry out the same job, and reveal problems that practitioners do not see so do not mention. For example, in one social work team, I was told that telephone messages were passed to social workers by means of a message board. During some observational time spent in the setting, I noticed that social workers not using the car park did not pass the message board and did not collect their messages; a small but very significant yet easily addressed breakdown in the flow of work.*

Table 9: Critical reflections on ethnography from a SPRINT practitioner's accreditation portfolio

A SPRINT practicum is also under development. The basic structure is currently envisaged as follows, consisting of the two key elements: Membership of an Action Learning Set and a Practitioner Accreditation workshop. Action Learning[109] Sets have proved themselves to be a very effective method for management development; they consist of a small group of individuals, drawn from the same or different organisations, who meet face-to-face several times a year to share experiences and to learn from one another. The purpose of the Sets is to support members in the development of their practice.

In the SPRINT practicum, it is envisaged that Sets will meet in person periodically, and between meetings will keep in regular electronic contact,

---

109 The concept of action learning was originally developed by Reg Revans, and is encapsulated by the formula: Learning = Programmed Knowledge + Questioning Insight (Pedler, 1996). It thus embodies the same spirit of reflective practice that informs SPRINT training and accreditation as a whole.

using a dedicated SPRINT forum supplemented by other methods, such as email. Each group will be supervised by an experienced SPRINT mentor, who attends face-to-face meetings and participates in the electronic communications. The Workshop will take place towards the end of the mentoring process. It will give members the opportunity to present their work and to gain feedback from peers and senior members of the SPRINT community. Following the workshop, candidates will have the opportunity to submit their applications for full accreditation formally and have the option of remaining in their action learning sets.

The design of the practicum also addresses the need to engage senior managers. Before anyone is admitted on the initial SPRINT training course, it is intended that they discuss with their senior managers how they will put their training into effect and agree an outline programme of work which will be carried forward in the practicum. Engaging senior management in this way is crucial if sustainable capacity is to be created.

APPENDIX 4

BINARY DIAGNOSTIC TESTS
AND BAYES THEOREM

A binary classifier is a test for discriminating objects into two groups on the basis of the possession of some property. They are widely used in medicine to determine if a patient has a certain disease. Wikipedia gives the example of the faecal blood test to screen for bowel cancer and I shall use this to introduce key concepts and terminology.

Consider the results presented below regarding the predictive efficacy of this test:

	Bowel cancer confirmed (by endoscopy)	No cancer present	Total
Positive test outcome	2	18	20
Negative outcome	1	182	183
Total	3	200	203

Table 10: predictive efficacy of the faecal blood test

Table 10 shows the test to yield 184 correct results made up of 2 'true positives' (TP) and 182 'true negatives'. Errors fall into two categories: 'false negatives' (FN) when a case is missed when the disease is present (FN = 1), and the generally more prevalent 'false positive', i.e. when there is a false alarm (FP = 18).

Two statistics are used to summarise the performance of binary tests: sensitivity (the proportion of predicted cases where the disease is actually present) and specificity (the proportion of cases where no disease is present and this is accurately indicated by the test).

Formally, we have:

Sensitivity = TP/(TP + FN) = 2/3 = 66.7%

Specificity = TN/(FP + FN) = 182/(18+182) = 91%

Both parameters are required to give a full appreciation of how well the test performs and mean different things. Sensitivity reflects how well the test predicts the disease whilst specificity reflects how effectively it indicates its absence. A high false positive rate compromises the latter, spuriously indicating the present of the disease. Here, sensitivity is relatively low, 1 of the 3 cancers is missed by the test, whereas specificity is high, 91%. High specificity is what we want in a screening test; its prime purpose is to provide reassurance. Here only 19 individuals are alarmed unnecessarily, compared with 182 who are correctly informed that they have no reason to fear.

The ratio between sensitivity and specificity is called the likelihood ratio and is defined as: the probability of a person with the disease testing positive divided by the probability of a person without the disease testing positive. Mathematically:

Likelihood ratio = sensitivity / (1 − specificity)

Here the ratio works out as: 66.7% / (1 − 91%) = 7.4. High values (above 5) are generally considered to indicate that the test has useful predictive value, but a value of 1 means it is worthless as a diagnostic test.

Bayes Theorem

On the subject of predictive validity, some remarks regarding Bayes theorem are apposite. Bayes theorem is generally concerned with the prediction of events on the basis of evidence. Importantly, it draws a crucial distinction between two forms of so-called 'conditional probability'. The concept of conditional probability denotes the probability that some state of affairs (event) of interest is likely to obtain in reality, given the availability of some evidence. For the disease example, there are two types of conditional probability: the probability of the disease being present given the test result and, conversely, the probability of the test result given the presence of the disease. Let us call these *pre hoc* and *post hoc* probabilities. They are quite different and confusion of the two is common and, potentially catastrophic, from a design perspective.

Consider the *post hoc* situation of positive test results in patients with the disease. The probability that patients with the disease will yield a positive test result is simply the sensitivity of the test, here 66.7%. Conversely, of those with a positive test result (20) only 2 actually have the disease, i.e. the *pre hoc* (advance) probability is 10%. And the reason for the disparity is simple, that the disease itself is relatively rare compared to the likelihood of a positive test result. The relative probability of the two types of event must thus be taken into account in making predictions, above and beyond the performance of the diagnostic test itself. The relationship between the two probabilities is mathematically very simple and is given by Bayes Theorem.

Pre hoc probability = (relative likelihood of event to evidence) x (*post hoc* probability)

Here we have: *Pre hoc* probability = (3/20) * 66.7% = 10%

The danger in confusing these two types of conditional probability is highly consequential in the design of formal systems to mitigate risk (and both health and social care come under this rubric). Typically in such systems, evidence of risk is sought with the aim of predicting and, therefore, preventing, some evil eventuality. The problem is that the evidence of risk is always so much more abundant than the likelihood of the evil occurring; nearly seven times more so for our bowel cancer example.

The situation with child protection is more problematic. In every child death, evidence is always there of neglect and delinquency on the family side and 'deficient' professional practice on the other. And the more we search, the more will be found; the probability of 'predictive' evidence once the death has occurred is doubtless close to 100%. This inevitably leads the public and politicians to the conclusion that had this evidence been heeded, the tragedy could have been forestalled, and calls are therefore made for tighter controls, better information sharing, and so on. But this is the wrong conditional probability; what we seek is the *pre hoc* probability not the *post hoc* one.

In terms of prediction in advance, i.e. the likelihood of the adverse event on the basis of the evidence, the situation is quite different and, the more extreme the event, the lower is the ability to predict. Ofsted figures, for instance, 2009/10 reveal 90 deaths in 147 serious case reviews (SCR) involving 194 children, with 119 known to children's services (as "children in need" or on child protection places). Using figures for 2008 as my nearest guide[110], around 30,000 children were on child protection plans in that year. Of the total of 540,000 referrals to social services, approximately 145,000 led to core assessments and/or initial child protection conferences. Some of these will be multiple referrals, so let us work on the nominal figure of 100,000 children per year being deemed significantly "at risk". In those

---

110 Taken from the national statistics for Child Protection and Children in Need referrals, furnished by Ofsted for England in 2008.

children known to social services who suffer serious harm, the *post hoc* evidence of such risk is, by definition, 119/119 (100%), whereas the advance probability of a child deemed at risk suffering extreme harm is 119/100,000 = 0.1%.

Given the relative abundance of evidence of risk to actual harm (approximately 1000:1), coming to the conclusion that harm can be predicted and, therefore, prevented, on the basis of evidence is highly problematic. Whatever the post hoc probability, the pre hoc probability, the probability that really matters, is actually very low; of every 1000 children deemed at significant risk, only 1 actually came to harm. The idea that risk can be predicted reflects a failure to distinguish the two types of conditional probability, and in so-ignoring the overwhelming impact of prior probabilities, it engenders a massively exaggerated sense that outcomes could be predicted if only more evidence had been gathered and acted upon.

Of course, no definitive claims are made for the validity of this analysis; it is shot through with improvised assumptions and part-formed questions. It is proffered merely as a *gedankenexperiment* to show what a little systems thinking might look like and to question the idea of predictive risk in the context of child protection.

BIBLIOGRAPHY

Alford, J. & Hughes, O. (2008). Public value pragmatism as the next phase of public management. *The American Review of Public Administration*, 38, 130-148.

Alter, S. (2003). 18 reasons why IT reliant work systems should replace "the IT artifact" as the core subject matter of the IS field. *Communications of the Association for Information Systems*, 12, 365-394.

Alter, S. (2008). Defining information systems as work systems: implications for the IS field. *European Journal of Information Systems*, 17, 448-469.

Argyris, C. (1999). *On Organizational Learning*. Oxford: Blackwell.

Ashby, W. R. (1956). *An Introduction to Cybernetics*. London: Chapman and Hall.

Avison, D. & Wood-Harper, A. T. (1990). *Multiview: An Exploration of Information Systems Development*. Henley: Alfred Waller.

Bacharach, S. B., Bamberger, P. & Sonnenstuhl, W. J. (1996). The organizational transformation process: the micropolitics of dissonance reduction and the alignment of logics of action. *Administrative Science Quarterly*, 41, 477-506.

Bauman, Z. (2004). *Wasted Lives – Modernity and Its Outcasts*. Cambridge: Polity Press.

Beck, U. (1998). Politics of Risk Society. In J. Franklin, *The Politics of the Risk Society* (pp.9-22). Cambridge: Polity Press.

Beer, S. (1979). *The heart of enterprise*. Winchester: John Wiley and Sons.

Bell, M. (2008, June). Put on ICS: research finds disquiet with ICS. *Community Care*, http://www.communitycare.co.uk/Articles/2008/06/05/108421/analysis-of-the-integrated-childrens-system-pilots.html (accessed 20/5/09).

Bennington, J. & Moore, M. H. (2011). Public value in complex and changing times. In J. Bennington & M. H. Moore, *Public value: theory and practice* (pp.1-30). Basingstoke: Palgrave Macmillan.

Bevan, G. & Hood, C. (2006). What get's measured is what matters: targets and gaming in the English public health care system. *Public Administration*, 84, 517-538.

Beynon-Davies, P. (1995). Information systems 'Failure': the case of the London Ambulance Service's Computer Aided Despatch Project. *European Journal of Information Systems*, 4, 171–184.

Beynon-Davies, P. (2009). *Business Information Systems*. Basingstoke: Palgrave Macmillan.

Binkley, S. (2000). Kitsch as a Repetitive System: A Problem for the Theory of Taste Hierarchy. *Journal of Material Culture, 5*, 131-152.

Blond, P. (2010). *Red Tory*. London: Faber and Faber.

Boland, R. J. & Collopy, F. (2004). *Managing as Designing*. Stanford: Stanford Business Books.

Borins, S. F. (1998). *Innovating with integrity: How local heroes are transforming American government* . Washington: Georgetown University Press.

Božilović, N. (2007). Political kitsch and myth-making consciousness. *Philosophy, Sociology and Psychology, 6*, 41-52.

Broadhurst, K., Wastell, D. & White, S. (2010). Performing 'initial assessment': identifying the latent conditions for error at the front-door of local authority children's services. *British Journal of Social Work*, 40, 2, 352-370.

Brooks, F. (1982). *The mythical man month: essays in software engineering*. Reading: Addison-Wesley.

Brown, I. D., Wastell, D. G. & Copeman, A. (1982). A psychophysiological investigation of system efficiency in public telephone systems. *Ergonomics, 25*, 1013-1040.

Brown, J. S. & Hagel, J. (2003, June). Does IT matter? An HBR debate. *Harvard Business Review 2003 (letters to the editor)*, 1-17.

Burns, C., Cottam, H., Vanstone, C. & Winhall, J. (2006). *RED PAPER 02 Transformation Design*. London: Design Council.

Carr, N. (2003, May). IT doesn't matter. *Harvard Business Review*, 41-49.

Carroll, J. M. (1995). *Scenario-based design: envisioning work and technology in system development*. Chichester: John Wiley.

Chan, Y. E. & Reich, B.H. (2007). IT alignment: what have we learned? *Journal of Information Technology, 22*, 297–315.

Chard, A. & Ayre, P. (2010). Managerialism – at the tipping point. In P. Ayre & M. Preston-Shoot, *Children's services at the cross-roads* (pp.95-106). Lyme Regis: Russell House.

Checkland, P. (1981). *Systems Thinking, Systems Practice*. Chichester: John Wiley.

Checkland, P. & Holwell, S. (2005). *Information, Systems and Information Systems*. Chichester: John Wiley.

Checkland, P. & Scholes, J. (1990). *Soft Systems Methodology in Action*. Chichester: John Wiley.

Cherns, A. (1976). Principles of sociotechnical design. *Human Relations, 29*, 783-92.

Christensen, C. M. (1997). *The Innovator's Dilemma: When New Technologies Cause Great Firms to Fail.* Boston, MA: Harvard Business School Press.

Ciborra, C. (1997). *De profundis?* Deconstructing the concept of strategic alignment. *Scandanavian Journal of Information Systems, 9*, 67-82.

Cleaver, H., Walker, S., Scott, J., Cleaver, D., Rose, W., Ward, H., *et al.* (2008). *The Integrated Children's System: enhancing social work and inter-agency practice.* London: Jessica Kingsley.

Clegg, C. W. (2000). Socio-technical principles for system design. *Applied Ergonomics, 31*, 463-477.

Cule, P. & Robey, D. (2004). A Dual-Motor, Constructive Process Model of Organizational Transition. *Organization Studies, 25*, 229-260.

Daft, R. L. (2004). *Organization Theory and Design* (8th ed.). London: Thomson.

Davenport, T. (1993). *Process Innovation: reengineering work through information technology.* Cambridge, MA: Harvard Business School Press.

Davenport, T. & Short, J. E. (1990). The New Industrial Engineering: Information Technology and Business Process Redesign. *Sloan Management Review, 31*, 11-27.

Davies, H. T., Nutley, S. M. & Smith, P. C. (2000). *What works? Evidence-based policy and practice in public services.* Bristol: Policy Press.

de Sitter, L. U., den Hertog, J. F. & Dankbaar, B. (1997). From complex organizations with simple jobs to simple organizations with complex jobs. *Human Relations, 50*, 497-534.

Deming, W. E. (1994). *The New Economics for Industry, Government, Education.* Cambridge: MIT Press.

Denhardt, J. V. & Denhardt, R. B. (2003). *The New Public Service – rowing not steering.* New York: M E Sharpe.

DCSF. (2008). *Integrated Children's system evaluation: Summary of key findings, Brief No: DCSF-RBX-02-08.* Department for Children, Schools and Families.

DCSF. (2009). *The Protection of Children in England: action plan. The Government's response to Lord Laming.* Department for Children, Schools and Families.

Department of Health. (1998). *LAC (98)28: The Quality Protects Programme: Transforming Children's Services.* London: Stationery Office.

Department of Health. (1999). *Government objectives for social services.* London: Stationery Office.

Department of Health. (2000a). *Learning the Lessons – The Government's response to Lost in Care.* London: Stationery Office.

Department of Health. (2000b). *Integrated Children's System: briefing paper number 1*. London: Department of Health.

Department of Health. (2002). *Integrated Children's System Working with Children in Need and their families: Consultation Document*. London: Department of Health.

Dewey, J. (1974). *John Dewey on Education: Selected Writings*. Chicago: University of Chicago Press.

Dillon, A. (2004). *Designing Usable Electronic Text*. New York: CRC Press.

Dillow, C. (2007). *The End of Politics: New Labour and the Folly of Managerialism*. Petersfield: Harriman House.

Dollery, B. & Akimov, A. (2008). Are shared services a panacea for Australian local government? A critical note on Australian and international empirical evidence. *International Review of Public Administration, 12*, 89-99.

Dorner, D. (1996). *The Logic of Failure*. New York: Basic Books.

Dorner, D. & Pfeifer, E. (1993). Strategic thinking and stress. *Ergonomics, 36*, 1345 – 1360.

Dowty, T. (2008). Pixie-dust and privacy: what's happening to children's rights in England? *Children and Society, 22*, 393-9.

du Gay, P. (2000). *In Praise of Bureaucracy*. London: Sage.

Dunleavy, P., Margetts, H., Bastow, S. & Tinkler, J. (2005). New public management is dead: long live digital-era governance. *Journal of Public Administration Research and Theory, 16*, 467-494.

Dunne, D. & Martin, R. (2006). Design Thinking and how it will change management eduction: an interview and discussion. *Academy of Management Learing and Education, 5* (4), 512-523.

Eason, K. (2007). Local socio-technical development in the National Programme for Information Technology. *Journal of Information Technology, 22*, 257-264.

Ellul, J. (1964). *The Technological Society*. New York: Vintage Books.

Farson, R. (1996). *Management of the Absurd: Paradoxes in Leadership*. London: Simon and Schuster.

Fitzgerald, G. & Russo, N. L. (2005). The turnaround of the London Ambulance Service Computer-Aided Despatch system (LASCAD). *European Journal of Information Systems, 14*, 244-257.

Fleck, L. (1979). *Genesis and Development of a Scientific Fact*. Chicago: University of Chicago Press.

Flood, R. L. & Jackson, M. C. (1991). *Creative Problem Solving: Total Systems Intervention*. Chichester: John Wiley.

Floyd, S. W. & Wooldridge, B. (1997). Middle Management's Strategic Influence and Organisational Performance. *Journal of Management Studies, 34*, 465-485.

Flyvberg, B. (2007). *Making Social Science Matter.* Cambridge: Cambridge University Press.

Frater, M. (2008). *Lifting the Burdens Task Force – Review of the Department of Children, Schools and Families.* London: LGA Publications.

Frazer, J. G. (1922). *The Golden Bough: a study in magic and religion.* London: Macmillan.

Galbraith, J. R. (1977). *Organization Design.* Reading: Addison-Wesley.

Gasser, L. (1986). The integration of computing and routine work. *ACM Transactions on Office Information Systems, 4*, 205-225.

Gibb, M. (2009). *Building a safe, confident future: The final report of the Social Work Task Force.* London: DCSF-01114-2009.

Gibson, C. B. & Birkinshaw, J. (2004). The antecedents, consequences and mediating role of organizational ambidexterity. *Academy of Management Journal, 47*, 209-226.

Goodsell, C. T. (1994). *The Case for Bureaucracy.* New Jersey: Chatham House.

Hackman, J. R. & Oldham, G. R. (1976). Motivation through the design of work: Test of a theory. *Organizational Behavior and Human Performance, 16*, 250-279.

Hackney, R. & Little, S. (1999). Opportunistic strategy formulation for IS/IT planning. *European Journal of Information Systems, 8*, 119-126.

Hammer, M. (1990, July-August). Reengineering work: don't automate, obliterate. *Harvard Business Review*, 104-112.

Hammer, M. & Champy, J. (1993). *Reengineering the corporation: a manifesto for business revolution.* London: Nicholas Brealey.

Hammer, M. & Champy, J. (2001). *Reengineering the corporation: a manifesto for business revolution.* (2nd Edition). London: Nicholas Brealey.

Hartley, J. (2008). The innovation landscape for public service organisations. In J. Hartley, C. Donaldson, C. Skelcher & M. Wallace, *Managing to Improve Public Services* (pp.197-218). Cambridge: Cambridge University Press.

Hartley, J., Donaldson, C., Skelcher, C. & Wallace, M. (2008). *Managing to improve public services.* Cambridge: Cambridge University Press.

Heinbokel, T., Sonnentag, S., Frese, M., Stolte, W. & Brodbeck, F. C. (1996). Don't underestimate the problems of user-centeredness in software development projects. There are many! *Behaviour & Information Technology, 15*, 226-236.

Hevner, A. R., March, S. T., Park, J. & Ram, S. (2004). Design science in information systems research. *MIS Quarterly, 28*, 75-105.

Home Office. (March 2010). *Vetting and Barring Scheme Guidance.* London: Home Office.

Hood, C. (1995). The "New Public Management" in the 1980s. *Accounting, Organizations and Society, 20,* 93-109.

Hood, C. & Peters, G. (2004). The Middle Aging of New Public Management: Into the Age of Paradox? *Journal of Public Administration Research and Theory, 14,* 267-82.

Hubbard, L., Mehan, H. & Stein, M. K. (2006). *Reform as learning: school reform, organisational culture and community politics in San Diego.* London: Routledge.

Hwang, M. I., & Thorn, R.G. (1999). The effect of user engagement on system success: A meta-analytical integration of research findings. *Information and Management, 35,* 229-236.

Irani, Z., Sharif, A. M. & Love, P. (2001). Transforming failure into success through organisational learning: an analysis of a manufacturing information system. *European Journal of Information Systems, 10,* 55-66.

Kaplan, R. S. & Norton, D. P. (2006). *Alignment: Using the Balanced Scorecard to Create Corporate Synergies.* Boston, MA: Harvard Busines School Press.

Kawalek, P. (2007). The bubble strategy: case study of dynamic, defensible processes in Salford. *International Journal of Public Sector Management, 20,* 178-191.

Kawalek, P. & Wastell, D. (2005). Pursuing Radical Transformation in Information Age Government: Case Studies Using the SPRINT Methodology. *Journal of Global Information Management, 13,* 79-102.

Kawalek, P. & Wastell, D. G. (1999). A case study evaluation of the use of the visable systems model in information systems development. *Journal of Database Management, 10,* 21-29.

Keil, M. (1995, December). Pulling the plug: management and the problem of project escalation. *MIS Quarterly,* 421-427.

Kelman, S. (2005). *Unleashing change: a study of organizational renewal in Government.* Washington: Brookings Institution Press.

Kotter, J. P. (1995). Leading change: why transformation efforts fail. *Harvard Business Review, 74,* 59-67.

Kovner, A. R., Elton, J. J. & Billings, J. D. (2000). Evidence-based management. *Frontiers of Health Services Management, 13,* 3-46.

Kuhn, T. S. (1962). *The Structure of Scientific Revolutions.* Chicago: University of Chicago Press.

Laming, L. (2003). *The Victoria Climbié Inquiry: Report of an Inquiry by Lord Laming.* Norwich: The Stationery Office.

Laming, L. (2009). *The protection of children in England: a progress report.* London: The Stationery Office.

Larsen, M. A. & Myers, M. D. (2000). 'When success turns to failure: a package-driven business process re-engineering project in the financial services industry. *Journal of Strategic Information Systems, 8,* 395-417.

Laudon, K. C. & Laudon, J. P. (2004). *Essentials of Management Information Systems: Managing the Digital Firm.* Harlow: Prentice-Hall.

Launer, J. (2008). Medical kitsch. *Postgraduate Medical Journal, 84,* 111-2.

Law, J. (1994). *Organizing Modernity: Social Order and Social Theory.* Oxford: Blackwell.

Learmonth, M. & Harding, N. (2006). Evidence-based management: the very idea. *Public Administration, 84,* 245-266.

Lin, C. (2007). Issues and recommendations in evaluating and managing the benefits of public sector IS/IT outsourcing. *Information Technology & People, 20,* 161-83.

Lipski, M. (1980). *Street-level Bureaucracy: Dilemmas of the Individual in Public Services.* New York: Russell Sage Foundation.

Locke, E. A. & Latham, G. P. (2002). Building a Practically Useful Theory of Goal Setting and Task Motivation: a 35-year odyssey. *American Psychologist, 57,* 705–717.

Luftman, J. & Brier, T. (1999). Achieving and Sustaining Business-IT Alignment. *California Management Review, 42,* 109-122.

Lugg, C. (1998). Political kitsch and educational policy. *AERA Annual Convention,* (pp.1-25). San Diego.

Lymbery, M. (2006). United We Stand? Partnership Working in Health and Social Care and the Role of Social Work in Services for Older People. *British Journal of Social Work, 36,* 1119–1134.

Lyotard, J.-F. (1979). *The Postmodern Condition: A Report on Knowledge.* Manchester: Manchester University Press.

MacIntosh, R. (2003). BPR: alive and well in the public sector. *International Journal of Operations & Production Management, 23,* 327-344.

Malinowski, J. (1932). *Argonauts of the Western Pacific.* London: George Routledge and Sons.

Markus, L. M. & Benjamin, R. (1997). The magic bullet theory in IT-enabled transformation. *Sloan Management Review,* 55-68.

Markus, M. L. (1983). Power, politics and MIS implementation. *Communications of the ACM, 26,* 430-444.

Marquand, D. (2004). *Decline of the Public.* Cambridge: Polity Press.

Martin, D. (2000). *Ethnomethodology and Systems Design. Interaction at the boundaries of organisations.* Unpublished Ph.D. thesis, University of Manchester, UK.

Martin, D. (2005). *An Ethnography of a Project to Introduce a New Mortgage Interview Application in a Leading UK Mutual Building Society.* NUBS Internal Teaching Case (DW1).

Martin, D., Bowers, J. & Wastell, D. G. (1997). The Interactional Affordances of Technology: An Ethnography of Human-Computer Interaction in an Ambulance Control Centre. *Proceedings of HCI on People and Computers XII* (pp.263-281). London: Springer-Verlag.

Martin, D., Wastell, D. & Bowers, J. (1998). An ethnographic systems design method: The development and evaluation of an Internet-based electronic banking application. *Proceedings of the 8th European Conference on Information Systems.* Aix-en-Provence, France.

Martin, J. (1992). *Cultures in organizations: three perspectives.* New York: Oxford University Press.

Martin, S. & Hartley, J. (2000). Best Value for all: an empirical analysis of local government's capacity to implement Best Value principles. *Public Management, 2,* 43-56.

Mauss, M. (2001). *A general theory of magic.* Abingdon: Routledge.

McAdam, R. & Donaghy, J. (1999). Business process re-engineering in the public sector: A study of staff perceptions and critical success factors. *Business Process Management Journal, 5,* 33-49.

McAfee, A., Dessain, V. & Sjoman, A. (2004). *Zara: IT for fast fashion.* Boston, MA: Harvard Business School Case Study 9-604-081.

McMaster, T. & Wastell, D. G. (2004). Success and failure revisited in the implementation of new technology: some reflections on the Capella project. In B. Fitzgerald & E. Wynn, *Innovation for Adaptability and Competitiveness* (pp.65-78). Boston: Kluwer.

McMaster, T. & Wastell, D. G. (2005). Diffusion or delusion? Challenging an IS research tradition. *Information Technology and People, 18,* 383-404.

Mehan, H. (1999). Oracular reasoning in a psychiatric team: the resolution of conflict. In A. Jaworski & N. Coupland, *The Discourse Reader* (pp.532-545). London: Routledge.

Mento, A. J., Jones, R. M. & Dirndorfer, W. (2002). A Change Management Process Grounded In Both Theory And Practice. *Journal of Change Management, 3(1),* 45-59.

Messer, S. B. & Wampold, B. E. (2002). Let's Face Facts: Common Factors Are More Potent Than Specific Therapy Ingredients. *Clinical Psychology: Science and Practice, 9*, 21-25.

Mintzberg, H. (1989). *Mintzberg on management.* New York: Free Press.

Moore, M. (1995). *Creating public value: strategic management in government.* Cambridge: Harvard University Press.

Moore, M. H. & Bennington, J. (2011). Conclusions: looking ahead. In J. Bennington & M. H. Moore, *Public value: theory and practice* (pp.256-274). Basingstoke: Palgrave Macmillan.

Mulgan, G. (2011). Effective supply and demand and the measurement of public and social value. In J. Bennington & M. H. Moore, *Public value: theory and practice* (pp.212-224). Basingstoke: Pagrave Macmillan.

Mumford, E. (2003). *Redesigning Human Systems.* Hershey: Information Science Publishing.

Munro, E. (2005). Improving practice: Child protection as a systems problem. *Children and Youth Services Review, 27*, 375-391.

Nichol, G., Detsky, A. S., Stiell, I. G., O'Rourke, K., Wells, G. & Laupacis, A. (1996). Effectiveness of Emergency Medical Services for Victims of Out-of-Hospital Cardiac Arrest: A Meta-analysis. *Annals of Emergency Medicine, 27*, 700-10.

Norman, D. A. (1998). *The Design of Everyday Things.* New York: Basic Books.

ODPM. (2002). *www.localegov.gov.uk: The national strategy for local e-government.* Wetherby: Office of the Deputy Prime Minister.

Ofsted. (2010). *Learning lessons from serious case reviews 2009-2010.* Manchester: Ofsted.

Orlikowski, W. & Hofman, J. D. (1997). An improvisational model for change management: The case of groupware technologies. *Sloan Management Review, 38*, 11-21.

Osborne, D. & Gaebler, T. (1993). *Reinventing Government.* New York: Plume.

Osbourne, S. (2006). Editorial: the new public governance. *Public Administration Review, 8*, 377-87.

Owen, R. (1967). *The Life of Robert Owen, written by Himself.* London: Frank Cass and Co.

Parsons, T. (1956). Suggestions for a sociological approach to the theory of organizations. *Administrative Science Quarterly, 1*, 63-85.

Pava, C. (1983). *Managing New Office Technology.* New York: Free Press.

Pava, C. (1986). New Strategies of systems change; reclaiming the synoptic methods. *Human Relations, 7*, 615-33.

Pava, C. (1986). Redesigning sociotechnical systems design: concepts and methods for the 1990s. *Journal of Applied Behavioral Science, 22*, 201-221.

Pedler, M. (1996). *Action Learning for Managers*. London: Lemos and Crane.

Penrose, E. (1980). *The Theory of Growth of the Firm*. Oxford: Blackwell.

Peters, T. (2005). *Design – innovate, differentiate, communicate*. New York: DK Publishing.

Petroski, H. (2006). *Success Through Failure: The paradox of design*. Princeton, NJ: Princeton University Press.

Pfeffer, J. & Sutton, R. I. (2006, January). Evidence-based management. *Harvard Busines Review*, 63-74.

Pichler, R. (2010). *Agile Product Management with Scrum*. Boston, MA: Pearson.

Popper, K. (1995). *The Open Society and its Enemies, Volume 1 – The Spell of Plato*. London: Routledge.

Ravishankar, M. N., Pan, S. L. & Leidner, D. E. (2009). Examining the strategic alignment and implementation success of a KMS: A Subculture-Based Multilevel Analysis. *Information Systems Research, Advance on-line access*, 1-23.

Reason, J. (2000). Human error: models and management. *British Medical Journal, 320*, 768-770.

Reich, B. H. & Benbasat, I. (2000). Factors that Influence the Social Dimension of Alignment between Business and Information Technology Objectives. *MIS Quarterly, 24*, 81-113.

Ritzer, G. (2004). *The McDonaldization of Society*. Thousand Oaks, CA: Pine Forge Press.

Rousseau, D. & McCarthy, S. (2007). Educating managers from an evidence-based perspective. *Academy of Management Learning & Education, 6*, 84-101.

Schön, D. A. (1987). *Educating the Reflective Practitioner*. San Fransisco: Jossey-Bass.

Schön, D. A. (1988, 41). Towards a marriage of artistry and applied science in the architectural design studio. *Journal of Architectural Education*, 4-10.

Schumacher, E. F. (1993). *Small is Beautiful: a study of economics as if people mattered*. London: Vintage.

Seddon, J. (2008). *Systems Thinking in the Public Sector*. Axminster: Triarchy Press.

Seden, J., Sinclair, R., Robbins, D. & Pont, C. (2001). *Studies informing the framework for the assessment of children in need and their families*. London: HMSO.

Seeger, M. W., Ulmer, R. R., Novak, J. M. & Sellnow, T. (2005). Post-Crisis Discourse and Organisational Change, Failure and Renewal. *Journal of Organizational Change, 18*, 78–95.

Senge, P. (1990). *The Fifth Discipline: the art and practice of the learning organization.* London: Century Business.

Serafeimidis, V. & Smithson, S. (2000). Information systems evaluation in practice: A case study of organisational change. *Journal of Information Technology, 15*, 93-105.

Shaoul, J., Stafford, A. & Stapleton, P. (2008). The cost of using private finance to build, finance and operate hospitals. *Public Money and Management*, 101-8.

Shaw, I., Bell, M., Sinclair, I., Sloper, P., Mitchell, W., Dyson, P., *et al.* (2009). An Exemplary Scheme? An Evaluation of the Integrated Children's System. *British Journal of Social Work (Advance Access April 8)*, 1-20.

Simon, H. (1966). *The Sciences of the Artificial.* Cambridge, MA: MIT Press.

Starkey, K. & Tempest, S. (2009). The winter of our discontent: the design challenge for Business Schools. *Academy of Management Learning and Education, 8*, 576-586.

Stivers, R. (2001). *Technology as Magic: the triumph of the irrational.* New York: Continuum.

Sullivan, H., Barnes, M. & Matka, E. (2002). Building Collaborative Capacity through 'Theories of Change: Early Lessons from the Evaluation of Health Action Zones in England. *Evaluation, 8*, 205–226.

Takeuchi, H. & Nonaka, I. (1986, January-February). The New New Product Development Game. *Harvard Business Review*, 137-146.

Tate, W. (2009). *The Search for Leadership: An Organizational Perspective.* Axminster: Triarchy Press.

Taylor, F. W. (1903). *Shop Management.* New York: Harper and Row (re-published by Kessinger Publishing's Rare Reprints).

The Cabinet Office. (2002). *Review of Major Government IT Projects: Successful IT – Modernising Government in Action.* London: HM Government.

Trist, E. & Bamforth, K. W. (1951). Some social and psychological consequences of the longwall method of coal-getting. *Human Relations, 4*, 3-38.

Unison. (2008). *Lord Laming Progress Report on Safeguarding: Summary of UNISON Memorandum.* London: Unison.

van Aken, J. E. (2005). Management research as a design science: articulating the research products of mode 2 knowledge production in management. *British Journal of Management, 16*, 19-36.

von Stamm, B. & van Patter, G. (2005). Organizational innovation: exploring avenues of approach. *NextD Journal – ReReThinking Design*, conversation 6.3.

Walker, R. M. & Damanpour, F. (2008). Innovation type and organizational performance: an empirical exploration. In J. Hartley, C. Donaldson, C. Skelcher & M. Wallace, *Managing to improve public services* (pp.217-235). Cambridge: Cambridge University Press.

Wallace, M. & Fertig, M. (2008). Orchestrating complex and programmatic change in the public services. In J. Hartley, C. Donaldson, C. Skelcher & M. Wallace, *Managing to improve public services* (pp.257-278). Cambridge: Cambridge University Press.

Wastell, D. (2007). The myth of alignment. In T. McMaster, D. Wastell, F. Ferneley & J. de Gross, *Organisational Dynamics of Technology-Based Innovation: Diversifying the Research Agenda.* (pp.513-518). Springer.

Wastell, D. (2010, March). The tragedy of ICS: social work's dogma-driven flight from paper records. *Community Care*, http://www.communitycare.co.uk/blogs/social-care-the-big-picture/2010/03/the-tragedy-of-ics-social-works-dogma-driven-flight-from-paper-records.html

Wastell, D. G. (1996). The fetish of technique: methodology as a social defense. *Information Systems Journal, 6*, 25-40.

Wastell, D. G. (1999). Learning dysfunctions in information systems development: overcoming the social defences with transitional objects. *MIS Quarterly, 23*, 581 – 600.

Wastell, D. G. (1999). The human dimension of the software process. *Lecture Notes in Computer Science, 1500*, 165-199.

Wastell, D. G. (2002). Organisational discourse as a social defence: taming the tiger of e-government. In M. Myers *et al. Global and Organisational Discourse about Information Technology* (pp.179-198). London: Kluwer.

Wastell, D. G. (2005). Enabling partnership work in crime reduction: tales from the trenches of evidence-based policy. *Evidence and Policy, 1*, 305-333.

Wastell, D. G. (2010). Managing as designing: "opportunity knocks" for the IS field? *European Journal of Information Systems, 19 *, 422-431.

Wastell, D. G. & White, S. (2010). Technology as magic: fetish and folly in the IT-enabled reform of Children's services. In P. Ayre & M. Preston-Shoot, *Children's Services at the Crossroads* (pp.107-114). Lyme Regis: Russell House.

Wastell, D. G., McMaster, T. & Kawalek, P. (2007). The rise of the Phoenix: methodological innovation as a discourse of renewal. *Journal of Information Technology, 22*, 59-68.

Wastell, D. G., White, P. & Kawalek, P. (1994). A methodology for business process redesign: experiences and issues. *Journal of Strategic Information Systems, 3*, 23-40.

Wastell, D. & Newman, M. (1996). Information systems design, stress and organisational change in the Ambulance Services: A Tale of Two Cities. *Accounting, Management & Information Technology, 6*, 283–299.

Wastell, D., White, S. & Broadhurst, K. (2009). The Chiasmus of Design: Paradoxical Outcomes in the e-Government Reform of UK Children's Service. In: Dhillon, G. *et al.* (2009). *Information systems – creativity and innovation in small and medium-sized encreativity and innovation in small and medium-sized enterprises.* (pp.257-272). London: Springer.

Wastell, D., White, S. & Broadhurst, K. (2010). Children's Services in the iron cage of performance management: street level bureaucracy and the spectre of Švejkism. *International Journal of Social Work, 19*, 310-320.

Weick, K. (1987). Organizational culture as a source of high reliability. *California Management Review, 29*, 112-127.

Weick, K. (1995). Organizational redesign as improvisation. In G. P. Huber & W. H. Glick, *Organizational change and redesign* (pp.346-379). New York: Oxford University Press.

Wenger, E. (2004). *Communities of practice: learning, meaning and identity.* Cambridge: Cambridge University Press.

White, S., Wastell, D. G., Broadhurst, K. & Hall, C. (2010). When policy o'erleaps itself: the tragic tale of the Integrated Children's System. *Critical Social Policy, 27*, 443-461.

Whitely, R. (1989). On the nature of managerial tasks and skills: their distinguishing characteristics and organization. *Journal of Management Studies, 26*, 209-224.

Wilson, D. & Game, C. (1998). *Local government in the United Kingdom.* Basingstoke: Macmillan.

Wren, D. (2005). *The History of Management Thought.* Hoboken, NJ: Wiley.

Yoo, Y., Boland, R. & Lyytinen, K. (2006). From organization design to organization designing. *Organization Science, 17*, 215-229.

Acknowledgements

To my partner, Sue White, who encouraged me to write this book in the first place and provided unstinting moral support. To the publishers, Triarchy Press, especially Imogen Fallows and Andrew Carey for their editorial support. I doff my hat to the various practitioners who have inspired me down the years; this book would not have been possible without them, and they make many appearances in its pages, especially the members of the Salford team. To my academic colleagues – Information Systems scholars in particular – who provided key theoretical insights; they are too numerous to mention, but I would single out Richard Boland, who co-organised the "Managing as designing" colloquium which provided the original intellectual stimulus that gave coherent shape (I hope) to my inchoate ideas.

Index

ABOUT THE AUTHOR

David Wastell is Professor of Information Systems at Nottingham University Business School. He began his academic career as a psycho-physiologist, sticking electrodes on people's heads trying to figure out how the brain works (the process is not dissimilar to the use of performance indicators for measuring organisational performance, but without the ability to go inside and work out what is really going on!). Following his PhD, he moved to the Applied Psychology Unit at Cambridge University in 1978 to carry out research on stress and technological innovation in collaboration with British Telecom. David's interests in technology and work developed during an extended period at Manchester University, first in the Medical School and then in the field of Computer Science. He was appointed Professor of the Information Society at Salford University in 2000 where he helped establish a leading international research group specialising in information systems. Subsequently he moved to UMIST, before transferring to Nottingham in 2005.

David has organised a number of international conferences. He has published widely in a spectrum of research journals, and has co-edited four books. His current interests are in public sector reform, innovation and design, and cognitive ergonomics. David is secretary of an international working group (IFIP WG8.6), which specialises in research on technology transfer and innovation. He has extensive public sector consultancy experience and was co-author of the SPRINT methodology, which provides a framework for service re-engineering and change management, and is widely used in the local government community. In 2001, he helped develop MADE, a multi-agency data exchange for crime policy which continues to support community safety partnerships across the whole of Lancashire. David has held a number of research grants, most recently an ESRC award to study governance and decision-making in child welfare. It was this grant which supported some of the key research reported in this book, and which led to his involvement in the ICT subgroup of the *Munro Review of Child Protection* (2010/11).

About Triarchy Press

Triarchy Press is an independent publishing house that looks at how organisations work and how to make them work better. We present challenging perspectives on organisations in short and pithy, but rigorously argued, books.

Through our books, pamphlets and website we aim to stimulate ideas by encouraging real debate about organisations in partnership with people who work in them, research them or just like to think about them.

Please tell us what you think about the ideas in this book at:

www.triarchypress.com/telluswhatyouthink

If you feel inspired to write – or have already written – an article, a pamphlet or a book on any aspect of organisational theory or practice, we'd like to hear from you. Submit a proposal at:

www.triarchypress.com/writeforus

For more information about Triarchy Press, or to order any of our publications, please visit our website or drop us a line:

www.triarchypress.com

We're on Twitter:

@TriarchyPress

and Facebook:

www.facebook.com/triarchypress

OTHER TITLES

JOHN SEDDON AND SYSTEMS THINKING FOR PUBLIC SERVICES

~ Systems Thinking in the Public Sector
John Seddon
The best-selling analysis of why public services in the UK and around the world so often don't work – and how to fix the mess. This is the book that made a laughing stock of the UK Audit Commission (now abolished), famously ridiculed the culture of targets and 'deliverology' that for years has characterised public services in England and set in train the conversion of the public sector to systems thinking. The reviews say it all:

> *"From trading standards to planning and housing repairs, all exhibit the same dysfunction, being forced to conform to a work design that starts from the wrong end – the requirements of government rather than those of the citizen."*
> **Simon Caulkin, The Observer**

> *"This book provides the public sector with the means to deliver higher levels of public value and the opportunity to be seen to be doing so in a robust way with measurable results, high customer satisfaction and high morale."* **Jim Mather, Scottish Govt. Minister for Enterprise, Energy & Tourism**

2008, 224pp., paperback, 978-0-9550081-8-4, £20.00

~ Delivering Public Services That Work: Systems Thinking in the Public Sector: Case Studies
Peter Middleton ~ Foreword by John Seddon
Six detailed and specific Case Studies which convincingly demonstrate that John Seddon's recipe (above) actually works and delivers the results he promised.

2010, 132pp., paperback, 978-0-9562631-6-2, £15.00

WILLIAM TATE AND APPLYING SYSTEMS THINKING TO ORGANISATIONS

~ The Search for Leadership: An Organisational Perspective
William Tate
This Systems Thinking approach to leadership asks us to look beyond individuals, managers, leaders and management training programmes. Using the analogy of an aquarium (where water quality determines the health of the fish), Bill Tate reviews a range of issues like:

Distributing authority ~ management vs. organisation development ~ the structural gaps that account for waste, rework, poor communication and failure ~ transferring learning ~ organisational competence ~ accountability ~ the organisation's culture and shadow-side.

> *"Full of practical tips and insights... a 'must read' book for any leadership or organisational development practitioner who wants to make a difference to business success."* **Linda Holbeche,** *CIPD*

> *"...offers a practical road map for understanding and improving organisations and the way they are led."* **Prof. John Storey,** *The Open University Business School*

2009, 324pp., paperback, 978-0-9557681-7-0, £28.00; hardback, 978-0-9557681-8-7, £40.00; e-book, £40.00

~Systemic Leadership Toolkit
William Tate
Designed for use in conjunction with *The Search for Leadership* (above) this toolkit presents nine self-assessment questionnaires in nine separate modules – designed to give any organisation a complete picture of itself: Management Development ~ Organisation Development ~ Learning ~ Competence ~ Culture ~ Decline ~ Systems ~ The Shadow ~ Accountability

2009, 152pp., paperback, 978-0-9562631-2-4, £55.00; e-toolkit, £95.00

RUSS ACKOFF

One of the founding fathers of Systems Thinking was Russ Ackoff, who died in 2009. An acknowledged genius, who often found himself in those lists of the most influential business thinkers and 'gurus', he was a pre-eminent consultant, practitioner, researcher and academic in this field.

Triarchy Press had the good fortune to publish four of his books:

~ Management f-Laws: How organisations really work
Russell Ackoff ~ with Herbert Addison. Responses by Sally Bibb
We've all heard of Sod's (or Murphy's) Law – if anything can go wrong, it will. Most of us know Parkinson's Law – work expands to fill the time available for its completion. Now *Management f-LAWS* brings together a collection of 81 of Professor Russell Ackoff's wittiest and most subversive insights into the world of business.

> *"If you ever need a reality check after stumbling out of some appalling management meeting, or just need cheering up on a long business trip, this is the book for you. Just about every myth or pompous delusion about management gets punctured..."* **Stefan Stern,** *The Daily Telegraph*

> *"This book is fun – not something one can often say about a management book. It's also a compact piece of distilled wisdom... Many of the 81 f-Laws are obvious when*

you think about them, but are too often ignored or neglected. Yet they matter. Take No. 4: 'There is no point in asking customers, who do not know what they want, to say what they want.'" **Charles Handy,** *Management Today*

2007, 180pp., paperback, 978-0-9550081-2-2, £18.00

~ Systems Thinking for Curious Managers: With 40 new Management f-LAWS
Russell Ackoff ~ with Herbert Addison and Andrew Carey
This more recent title added 40 new f-LAWS to those previously published as *Management f-Laws.* The book also includes plus an insightful, extended introduction to Systems Thinking as developed by Russ Ackoff.

2010, 96pp., paperback, 978-0-9562631-5-5, £18.00

> **For managers, leaders and their victims as well as MBA students, these two books of *f*-Laws offer the essence of Ackoff at his sparkling and most digestible best.**

~ Memories
Russell Ackoff ~ Foreword by Peter Senge
You might think *Memories* would be the fond autobiography of a grumpy old guru. Not a bit of it! There <u>are</u> stories of his chats with the Queen of Iran, his introduction of theme parks to the US, appearing naked in front of his commanding officer in World War II… but they're all there to do a serious job. Ackoff knew his students remembered stories better than teachings, so he uses them to deliver a succession of principles and aphorisms relating to management, organisations and work that he had developed during his life.

> *"Russ was an incisive, lifelong critic of the modern organizational form... He was an advocate for major re-visioning and processes of change that started with helping people see what they truly valued and where they truly wanted to get – and then working backwards to see what it would take to get there."* **Peter Senge,** *from his Foreword to Memories*

2010, 120pp., paperback, 978-0-9565379-7-3, £16.00; hardback, 978-0-9565379-9-7, £25.00

~ Differences that make a Difference: An annotated glossary of distinctions important in management
Russell Ackoff ~ Foreword by Charles Handy
Towards the end of his life, Russ Ackoff determined to explain how some of the apparently insignificant misinterpretations of language and meaning he observed during his long years of research can, in practice, have far-reaching consequences. His aim was to **dissolve** (not **solve** or **resolve**) some of the many disputes in professional and private life that revolve around such misunderstandings. In this last manuscript that he was to complete before his death he does exactly that.

2010, 144pp., paperback, 978-1-908009-01-2, £14.00

Lightning Source UK Ltd.
Milton Keynes UK
UKOW040630161011

180356UK00001B/3/P